Beneath the Cross

Essays and Reflections on the Lord's Supper

Edited by Jady S. Copeland and Nathan Ward

DEWARD
PUBLISHING COMPANY

Beneath the Cross: Essays and Reflections on the Lord's Supper
© 2008 by DeWard Publishing Company, Ltd.
P.O. Box 6259, Chillicothe, Ohio 45601
800.300.9778
www.dewardpublishing.com

Cover design by Jeff Angelo.

For copyright information on previoulsy published material, please see
the acknowledgments on pages 323–324, which consitute a continua-
tion of this copyright page.

Reasonable care has been taken to trace original sources for any
excerpts and quotations appearing in this book and to document such
information in the footnotes. For material not the public domain, fair-
use standards and practices were followed. Should any attribution be
found to be incorrect or incomplete, the publisher welcomes written
documentation supporting correction for subsequent printings.

Printed in the United States of America.

ISBN: 978-0-9798893-3-2

Contents

Part Three: Meditating on the Cross

Editors' Preface

You hold in your hand a book devoted to the Lord's Supper and to the sacrifice of Christ it commemorates. This is not a book of Lord's Supper talks, though it contains articles appropriate for using at the Lord's table. This is not a book of scholarly essays, though it contains essays of excellent scholarship. This is not a book of devotionals, though it contains meditations suitable for deep, personal reflection. This is a book of *all these things*, written and compiled with the hope of bringing focus to the memorial feast so important to Christians.

Several years ago, a preacher shared a goal of his with a group in a Bible study. His goal: to read through the entire Bible looking for passages that relate to Christ, His sacrifice, and the Lord's Supper. He told us that he was astounded with what he had discovered so far in his reading. Though he had not gone through much of the Old Testament at all, he was seeing Christ everywhere. The preacher challenged us with the same exercise; this book, we hope, is a step in that direction.

The direct inspiration for this book is a series of Bible classes that happened not long ago. These classes—in their wide, biblical scope—introduced the editors of this book to a whole series of Scriptures about the Lord's Supper. These classes showed us that the Scriptures used for most Lord's Supper talks—Isaiah 53, Matthew 26, 1 Corinthians 11, perhaps a handful more—covered good, basic groundwork, but were insufficient in covering all that the Bible said concerning the Lord's Supper. Other passages—neglected passages—should similarly receive our attention. The old standby verses are crucial, of course, to understanding what the Lord wants us to know and to do when we come to His table. But the Bible contains much more that should be shared and contemplated by His children.

We read from God's word that the Lord's Supper is central to what the Lord's disciples are to do together as Christians. Luke tells us in Acts 20.7 that he and Paul gathered together with saints on the first day of the week *to break bread.* In 1 Corinthians, Paul seems to equate the brothers' coming together with their partaking of the Lord's Supper (1 Cor 11.17–20). Clearly, fellowship at the Lord's table was an important part of early Christian practice. If this fellowship is as central to Jesus' disciples today as it was to His disciples then, we ought to be diligent in making our communion with Christ at His table as meaningful and significant as possible.

Beneath the Cross is an attempt to do this. It is not an attempt to make a catechism, canon, or statement of creed. This book serves no other purpose than to help us partake of the Lord's Supper more thoughtfully, more scripturally, and with deeper understanding. That may mean paying closer attention to the songs we sing around the table. It may mean thinking more deeply about what Christ's sacrifice means to our life. It may mean growing in our knowledge of Christ as He is found throughout Scripture. It may even mean learning more about the Lord's Supper itself and what it meant to Christ's first-century audience.

Join us as we explore these things.

It should be said that a wide variety of men have contributed essays to this book. We think it only appropriate for a book on this topic to be written by brothers of all ages, occupations, and backgrounds. Just as we are all partakers, we all—elders, teachers, college students, lawyers, businessmen, doctors, retirees, and more—have something to share from the word. As a result, the style of writing varies from one essay to the next. Some are more scholarly, others are more pithy; one is an instructive allegory.

The essays included in this collection cover a variety of topics, and we have tried to minimize overlap within the manuscript. We think you'll find that each entry focuses on a unique theme or message that distinguishes it from the surrounding essays.

We hope you are encouraged and strengthened by what you read in all of the following articles. We know we have grown from our work on this project, and we look forward to reading these men's thoughts for years to come.

There are several men to whom we would like to offer a special thanks. To Brent Lewis, Gary Henry, Mark Bingham, and Tack Chumbley, who served as advisors and proofreaders to this book: thank you for your wisdom, insight, and excellent editing skills. To Marty Broadwell, who was unable to contribute an essay, but provided a long list of helpful topics, many of which you will find herein: thank you for playing a vital behind-the-scenes role in broadening the scope of this book. To Matt Harber, who served as something of an associate editor and took on the mind-numbing task of double-checking every Scripture reference: thank you for your help in that regard and for offering your thoughts in other editorial issues as they arose. To Brooke Ward and Katie Harber: thank you for giving up your husbands a few evenings each month for the past half year. To Jeff Angelo, who designed the cover and taught Nathan the skill needed to turn these essays into an attractive book: thank you for sharing your expertise.

Finally, a word of thanks is in order to the authors who contributed to this work. Thanks for volunteering your time and energy to this project, especially those of you who really didn't have the time to contribute, but did anyway. Thanks for being willing to work with short deadlines and almost entirely by e-mail communication. Thanks especially to those of you who were cooperative and congenial through our editorial suggestions, and to those of you who were willing to write by assignment to help fill some of the subject gaps left after our first round of volunteer essays. To all of you, we offer our sincerest thanks. Without your excellent work, this book would not exist in any form. Because of your excellent work, we now have what we believe will be an edifying and enduring resource for Christians.

Jady S. Copeland
Nathan Ward

In the beginning was the Word, and the Word was with God, and the Word was God. He was in the beginning with God. All things were made through him, and without him not anything was made that has been made. But though he was in the form of God, he did not count equality with God a thing to be grasped, but made himself nothing, taking the form of a servant. Being born in the likeness of men, he became flesh, and dwelt among us, and we have seen his glory, glory as of the only Son from the Father, full of grace and truth.

And being found in human form, he humbled himself by becoming obedient to the point of death, even death on a cross. For it was fitting that he, for whom and by whom all things exist, in bringing many sons unto glory, should make the author of their salvation perfect through suffering. Since therefore the children share in flesh and blood, he himself likewise partook of the same things, that through death he might destroy the one who has the power of death, that is, the devil, and deliver all those who through fear of death were subject to lifelong slavery. While we were still weak, at the right time Christ died for the ungodly. One will scarcely die for a righteous person—though perhaps for a good person one would dare even to die—but God shows his love for us, in that, while we were still sinners, Christ died for us. By the grace of God he tasted of death for every man.

Surely he has borne our griefs and carried our sorrows; yet we esteemed him stricken, smitten by God, and afflicted. But he was wounded for our transgressions, he was crushed for our iniquities; upon him was the chastisement that brought us peace, and with his stripes we are healed. All we like sheep have gone astray; we have turned every one to his own way; and the Lord has laid on him the iniquity of us all. He was oppressed, and he was afflicted, yet opened not his mouth; like a lamb that is led to the slaughter, and like a sheep that before its shearers is silent, so he opened not his mouth.

And between the throne and the four living creatures and among the elders I saw a Lamb standing, as though it had been slain. Then I looked, and I heard around the throne and the living creatures and the elders the voice of many angels, numbering myriads of myriads and thousands of thousands, saying with a loud voice, "Worthy is the Lamb who was slain, to receive power and wealth and wisdom and might and honor and glory and blessing!" God has highly exalted him, and bestowed on him the name that is above every name, so that at the name of Jesus every knee should bow, in heaven and on earth and under the earth, and every tongue confess that Jesus Christ is Lord, to the glory of God the Father.

And I heard every creature in heaven and on earth and under the earth and in the sea, and all that is in them saying, "To him who sits on the throne and to the Lamb be blessing and honor and glory and might forever and ever!"

Therefore, whoever eats the bread or drinks the cup of the Lord in an unworthy manner will be guilty of profaning the body and the blood of the Lord. Let a person examine himself, then, and so eat of the bread and drink of the cup. For anyone who eats and drinks without discerning the body eats and drinks judgment on himself.

Excerpted and adapted from Isaiah 53, John 1, Romans 5, 1 Corinthians 11, Philippians 2, Hebrews 2 and Revelation 5 (ESV).

Part One

Approaching the Lord's Table

The Last Passover Meal

Daniel W. Petty

During the last weeks of His earthly ministry, Jesus often directed His disciples' attention to His approaching suffering and death. "Behold, we are going up to Jerusalem, and all things which are written through the prophets about the Son of Man will be accomplished" (Luke 18.31 NASB; *cf.* 9.51). He was fully aware of the way of suffering that awaited Him. Jesus chose voluntarily and purposefully to lay down His life as a sacrifice.

So, on the eve of His crucifixion, Jesus made definite preparations in anticipation of His death and departure—preparations that would be necessary for Him to carry out His plan to save man. "My time is near" was the message Jesus sent by the disciples to the man at whose house they would meet for the Passover meal. "I am to keep the Passover at your house with My disciples" (Matt 26.18). His message here underlines the sense of urgency Jesus must have felt. He was conscious of His destiny. Our Lord was rapidly approaching the goal and purpose of His life on this earth.

The preparation of the Passover involved removing all the leaven from the house (Exod 12.14–22). Unleavened bread would be prepared for the Passover. The Passover lambs would be slaughtered. So, on the day before Jesus' crucifixion—"the first day of Unleavened Bread"—He directed Peter and John to "Go and prepare the Passover for us, so that we may eat it" (Luke 22.8).

But even as the Passover was approaching, one of Jesus' disciples had already made arrangements with the Jewish authorities to deliver Him into their hands for a sum of money (Luke 22.1–6). Perhaps Jesus intended to keep secret right up to the end the place where they would gather to eat the Passover. The eve of the Passover might provide a "good opportunity" for them to take Jesus. Arrangements had been made in advance with the owner of the house. Peter and John were to find a man carrying a pitcher of water at a certain place and follow him to the house.

In the large, furnished upper room of the house, Jesus and His disciples observed the Passover meal together. How fitting! God's redemption of Israel from Egyptian bondage was commemorated every Passover (Exod 12.23–27). That historic event foreshadowed Jesus' own redemptive sacrifice. So it was necessary for Him to eat the Passover meal with His disciples the night before His death. The Passover was perhaps the most appropriate setting for Him to convey to them the meaning of His impending death for all men. John the Baptist had already proclaimed this truth: "Behold, the Lamb of God, who takes away the sin of the world!" (John 1.29).

The bitterest of ironies in these events was about to be revealed. Jesus announced to His disciples the solemn and shocking news that His betrayer was one of them! They were deeply grieved. "Surely not I, Lord?" they each asked. Jesus' answer seems deliberately vague, for they all had dipped their hand with Him in the dish. Here we see the painful reality that one of those who were gathered there to participate with Jesus and His disciples in such a holy feast would also now betray Him. Yet Jesus used the occasion to emphasize the necessity that the Son of Man suffer as written of Him in the prophets: "All of us like sheep have gone astray, each of us has turned to his own way; but the LORD has caused the iniquity of us all to fall on Him" (Isa 53.6). "Surely it is not I, Rabbi?" Judas, it seems, asked the question only after Jesus had also revealed the tragic fate of His betrayer. Jesus answered, "You have said it yourself" (*cf.* Matt 26.24–25).

This was not the only tragic irony. After supper, as Jesus and the disciples went out to the Mount of Olives, Jesus warned them of what the immediate future held in store for them as well as for Himself. Because of what was about to happen to Him, they would all become disheartened and lose faith before the night had passed. Using Zechariah's words, Jesus made a dire prediction: "I will strike down the shepherd, and the sheep of the flock shall be scattered" (Matt 26.31; *cf.* Zech 13.7). He was their shepherd and they were His flock. The sheep would be temporarily scattered even while the shepherd laid down His life for them. Then He would be raised (Matt 26.32).

In the midst of all these revelations, Jesus instituted the Lord's Supper. As they observed the Passover, Jesus took some of the unleavened bread, offered a blessing, broke it, and gave it to the disciples. "Take, eat; this is My body." In the same way He took a cup, gave thanks, and said, "Drink from it, all of you." The significance of His impending death was revealed to them when He said, "This is My blood of the covenant, which is poured out for many for remission of sins" (Matt 26.26–28). Jesus knew that the shedding of His blood would mark the inauguration of a new covenant—the new covenant prophesied by Jeremiah, through whom God said, "For I will forgive their iniquity, and their sin I will remember no more" (Jer 31.31–34). He would suffer *for many* just as Isaiah said that God's Servant would "justify the many and bear their iniquities" (Isa 53.11).

Jesus intended that the events of that night be repeated by His disciples as a perpetual memorial. "Do this in remembrance of Me," He said (1 Cor 11.23–26). It was their last Passover together, but it was also the beginning of something new and wonderful. We who are disciples of Jesus Christ continue to observe the Lord's Supper every first day of the week (Acts 20.7). By doing so, we share in the body and blood of Christ, offered as our sacrifice (1 Cor 10.16). Our fellowship with Christ and His sufferings (Phil 3.10; *cf.* Rom 8.17) is enriched by the privilege of communing with Him in His death. His suffering on the cross on our behalf becomes real to us as we relive that scene. At the same time, we are drawn together in fellowship with one another, "for we all partake of the one bread" (1 Cor 10.17). The unity of all disciples is enhanced as our minds are brought to dwell on that sacrifice that reconciles us to God and to one another (Eph 2.13–16).

Through the perpetual observance of the Lord's Supper, we "proclaim the Lord's death until He comes" (1 Cor 11.26). We declare our faith in the redeeming power of His death. Just as the yearly observance of the Passover retold an old, old story of redemption, our gathering around the Lord's table every Lord's day becomes our proclamation and confirmation of the words of Jesus: "This is My blood of the covenant, which is poured out for many for forgiveness of sins" (Matt 26.28). And that is the greatest story ever told.

Communion

Melvin D. Curry

The Lord's Supper is not only a memorial but also a communion. It is a time to participate as well as remember. We frequently prepare our minds by reading 1 Corinthians 11.23–26, especially verse 26: "As often as you eat this bread and drink this cup, you proclaim the Lord's death till He comes" (NKJV). But Paul reveals a truth in 1 Corinthians 10.14–22 about the Lord's Supper that is often overlooked. In this passage the apostle warns the Corinthians about provoking the Lord to "jealousy" by eating and drinking in an idol's temple. A Christian's allegiance cannot be divided: "You cannot drink the cup of the Lord and the cup of demons; you cannot partake of the Lord's table and of the table of demons" (v 21). One cannot have a divided loyalty when partaking of the bread and fruit of the vine.

The Lord's Supper is communion between Christians and Christ. Notice how pointedly Paul says this: "The cup of blessing which we bless, is it not the communion of the blood of Christ? The bread which we break, is it not the communion of the body of Christ?" (1 Cor 10.16). The term *communion (koinonia)* represents "a relationship characterized by sharing in common fellowship, participation."[1] Normally we think of fellowship among Christians, but here the fellowship is with the Lord's body and blood. The basis of this fellowship with Christ is obvious: "For we though many, are one bread and one body; for we all partake of that one bread" (v 17). One "partakes" *(metecheo)* by sharing with someone in something. As Jesus literally "shared" *(metecheo)* with us in flesh and blood (Heb 2.14), so we both spiritually and symbolically "share" with Him in flesh and blood. The apostle then provides an illustration: "Observe Israel after the flesh: Are not those who eat of the sacrifices partakers of the altar?" (v 18). Here the word *partakers* is the same term that was translated *communion* in verse 16 (see v 20). When the priests ate the sacrificial meat, they were doing more than having a common meal. Their action was an expression of fellowship with God. Likewise, the church is the body of Christ, and each Christian is a member of the body. The communion, therefore, represents the close union that each one has with the death, burial, and resurrection of the Lord. As we were baptized into Christ, so we are united with Him in the Supper. Neither action is a mere ritual; each one involves an intimate relationship. We must think about what we are doing. "For he who eats and drinks in an unworthy manner eats and drinks judgment to himself, not discerning the Lord's body" (1 Cor 11.29).

The Lord's Supper demands undivided loyalty. It should remind us that if we are yoked with Christ, we must not be "unequally yoked together with unbelievers" (see 2 Cor 6.14–7.1). It reminds us that we are a separated and sanctified people (7.1). One must not compromise with the world. "For what fellowship [*metoche*, "sharing"] has righteousness with lawlessness? And what communion [*koinonia*, "participation," "fellowship"] has light with darkness? And what accord [*symphonesis*, "agreement," "harmony," "symphony"] has Christ with Belial? Or what part [*meris*, "part," "portion"] has a believer with an unbeliever? And what agreement [*synkatathesis*, "joint arrangement," "consent"] has the temple of God with idols?" (6.14–16). The cluster of nouns in these verses should help us to understand our relationship to Christ in the Supper.

When we are baptized into the body and blood of Christ, we covenant to die with the Lord to sin and rise with Him to walk in newness of life (Rom 6.3–4). Likewise, when we commune with Jesus, we remember this sacred commitment to the *"blood of the new covenant"* (Matt 26.28). Christians belong to the Lord and eat *the Lord's Supper* (1 Cor 11.20) on *the Lord's Day* (Rev 1.10), *the first day of the week* (Acts 20.7; 1 Cor 16.2). We commune with our Lord.

Man Does Not
Live by Bread Alone

Patrick N. Halbrook

As the Israelites endured the long, hot, dry journey from Egypt to Mount Sinai, they began to run out of food. The days passed, their hunger grew more intense, and they wondered whether God even noticed. They grumbled against Aaron and Moses: "Would that we had died by the LORD's hand in the land of Egypt, when we sat by the pots of meat, when we ate bread to the full; for you have brought us out into this wilderness to kill this whole assembly with hunger!" (Exod 16.3 NASB). But despite their lack of faith, the Lord refused to give up on them. He had not brought them out of Egypt to kill them, but to show them that He would take care of them; He wanted them to understand that He is "compassionate and gracious, slow to anger, and abounding in lovingkindness and truth" (Exod 34.6). God answered their cries by raining down bread from heaven, the miraculous food they came to call *manna* (16.4). God had shown them His power and love, and no longer would they need to worry about what they would eat.

Many years later, when the promised land was within sight and their years of wandering had come to an end, Moses reminded the Israelites of the wonders God had done for them during the previous forty years. The provision of manna, he said, was intended to teach a lesson about the nature of God: "He humbled you, causing you to hunger and then feeding you with manna, which neither you nor your fathers had known, to teach you that man does not live on bread alone but on every word that comes from the mouth of the LORD" (Deut 8.3 NIV).

Like Jesus' parables, manna represented a higher spiritual truth intended to bring God's people to a fuller understanding of their relationship with Him. God became the direct source of His people's physical nourishment because He wanted them to understand that He could also be the source of their spiritual nourishment.

The lie the Israelites were tempted to believe was the same one to which people have always been susceptible: the belief that life can be sustained by "bread alone." Perhaps the Israelites believed that once they had bread in their stomachs, their needs would be met and God would become irrelevant. This belief is not wholly irrational; anyone who consistently eats will not starve to death, as we learn from those who exclude God from their lives. But life in its fullest expression is available to us only when we find in God the spiritual nourishment that can sustain our souls. God created us as physical and spiritual beings, designed to crave both physical and heavenly bread. Neglecting either will leave us hungry.

When Jesus endured His own wilderness wandering—forty days of fasting at the beginning of His ministry—Satan tempted Him as he had the Israelites. He taunted Jesus: "If you are the Son of God, command this stone to become bread" (Luke 4.3 ESV). After going without food for so many days, Jesus' body must have cried out to Him with an intensity we can scarcely imagine.

Yet Jesus resisted Satan, turning for strength to the words of Moses: "It is written, 'Man shall not live by bread alone'" (4.4). While there may have been no bread in Jesus' stomach, His spirit was full and satisfied. He had spent forty intimate days with His Father, praying and meditating and seeking Him. Jesus was living on "every word that comes from the mouth of God," and this spiritual food provided Him with just the nourishment He needed.

Jesus' teachings also reflected this idea. He said that God's coming Kingdom would be a realm in which His provision would cause man's fundamental hungers to cease (Matt 5.6; Luke 6.21), and at the heart of this provision would be Jesus Himself. On one occasion, after miraculously feeding a large crowd by the Sea of Galilee with five barley loaves and two fish, the people began to follow Jesus because they were looking for another handout of food. Jesus rebuked them, describing what they ought to have sought instead:

> Truly, truly, I say to you, you are seeking me, not because you saw signs, but because you ate your fill of the loaves. Do not labor for the food that perishes, but for the food that endures to eternal life, which the Son of Man will give to you. For on him God the Father has set his seal. (John 6.26–27)

The crowd then asked, "Then what sign do you do, that we may see and believe you? What work do you perform? Our fathers ate the manna in the wilderness; as it is written, 'He gave them bread from heaven to eat'" (6.30–31). Jesus again reminded them that they ought to look for something greater than physical food: "Truly, truly, I say to you, it was not Moses who gave you the bread from heaven, but my Father gives you the true bread from heaven. For the bread of God is he who comes down from heaven and gives life to the world" (6.32–33). In a twist of irony, the very thing the people were asking for was standing before them. They needed to understand that Jesus had come "that they may have life and have it abundantly" (John 10.10), and that the abundant life is sustained by the *true* Bread of Life.

The night before His death, Jesus described to His disciples the type of ceremony by which they should remember Him. There are many ways we remember people: we build monuments; we observe moments of silence; we take days off work; we celebrate festivals. Jesus chose none of these. His memorial service would consist of eating bread and drinking the fruit of the vine:

> And He took bread, and when He had given thanks, He broke it and gave it to them, saying, "This is my body, which is given for you. Do this in remembrance of me." And likewise the cup after they had eaten, saying, "This cup that is poured out for you is the new covenant in my blood." (Luke 22.19–20)

From a purely physical perspective, this act of remembrance is rather unfulfilling. For someone who skipped breakfast, a small piece of bread and a sip of grape juice will not leave him feeling very satisfied. But spiritually and symbolically, the Lord's Supper is a royal banquet because it is about Christ, our source of true bread and true nourishment. By eating Christ's "body" and drinking Christ's "blood," we are showing our desire for God to provide us with spiritual nourishment; we are proclaiming that there is something deeper and more fulfilling to life than mere food and drink; we, like our Israelite forefathers, are learning that "Man does not live on bread alone, but on every word that comes from the mouth of the LORD" (NIV).

Our earthly bodies, sustained by bread, will endure for only so many years. No matter what we do to slow or prevent their end, they inevitably decay. But through Christ we may find "the living bread that came down from heaven" (John 6.51). Even those who ate manna in the wilderness eventually died. "But he who feeds on this bread," the Word of God promises us, "will live forever" (6.58).

The Meal Format of the Communion

Martin Pickup

As Christians we commemorate the Lord's death every first day of the week. Yet ironically, we may tend to overlook the most significant aspect of the memorial that the Lord instituted: the fact that He designed it to be in the form of a meal.

Human beings have come up with numerous ways to commemorate great heroes and key events of history, and surely there are any number of ways in which God might have structured a commemoration of His Son's death. But He fashioned it in the form of a meal. Paul called this memorial the Lord's *deipnon* (1 Cor 11.20), a Greek word that referred to a supper or feast, and that normally designated the main meal of the day. Though the Corinthians went to a carnal extreme by turning this memorial into an opportunity to feed their stomachs and foster division, it is clear that Paul did not object to the meal format of their communion itself, for this was the format that Jesus established originally (vv 20–34). The pinch of bread and the tiny cup that we see most often in our communion services today may have emerged as a way of preventing a reoccurrence of the Corinthians' carnality (certainly a noble goal). But regardless of the size of the portions we consume when we partake of the Lord's Supper, we must not lose sight of the significance of the meal format of the memorial Jesus established.

Jesus even instituted His memorial on the occasion of another commemorative meal: the Passover (Luke 22.14–20). But unlike the Passover, the supper of the Lord does more than mark the anniversary of an historical event. Jesus' new meal consists of two items that He declared symbolic of Himself. Meals comprise food and drink, the two elements necessary to sustain life. The supper that Jesus established likewise consists of food and drink, but of a most remarkable kind. He said of the bread, "This is My body"—and of the fruit of the vine, "This is My blood." Whenever we partake of the Lord's Supper, we are symbolically consuming the flesh and the blood of our Lord!

Powerful Imagery

Jesus' imagery is quite graphic—one might even say gruesome. Our Lord was obviously speaking metaphorically, for His apostles surely understood on that occasion that they were not literally consuming the flesh and the blood of the man who sat before them. Yet many people have misunderstood this kind of language. There is evidence that the early Christians were suspected by non-Christians of practicing cannibalism, due in part perhaps to reports that Christians ate flesh and drank blood in their weekly assemblies.[1] A failure to appreciate Jesus' use of figurative language has caused Catholicism to concoct the false idea of transubstantiation—a doctrine that claims that when a priest prays over the elements of the Eucharist, the bread and wine are miraculously transformed into the actual body and blood of Jesus, while still maintaining their original appearance.

In our desire to avoid any appearance of the Catholic misconception in our communion (or perhaps to blunt the gruesome imagery of Jesus' words a bit?), we tend to avoid the metaphorical language that Jesus used. In communion services today one rarely hears men at the table repeat Jesus' original statement. Instead, they insert terms like *represents* or *symbolizes,* as in "This bread represents His body" or "This cup symbolizes His blood." Now, of course, we must not mandate the use of some particular phraseology. But in our reticence to use Jesus' precise language we may unwittingly be hindering people from appreciating the fact that the Lord designed this memorial to be in the form of a meal consisting of the most astonishing of food items. Symbolically, to be sure—but, nevertheless, in a true sense Christians eat the crucified flesh of Jesus and drink His sacrificial blood every first day of the week.

Purpose of the Meal Format

But why? What was the Lord's purpose in having His disciples engage in such a startling practice? I would suggest several reasons. First, metaphor—speaking of one thing as if it were something else—is the strongest possible means of associating two concepts. Jesus wants us to see a connection between bread, the staple of life, and His body that was nailed to the cross as an atonement for sin. He wants us to see a connection between our need to quench physical thirst and our need for the life-sustaining blood that He shed on the cross. Jesus wants us to engage in the physical act of consuming these symbolic elements just as we would consume physical food and drink, so that we will grasp the spiritual significance of His death in a very personal and powerful way.

Observing the Lord's Supper each week reminds us that Jesus is our spiritual food. Just as our bodies will die without physical sustenance, so our souls will die without the spiritual sustenance of Christ. The Lord taught the same lesson in John 6 when He said,

> I am the living bread that came down out of heaven; if anyone eats of this bread, he will live forever; and the bread also which I will give for the life of the world is My flesh. ...Truly, truly, I say to you, unless you eat the flesh of the Son of Man and drink His blood, you have no life in yourselves. He who eats My flesh and drinks My blood has eternal life. (vv 51–54 NASB)

Jesus wasn't talking about the Lord's Supper in this passage, but He *was* teaching verbally the lesson that the Lord's Supper teaches non-verbally: He is our one and only spiritual food and our only source of eternal life.

The blood that Jesus shed on the cross is the means by which we receive eternal life. "The life is in the blood," God declared in the Old Testament (Lev 17.11; *cf.* Gen 9.4). In other words, the life force of an animal or a human being is the blood that runs throughout their bodies. It was for this reason that many ancient cultures associated consuming the blood of an animal with ingesting its power. What more graphic reminder could Jesus give that His blood is the means of our life and strength than in a memorial meal like this one in which we imbibe, so to speak, our Master's blood?

Another startling thing about this memorial meal is that we are engaging in a figurative action that would be reprehensible in a literal sense. Eating human flesh is unthinkable. Drinking the blood of an animal was condemned by God from the very beginning (Lev 17.11–14), and certainly the idea of drinking our Savior's blood is, on the surface, a revolting contemplation. But such is the nature of the actual sacrifice of Jesus on the cross. The sacrifice of a human being was always reprehensible to God (Jer 19.5). Yet it was the sacrifice of a human being—the incarnate Son of God—that was necessary to take away the sin of the world. The unthinkable nature of the acts of communion if performed in real life serves to highlight how extraordinary the sacrifice of Christ really was.

Every Sunday as we partake of the body and the blood of the Lord, it should be a sober reminder of the magnitude of Jesus' sacrifice and how absolutely vital He is to us. Partaking of the Lord's Supper should shake us out of our spiritual lethargy and motivate us to renewed dedication and service. What an amazing memorial the Lord established!

The Lord's Supper
Four Meals in One

Edwin L. Crozier

The Lord's Supper: A Memorial Meal

If there is anything we remember about Jesus' institution of His supper, it is His statement, "Do this in remembrance of me" (Luke 22.19). Paul highlighted the memorial nature of the Supper in 1 Corinthians 11.24–25, twice repeating that we eat this meal not to assuage our hunger but to remember Jesus' death.

The concept of *memorial* was not new in the New Testament, which itself was not written in a vacuum. Rather, the concept of memorial was well known throughout the Old Testament and the Lord's Supper was established within this well-known context.

Most are familiar with the Passover, the Old Testament meal in which the Jews participated yearly to memorialize their deliverance from Egyptian bondage. According to Exodus 12.14, the Passover meal was a day of memorial: "You shall keep it as a feast to the LORD; throughout your generations, as a statute forever, you shall keep it as a feast" (ESV). Exodus 13.9, speaking of the annual Feast of Unleavened Bread that accompanied the Passover, provides a great word picture for the purpose of these memorials. "It shall be to you as a sign on your hand and as a memorial between your eyes, that the law of the LORD may be in your mouth. For with a strong hand the LORD has brought you out of Egypt." These feasts—these memorial meals—were to serve as a reminder like something written on the rememberers' hands or planted between their eyes. But there was a greater purpose. The memorial was not just a reminder of what God had done, but of what the participants were to do in response to God's work. The law of the Lord must be in our hearts and minds. Thus, each Sunday we participate in this Supper to remind us of God's deliverance but also of our need to obey Him.

Joshua 4.1–7 provides another reason for memorials. The Israelites took 12 stones from the Jordan as they crossed, under Joshua's lead, and set them up as a memorial. This memorial was not just for the people who crossed the Jordan but for their descendants. It reminded each new generation of what God had done for their nation and their ancestors. The memorial was a proclamation of God's good news for each new generation. No wonder Paul speaks of the Lord's Supper as a proclamation in 1 Corinthians 11.26. The memorial for us becomes evangelism for our children and for others in our assemblies. Through reminding ourselves of the 'old, old story,' we teach others a new story of grace, love and forgiveness. As they wonder why we eat that bread and drink that juice, we proclaim to them the story of Jesus Christ who died for them.

Finally, when we recognize the Lord's Supper as a memorial meal, we find an interesting contrast in Hebrews 10.1–3. For years, under the Old Covenant, the Jews traveled to Jerusalem to offer and eat of sacrifices that atoned for their sins. However, the Hebrew author explains that each sacrifice provided a different memorial for them. If their sacrifices had actually forgiven them, they could have ceased offering them. However, their sacrifices offered "a reminder of sins every year." As they ate their sacrifices, they were reminded of their sins. They were reminded they needed a Savior to come because the blood of bulls and goats could not save them. However, according to Hebrews 10.10–18, the sacrifice of Jesus, offered once for all, truly provides forgiveness. No more sacrifice is needed. We do not sacrifice Jesus again with each participation in this meal. Rather, we remind ourselves of that which our Old Testament counterparts were never able to enjoy fully. We do not have a weekly reminder that we are still in our sins. We have a weekly reminder that we have a Savior whose sacrifice has cleansed us. We have a weekly reminder of forgiveness.

As we partake in the Lord's Supper, it must not be a casual snack in the middle of our assemblies. It must be a memorial. Let us remember what God has done for us. Let us remember forgiveness. Let us remember deliverance. Let us proclaim our faith to our children and others through our remembrance. Do this in remembrance of Jesus.

The Lord's Supper: A Sacrificial Meal

When Jesus instituted the Lord's Supper, He said of the bread, "This is my body, which is given for you" (Luke 22.19). He said of the fruit of the vine, "This cup that is poured out for you is the new covenant in my blood" (Luke 22.20).

A body given for us. Blood poured out for us. Jesus was speaking of sacrifice. A body would be slain and lifeblood poured out on the ground, just as the Jews had done for years at the temple in Jerusalem. No wonder Jesus' cousin John, recalling a millennium of sacrifices, said of Jesus, "Behold, the Lamb of God, who takes away the sin of the world!" (John 1.29).

One commonly overlooked aspect of Old Testament sacrifices is that they were often eaten by the priests and those who offered them. Most of us recognize this with the Passover sacrifice. Exodus 12.6–10 describes how the Israelites were to slay and then eat the Passover lamb. However, few recognize that many of the other sacrifices were also eaten. Deuteronomy 12.6–7 and 17–18 both explain that burnt offerings, tithes and other sacrifices were to be brought to the Lord and eaten before Him. According to 1 Corinthians 10.18, those who ate the sacrifices were participants in the altar. Eating the sacrifice was a visible representation of taking the atonement into their bodies.

Perhaps two Old Testament sacrifices most often come to mind when we think of Jesus' sacrifice. The Passover we have already mentioned. First Corinthians 5.7 says Jesus is our Passover. As the Israelites ate the Passover sacrifice in that first observance and the blood of the lamb was painted on their doorpost to ward off the death of their first born, so do we, in a sense, ward off the wrath of God by faithful participation in the Supper. Not that the Supper is a sacrament, but that when faithful Christians participate faithfully in this sacrificial meal, they declare their participation in the atonement of the sacrifice.

The annual atonement sacrifice, first taught in Leviticus 16–17, clearly relates to Jesus' sacrifice as seen in Hebrews 10.1–18. On that one day of the year, the High Priest would carry the sins of the nation into the Most Holy Place of the temple and seek atonement from God for them. We, however, participate in the sacrifice of our High Priest as we eat His body and drink His blood each first day of the week. We are all priests who may come into the presence of the Holy God by the blood of His Son. Each week we participate in a sacrificial meal that reminds us of this confidence we have (Heb 10.19–25) to enter God's presence because we have participated in the altar of Jesus' sacrifice.

Considering the nature of sacrificial meals, we cannot help noticing one significant difference between the sacrificial meals of the Old Testament and that of the New. We do something completely different with the blood of our sacrifice. Under the Old Covenant, the flesh of the sacrifice was eaten, but the blood was not to be drunk. It was to be poured out (Deut 12.16, 26–27). Under the Old Covenant, those who drank the blood of their sacrifice would be cut off from among the people (Lev 17.10). We, however, drink the blood of our sacrifice. The fruit of the vine is Jesus' blood of the New Covenant. According to Leviticus 17.11, "The life of the flesh is in the blood, and I have given it for you on the altar to make atonement for your souls, for it is the blood that makes atonement by the life." Under the Old Covenant, the blood which contained life was not to be drunk. Yet we, figuratively, drink the blood of our sacrifice, imbibing the life contained in the blood of Jesus Christ.

As we participate in the Lord's Supper, we are eating the flesh of our sacrifice, participating in the altar of atonement He provided. We are also drinking the blood of our sacrifice, taking His life to ourselves. Yes, this is all a figure. The Lord's Supper is not a sacrament that mystically provides grace when we eat the sacrifice. It is, however, a figure that tells us exactly what Jesus has done for us. He sacrificed His body that we might have atonement. He has poured out His blood that we might have life.

Let us share in the altar of Jesus Christ and celebrate the life we have in His name.

The Lord's Supper: A Covenant Meal

When Jesus instituted the Lord's Supper, He said, "This cup that is poured out for you is the new covenant in my blood" (Luke 22.20). One aspect of the Lord's Supper we often overlook because of our cultural background is the covenant meal. Covenants, for us, are a matter of papers, lawyers and courts. For our biblical counterparts, participating in a covenant was a very special activity. As with the other meal concepts, the Old Testament provides an instructive background for this.

According to the *International Standard Bible Encyclopedia*, an ancient covenant between two parties had four parts.

1. *A statement of the covenant's terms:* For example, the covenant between Laban and Jacob in Genesis 31.44–54 stipulated that Jacob would not mistreat Laban's daughters or marry anyone else. Additionally, neither Jacob nor Laban would ever pass the heap of stones they were setting up in order to harm the other.

2. *An oath or commitment to the covenant:* Notice in Genesis 31.53 that Jacob took an oath to abide by the covenant.

3. *A curse upon the parties if they violate the covenant:* In Genesis 31.53, Laban stated the curse of breaking their covenant. If either of them broke it, then the God of Abraham would judge between them. Another example is God's covenant with Old Testament Israel. Upon making that covenant with them, He pronounced the curses upon them if they would not obey. See Deuteronomy 27.15–26; 28.15–68.

4. *An external act of ratification:* In the Old Testament, this usually took the form of a sacrifice and sharing in that sacrifice in some way. In some cases, they would cut the animal in two and the covenanters would walk between them (Jer 34.18). In

others, they would sprinkle the blood of the sacrifice on the covenanters (Exod 24.6–8). In some cases, they would eat a sacrificial meal together, that is, they would have a covenant meal (Gen 31.54).[1]

The Lord's Supper is our covenant meal. The Lord's Supper is our external act of ratification of the covenant agreement we have with God.

1. The agreed upon terms are that God grants us forgiveness and we agree to live as new men, dead to sin and alive to Him (Rom 6.1–23).

2. Our commitment to the covenant took place in baptism, when our consciences were sprinkled clean by the blood of Christ (Heb 10.19, 22). When we eat the Lord's Supper covenant meal, partaking in the body and blood of our covenant sacrifice, we are remembering the commitment we have made to obey the Lord always. Further, we are continually reminded of the promises God made on His end of our covenant agreement.

3. At the same time, we are reminded of the curse we are under if we trample under foot the blood of the covenant, violating the covenant agreement. According to Hebrews 10.29–31, if we drink this cup on Sunday but on Monday go about sinning willfully in rebellion to God, we will fall into His terrifying hands. Eating this meal does not make us clean; it reminds us of God's cleansing and what we are to do for Him.

4. This meal, the Lord's Supper, is our ratification and agreement to the covenant. Unlike the covenant meal between Jacob and Laban which took place once, and after which they parted ways, we participate in this covenant meal every week. It is a weekly reminder of the covenant to which we have agreed. It is a weekly reminder of both sides of the covenant agreement, God's side and ours. It is a weekly re-ratification of our agreement to serve the Lord because He has forgiven us.

Here is the great thing about our covenant. We can trust God to keep His end of the covenant. He cannot lie (Heb 6.17–20). As we partake, let us allow this reminder to be a motivator for us to serve the Lord all week long. Jesus sacrificed Himself to establish this covenant. Let us remember not just to take the Supper, but also to keep the covenant.

The Lord's Supper: A Communion Meal

Perhaps our most common concept of the Lord's Supper is found in the word *communion*. First Corinthians 10.16 calls the supper a communion in the body and blood of the Lord. Thus we have adopted the word *communion* as another title for the meal. The idea of communion is sharing or fellowship. It highlights the fact that through this supper we are a community, separate from the rest of the world. Through the supper we have fellowship, not because we are eating, but because of our spiritual connection.

The concept of communion through this kind of memorial has its roots in the Old Testament, as do all the meal concepts of the Supper. When the Israelites ate their sacrificial meals they were not simply doing so by themselves. They were commanded to do so in the place where God desired His presence to be (Deut 12.5–7, 18; 14.23). They were eating with God. The people ate their portion of the sacrifice in God's presence as He consumed His portion of the sacrifice in the fires of the altar. As Paul stated in 1 Corinthians 10.18, those who ate the sacrifices were participants in the altar. That is, they were in fellowship with the altar, sharing in the blessings of the altar's sacrifice and doing so in fellowship with God as He also shared in the altar.

There is, perhaps, no better illustration of this communion with God than the story found in Exodus 24. On the heels of their covenant ratification, the leaders of national Israel went up on the forbidden mountain to commune with God. These 74 men ate in God's presence, even seeing some kind of visible representation of Him. I can only imagine what that must have been like. Why were they able to commune with God? On their own merits, they were not allowed to touch the mountain; doing so meant death (Exod 19.12–13). All things being equal, this should not have been allowed. However, all things were not equal; God's mercy and grace were part of this equation. These men had been party to the sacrifices just offered, they had received the sprinkled blood, they had confirmed their willingness to obey (Exod 24.5–7), but they had not earned the right to commune with God. They had not climbed the heights of personal strength and worth to be on a level with God. Rather, God condescended to these men and communed with them. They deserved death. Instead, they received a confirmation of the life God gave them through His covenant. What a great God they served!

As we partake in the Lord's Supper, we are also participating with God, communing with God, especially in the person of Jesus, God the Son. First Corinthians 10.16 says we are in fellowship with the body and blood of the Lord as we partake. Just as the Jews shared in their altar by their meal, we share in the cross of Christ through this meal. We are further participating in communion with Christ as He promised in Matthew 26.29 (*cf.* Luke 22.16). Now that God's kingdom is established, Jesus is eating with us when we share the communion. We do not see a visible representation of Him, but He is there as we partake. As the Israelites ate in the presence of God, we eat in the presence of Jesus Christ. Yet, we must not forget the lessons of Exodus 24. We are not communing with Christ because we have gained worthiness through our baptism. Rather, our great and glorious God is condescending to commune with us through the Supper. We have come to the forbidden mountain to connect with God. All things being equal, we deserve death for even presuming to sit at the table with Jesus Christ. Yet all things are not equal; we do not die. The very sacrifice we celebrate through this communion has provided us the grace and mercy we need to commune with God. Instead of death, we receive confirmation of the life we have through Jesus. We do not come to this table because we presume any great prominence, but because we have humbly accepted the invitation of our Gracious Host. What a great God we serve!

In addition to communion with the cross, with God and with Jesus, we are also in communion with one another. According to 1 John 1.7, every person who walks in the light is in fellowship with every other Christian who walks in the light. As we commune with one another in the Supper, we are reminded of our constant communion with one another through the forgiving blood of Jesus Christ. As Paul said in 1 Corinthians 10.17, because every Christian participates in the same bread, which represents Christ's body, we who are many are one body. We are all in fellowship with one another through the body and blood of our Lord Jesus Christ, and the meal represents that communion, not because we are eating together, but because we are sharing in the same Savior. The fact that we Christians of all races, countries, cultures, backgrounds and classes participate in the same Supper, in fellowship with the same Sacrifice and Savior, demonstrates our sharing with one another not only in the body of Christ that hung on the cross, but also in the body of Christ that is present in the world today—His church (Eph 1.22–23). In Christ, there is neither Jew nor Greek, slave nor free, male nor female, black nor white, rich nor poor, American nor Russian, Republican nor Democrat; all are one in Christ Jesus (Gal 3.28).

I am reminded of 1 Peter 1.2. Peter was writing to Christians dispersed throughout multiple geographical locations. Each region would have its own norms, dialects, traditions, and culture. Each region was its own community. As people moved between these regions, it would be obvious that they were from a different community. Yet the Christians dispersed throughout these different cultures all had their own culture—their own community. Geographical barriers or lines of governmental demarcation did not bind this community; the body and blood of Jesus Christ bound this community. Whether they traveled far and wide or stayed in the land of their physical birth, they were distinct and different, part of a foreign community. Their citizenship was in heaven (Phil 3.20). They were in communion with Jesus Christ, His cleansing blood and His cleansed people. The Supper reminded them of their community every week.

As we partake in this communion meal, let us remember our true community and with whom we are to be in communion. In 1 Corinthians 10, Paul's concern was with Christians eating of Christ's altar on Sunday and the idols' altars throughout the week. While we are not in danger of eating from the altar of Zeus, this communion meal reminds us to be in communion with God all the time. We are not to be in fellowship with unrighteousness throughout the week and then try to claim fellowship with Christ through this meal on Sunday. We learn this lesson also from Exodus 24. What a glorious event it was for the 74 men to eat in the presence of God. Yet, in less than 40 days, 72 of these men (assuming Joshua was one of the 70 leaders) were involved in idolatry (Exod 32). Even Aaron, Israel's interim leader (Exod 24.14), made the calf. The communion meal of the leaders with God did not simply cover this breach as if it had been the sacramental means by which they received God's grace. The communion meal was not a grace-filled license to turn from God, but a reminder to submit to the gracious God. Sadly, the leaders did not allow that communion meal to stay with them. The reminder was forgotten. They communed in the meal, but not all the time.

Our communion meal is not a sacrament. We do not live how ever we want and then receive grace through the Supper. Rather, our communion in this meal should represent and remind us how to live at all times, in communion with God, with Christ, with the cross and with Christ's people. We must not let it be an event that affects us only on Sundays. Rather, we must let it be a governing principle of our lives. Perhaps this is why a weekly observance is so important. We need to be reminded of our community. We need to be reminded of our common Savior. We need to be reminded of our common God. We need to be reminded of our common forgiveness. We need to be reminded of our communion. Glory and revel in this communion today, but do not leave it here. Carry this communion meal with you in your heart throughout the week.

When we partake, let us remember our true Communion.

In Remembrance of Me

Nathan Quinn

He was a great pioneer in the Midwest from the middle of the 19th century. He led a train of people across the Prairie Lands and settled just east of the Rockies in an area that is now a small Colorado town. This man was known for his courage, integrity, and great leadership abilities, along with his deep concern for every person, from the least to the greatest, in his particular wagon train. During this journey, he single-handedly made peace with the Native Americans and established good relations with those who had lived off the land before his company's arrival. He was involved in nearly every family's construction project as they broke ground for the first time. He made sure that everyone was equally satisfied with his lot. He was a man among men, one who loved life, loved his fellow man, and did all he could to improve the world in which he lived.

The modern town is now full of middle class Americans pursuing the American dream, a town full of two-car garages with two-and-a-half kids playing in every yard, with a little league and a successful high school football program (they placed second in state last year!). This budding community is the type of place in which you would want to raise your kids. In the City Square there is an old oak tree which was planted long ago, and at the foot of the tree sits a small plaque. Inscribed on the plaque is the name of the man after whom this community is named. Children occasionally read the short epitaph, but then continue playing. The adults no longer read the plaque at all, but if you asked them if they knew the man's full name they would be quick to refer you to "that tree in the square." The sad thing is that this once-great man has now been reduced to a name on a tree. His works have been forgotten, his courage is unknown—and all are unaware of the sacrifices he made for that community. The memorial failed because someone forgot to tell his story, and now he exists only as a tree in a park.

When people observe something regularly, they tend to turn off their minds, not seeing the significance of what is set before them. When a ritual becomes familiar, people may simply go through the motions, and all significance of what they do can be lost. This often happens to memorials. Veterans Day becomes a day off school or work, and Independence Day becomes a spectacular fireworks display. Too many of these memorials have lost the meaning they were intended to have.

Christians are given a memorial to "do this in remembrance of me" (Luke 22.19). Sometimes I fear that this memorial is done in the memory of having a memorial—in other words, 'We still do this today as the disciples did in the first century.' But did the disciples break bread to remember they had a memorial? Or did they break bread to remember Christ and proclaim His death until He comes?

What is your focus when you break bread? Is it solely to fulfill a religious duty to appease a temperamental god? Do we break bread out of tradition? Or is the supper an opportunity to honor the Lord's Son by focusing on and remembering the man, Jesus Christ? If all you ever think about in breaking bread is the fact that the disciples gave us an example to break bread, then you may have substituted the memorial for the One who is to be remembered.

Once we have committed ourselves to remembering Jesus, we may ask ourselves, 'What about Jesus is to be remembered?' Jesus' life was full of moments about which we could meditate. But as we gather around the table to partake of the Lord's memorial, the primary focus should be on remembering Jesus' death, burial and resurrection.

Paul wrote, "For as often as you eat this bread and drink the cup, you proclaim the Lord's death until He comes" (1 Cor 11.26 NASB). The Lord's death is the focal point for this memorial supper. As we break bread we are announcing what Jesus did for our sins. We are proclaiming the Lord's death and showing our belief in this sacrifice. We are boldly stating our confidence in Jesus' broken body, the pouring out of His blood for our forgiveness, and the victory He shares with us: His rising from the grave. The supper is an opportunity to shout out unashamedly our conviction of Jesus' redeeming work on the cross.

There are many impressive aspects of Jesus' life, but none of them have the same importance or relevance during the Lord's Supper as what Jesus did for us on the cross. Consider the miracles when Jesus fed the multitudes. We may remember those moments in Jesus' life because they impress us and teach us how Jesus provides. They reveal Jesus to have the same power God once showed in the wilderness as He rained bread from heaven—but do they save us? Consider the faith-building miracle when Jesus walked on the water. Again, we may be amazed at the Jesus' power over nature, but without the cross, what good does walking on the water do? Jesus performed many miracles, but none of them could bring about our salvation from sin, except the cross. The cross is where we make our boast (Gal 6.14) because without the events which occurred on the three days beginning with the day of the crucifixion, we would still be hopelessly lost.

The Lord's Supper is a time for God's people to consider the body of the Lord and "judge the body rightly" (1 Cor 11:29). The church at Corinth had failed to do this, and as a result many were weak in faith and were dying spiritually (1 Cor 11.30). We need to be sure we understand what we are telling each other when we partake of this feast. Every memorial has its purpose; the Lord's memorial is no different. The Lord commanded us to break bread for a reason, and it must be done according to truth and in a manner that honors God. It should never be old or mundane. Though the feast is observed each week, it must be fresh and significant each time God's people come together to observe it. When we remember Jesus, the feast will help us draw closer to God and become more spiritually minded. This feast helps us remember the single greatest mission ever accomplished, the basis for our hope, and the reason we can have forgiveness. In this supper we joyfully and soberly remind ourselves of the moment when Christ breathed His last and yielded up His Spirit so we could live. We tell the world that Jesus died on the cross and purchased our redemption (1 Pet 1.18–19). May we praise God for this tremendous blessing, and may we remember.

Communing in Memory of Him

Reagan Allen McClenny

When Jesus instituted the Lord's Supper, it was no coincidence that He did so during the Passover feast. The Communion is the New Testament equivalent of the Jewish Passover, the feast that commemorated the freedom of the Hebrew nation from Egyptian bondage. While the Passover feast called to remembrance a physical emancipation, this Feast memorializes the freedom we can receive from the spiritual bondage of sin and death through the crucifixion of Christ.

Few Christians question the importance of the Lord's Supper. However, it is easy to forget exactly what we are doing. In a spirit of restoration, let us examine the Lord's Supper as it was instituted by Christ and observed by the New Testament church to determine some common mistakes to avoid when we partake of it.

Mistakes to Avoid When Partaking of the Lord's Supper

Partaking in an Unworthy Manner

When we strive to avoid mistakes concerning the Lord's Supper, the obvious place to begin is by eliminating the mistakes made by the early church. First Corinthians 11.27–29 says,

> Therefore whoever eats this bread or drinks this cup in an un-
> worthy manner will be guilty of the body and blood of the Lord.
> But let a man examine himself, and so let him eat of that bread
> and drink of that cup. For he who eats and drinks in an unwor-

thy manner eats and drinks judgment to himself, not discerning the Lord's body. (NKJV)

First, we partake in a worthy manner by examining ourselves before we partake. Do we have a right state of mind? Are we living as we should as Christians? We need to make sure we are right before God and focused on Christ before we partake.

Second, the Lord's Supper cannot become common if we partake in a worthy manner. By apostolic example, we see that the Communion is to be taken by believers, on every first day of the week, wherever the disciples are gathered. Acts 20.7 says, "Now on the first day of the week, when the disciples came together to break bread, Paul, ready to depart the next day, spoke to them and continued his message until midnight." While the New Testament shows us that the early church also performed other acts of worship while assembled, the disciples assembled on the Lord's Day with the express purpose of partaking of the Lord's Supper. This does not mean that the Lord's Supper was more important than the other acts of worship, but it does show an emphasis that is often lacking in the church today. Among some followers of Christ, when we "come together in one place, it is not to eat the Lord's Supper" (1 Cor 11.20) because the Communion has become something we fulfill as swiftly as possible in order to leave enough time for the "weightier matters" like the sermon. It is difficult to partake as we should when we have not invested time, thought, and energy, both before and during the partaking.

Even though we partake every week, we should see our communion—our fellowship with the Lord—as the awesome privilege it is, every time we have the opportunity. Nichol and Whiteside comment,

> The church at Corinth had corrupted the Lord's Supper till it was no longer the Lord's Supper. It was a common meal; each took his own supper. Some were full, others were hungry. For this reason Paul said, "When therefore ye assemble yourselves together, it is not possible to eat the Lord's Supper" (1 Cor 11.20). They were eating and drinking in an unworthy manner.

It is not likely now that any will imitate their excesses, but it is yet possible to commit the same sin, possible yet to eat in an unworthy manner. In their eating they failed to discern the Lord's body—they made no difference between this eating and a common meal. May we not eat the bread and drink the cup with no thought of its significance, not discerning in them the representations of his body and blood? "For he that eateth and drinketh, eateth and drinketh judgment unto himself, if he discern not the body" (1 Cor 11.29). Do you eat and drink in a light, flippant way? If so, you eat and drink in an unworthy manner.[1]

This flippancy can be the byproduct of the way the Lord's Supper is administered. Two main contributors to this problem are a lack of preparation by those serving the Lord's Supper and an overly-condensed time to partake. The Lord's Supper should be treated as the important part of the worship service that it is. This includes not only using songs, prayers, and talks to prepare the minds of those who partake, but also allotting enough time for them to meditate on the Suffering Savior—regardless of how long it takes to pass around the emblems. While "expediency" should be considered, our chief concern in serving the Lord's Supper is to create an environment most conducive to partaking in a *worthy manner.*

Failing to Concentrate on Christ
Perhaps the most common problem faced by the Christian partaking of the Lord's Supper is the wandering mind. The following story illustrates the attitude of many "mature" Christians:

As the young man considered the meaning of the Lord's Supper, a tear slipped silently down his face. His mother, trying to remember if she had turned off the roast, noticed and asked, "What's wrong son?" He hesitated—"The greatness... what Jesus has done for me... it gets to me." "Well," she replied, "don't take it so seriously."[2]

How often do Christians allow their minds to drift to things other than Christ while partaking of the Lord's Supper? How seriously do we take this sacred rite?

There are some things that simply take precedence over everything else, and communing at the Lord's Table is one of those things. I am not suggesting that we need to cry to prove our emotional involvement in the moment, but we should have the strength of mind to focus for the brief time we are partaking. If we struggle with wandering minds, then we can read from the Bible the accounts of His suffering, we can think about the words to the song we have sung before the Lord's Supper, or we can consider the things said by those who are serving, in their comments or their prayers. However we accomplish it, we should do whatever it takes to focus on Him.

Focusing on 'How It Makes Me Feel,' Rather Than on Christ
In an apparent attempt to combat the common mistakes of de-emphasizing the Lord's Supper and drifting thoughts, many Christians have changed how the Lord's Supper is carried out. In many groups, the time of silence and personal reflection has been replaced by a period of sharing where individuals express their personal feelings regarding Christ's sacrifice. During this time of group discussion, those in attendance are asked questions like, "How do you feel about Christ's sacrifice?" or "What does the crucifixion mean to you?" There are at least two inherent dangers in this non-traditional format.

First, our focus should always be on Christ, not on the way the Supper 'makes me feel.' While I agree that we need to be examining ourselves before we can partake properly, and that the Lord's Supper should certainly involve great emotion, our emotion should be a result of focusing on Christ rather than focusing on an emotional experience. In other words, the emphasis should not be on emotions; emotions will result from a proper focus on Christ's sacrifice. His Supper, His Communion, is about what He did. By focusing on my feelings and my thoughts—proper though that may be in another context—I remove the focus from Christ.

This Supper is the Christian memorial of Christ's sacrifice. When we think of a memorial, be it a physical monument like the Lincoln Memorial or a memorial-holiday like Veterans Day, we see that its purpose is to proclaim the greatness of something or someone. We commemorate what they did—their actions, their work, or their sacrifice. The same is true of the Lord's Supper. First Corinthians 11.23–26 says,

> For I received from the Lord what I also delivered to you, that the Lord Jesus on the night he was betrayed took bread, and when he had given thanks, he broke it, and said, "This is my body which is for you. Do this in remembrance of me." In the same way also he took the cup, after supper, saying, "This cup is the new covenant in my blood. Do this, as often as you drink it, in remembrance of me." For as often as you eat this bread and drink the cup, you proclaim the Lord's death until he comes. (ESV)

We perform this act "in remembrance" of Him so that we do not forget how great a sacrifice He gave and what it means to our soul. It commemorates His life and His death, and we "proclaim His death until He comes." We proclaim how great His death was in that it provided a way for us to be saved. The Lord's Supper is declarative in nature; it is a witness of the greatest sacrifice of all the ages. The Lord's Supper is our memorial of Christ and of His willingness to die on our behalf.

Therefore, the Lord's Supper is only about me in that Christ's sacrifice was for me, and for each one of us, and that we can have fellowship with Him because of that sacrifice. The focus, however, should remain on Him.

Second, having an oral "sharing period" during the meal destroys the privacy and intimacy we should have with the Lord while partaking. First Corinthians 10.16–17 says, "The cup of blessing which we bless, is it not the communion of the blood of Christ? The bread which we break, is it not the communion of the body of Christ? For we, being many, are one bread and one body; for we all partake of that one bread" (NKJV).

Webster defines *commune* as "to be in intimate communication or rapport." It is a private fellowship, or sharing, with Christ and other Christians. In the ancient world, eating at another's table was a sign of fellowship and intimacy. In fact, verse 21 shows this connection between being at the table and having fellowship when it says, "You cannot drink the cup of the Lord and the cup of demons; you cannot partake of the Lord 's table and the table of demons." When we partake of the emblems of the communion, we are at the Lord's table, and thus we are in very close fellowship with Him. This fellowship is attainable only by believers who have a covenant relationship with Him—the saved ones of Christ's church—as evidenced by the "one body" mentioned in verse 17. The saved are the ones invited to the feast at His table, where we have communion with Him and one another.

Clearly, we have no more intimate, direct fellowship with the sacrifice of Christ than in the communion feast. We are partaking of His body, figuratively putting Christ into ourselves through eating the bread and fruit of the vine that symbolize His flesh and blood. When we partake in a right manner, our hearts and minds are consciously centered upon the suffering, crucified Savior and the blessings derived from His loving sacrifice. Perhaps most importantly, we have a foretaste of heavenly glory when our fellowship with Christ will be full and unending. That is part of what Jesus is saying in Matthew 26.29: "But I say to you, I will not drink of this fruit of the vine from now on until that day when I drink it new with you in My Father's kingdom." While the Lord's Supper is the fulfillment of the Passover, it is just a small taste of the things to come in Heaven.

This foretaste of heavenly communion is not a public fellowship, but one of the most private interactions we have with our Lord. Therefore, we should do all that we can to make sure our undivided attention is on Him and Him alone. Listening to the thoughts of others *during* Communion diverts our attention from Him, while having a period of quiet reflection allows us to think back to His sacrifice. The difference is between reflecting on the meaning of the emblems, on the one hand, and talking about your responses, on the other. It is the difference between listening to a song's lyrics and talking about how the song makes you feel. During the Lord's Supper, we are to remember and focus on Christ, not talk about how we remember and focus on Christ.

While there is great value in preparing our minds for the partaking through talks, Scripture readings, songs, and prayers, the Lord's Supper itself should be characterized by our personal contemplation on Christ's death. When this occurs and we all have communion with Him, we also achieve a great unity and fellowship with one another—as Christ intended.

Hebrews 9.22 says, "Without the shedding of blood there is no forgiveness of sins" (ESV). Jesus Christ shed His perfect blood, while we were yet sinners, so that we might have the hope of everlasting life. The Lord's Supper, the Communion of the body and blood of Christ, is a needed reminder of the magnitude of that awesome sacrifice. What indescribable love! What humbling mercy! What awesome communion! It should be the goal of every Christian to partake in a manner well-pleasing unto Him—for He is what it is all about.

The Feast of Unleavened Bread

Ethan R. Longhenry

Now as they were eating, Jesus took bread, and after blessing it broke it and gave it to the disciples, and said, "Take, eat; this is my body." (Matt 26.26 ESV)

Thus Jesus inaugurates the observance of the Lord's Supper that Passover night so many years ago. We can be sure that the bread that Jesus took up that night was unleavened, for the Passover night led into the Feast of Unleavened Bread, memorializing Israel's deliverance accomplished in Moses' day.

We learn of the Feast of Unleavened Bread from Exodus 12. The observance began with a complete purging of leaven (or yeast) from every Israelite house, and the Israelites were then not to eat anything leavened for seven days (Exod 12.15–20). The event is described in Exodus 12.39: "And they baked unleavened cakes of the dough that they had brought out of Egypt, for it was not leavened, because they were thrust out of Egypt and could not wait, nor had they prepared any provisions for themselves."

God initiates the memorial and provides the reason for the observance in Exodus 13.3: "Then Moses said to the people, 'Remember this day in which you came out from Egypt, out of the house of slavery, for by a strong hand the LORD brought you out from this place. No leavened bread shall be eaten.'"

The Feast of the Unleavened Bread memorialized Israel's flight from Egypt and their deliverance from bondage. The bread was to be unleavened since the Israelites had needed to depart quickly with no time to wait for the bread to rise. Israel was a people on the move.

Thus it came to pass that when Jesus broke bread on the night of His betrayal, the bread He and His disciples ate was not leavened. While some may believe that the lack of leavened bread is merely incidental to the story, the imagery of the Feast of Unleavened Bread and the subsequent use of the image of unleavened bread in 1 Corinthians 5.5–8 indicates that it was significant that the bread was without leaven.

The Feast of Unleavened Bread was a memorial both of the great act of God in His delivering Israel from bondage in Egypt and of the beginning of Israel's journey to the Promised Land. The Israelites were quickly thrust out of their homes and everything they had ever known to begin a long and perilous journey in a harsh desert.

Christians find themselves in a remarkably similar situation. The Lord's Supper is our memorial of the great act of God in delivering all of us from the bondage of sin (Rom 6.14–23). When we put on Christ, we are quickly thrust out of our 'homes'—the familiar world of sin and death—and begin our long and perilous journey in the midst of a wicked world (Rom 6.3–7; Matt 7.13–14). Likewise, as the Feast of Unleavened Bread memorialized the beginning of Israel's journey to the Promised Land, so we are now in the midst of our sojourning on the earth, awaiting our promised home of rest (Heb 4.1–11).

Paul finds great value in the imagery of the Feast of Unleavened Bread, especially in the purging of the house of all leaven, as it is written:

> Your boasting is not good. Do you not know that a little leaven leavens the whole lump? Cleanse out the old leaven that you may be a new lump, as you really are unleavened. For Christ, our Passover lamb, has been sacrificed. Let us therefore celebrate the festival, not with the old leaven, the leaven of malice and evil, but with the unleavened bread of sincerity and truth. (1 Cor 5.6–8)

Paul applies the idea of the Passover and the subsequent Feast of Unleavened Bread to Christians and sin. In Galatians 5.9, Paul likens sin to leaven, both in terms of immoral practice and false teachings. Just as a little bit of yeast is able to spread throughout the whole lump of dough, so even just a little bit of sin can spread throughout the entire church. Paul has no desire for this to occur. As the Israelites were to purge their houses of leaven in order to celebrate the Feast of Unleavened Bread, so Christians must purge the sin out of their lives (and out of the church) in order to be found pure and faithful to God.

Jesus did not inaugurate the Lord's Supper during the Passover and Feast of the Unleavened Bread by chance. Just as God delivered the Israelites from bondage and set them on the path toward the Promised Land, He has now delivered us from the bondage of sin through Christ's death, setting us on the path toward the promised rest. Just as Israel was to purge leaven from their houses, so Christians must be diligent to purge sin from their lives. We ourselves must be unleavened and pure. Christ has been sacrificed for our sins; we who have been made holy can now observe our own feast of unleavened bread in the Lord's Supper.

The Hallel Psalms and the Passover

Lucas Ward

Growing up, I thought of the Passover Feast as primarily a memorial of God's mercy. God sent the Angel of Death to punish the wicked, and the righteous marked themselves by putting blood on the doorposts of their houses. When the angel saw the blood, he passed over that house, sparing those inside. The Passover feast would therefore be a quiet feast, a somber feast commemorating God's great, and undeserved, mercy.

Reading through the Hallel Psalms (113–118)—the psalms that were traditionally sung at the Passover feast—shows us that the ancient Hebrews saw this feast very differently. The Passover feast was a time to rejoice, a time to remember a great victory and to praise God for a great salvation. For example, in Psalm 116.3: "The cords of death compassed me and the gates of Sheol got hold of me" (ASV). Then the writer records their plea for help, and we see God's response:

> Gracious is Jehovah, and righteous;
> Yea, our God is merciful.
> Jehovah preserveth the simple:
> I was brought low, and he saved me.
> Return unto thy rest, O my soul;
> For Jehovah hath dealt bountifully with thee.
> For thou hast delivered my soul from death,
> Mine eyes from tears... (vv 5–8)

Verses 12–13 then praise God for His salvation.

Psalm 118 is nothing but a paean to God for the victory He brings. "Out of my distress I called upon Jehovah, Jehovah answered and set me in a large place" (v 5). Verses 10–13 speak of being surrounded by enemies, but easily destroying them: "They compassed me about like bees; they are quenched as the fire of thorns: in the name of Jehovah I will cut them off" (v 12). God is joyfully praised throughout this Psalm for the salvation He brings to His people.

Psalm 114 portrays the almost arrogant boasting of a people who had just escaped from generations of slavery because their God had set them free. God was on their side, they knew it, and no one could stand in their way:

> When Israel went forth out of Egypt,
> The house of Jacob from a people of strange language;
> Judah became his sanctuary, Israel his dominion.
> The sea saw it, and fled;
> The Jordan was driven back.
> The mountains skipped like rams,
> The little hills like lambs.
> What aileth thee, O thou sea, that thou fleest?
> Thou Jordan, that thou turnest back?
> Ye mountains, that ye skip like rams;
> Ye little hills, like lambs?
> Tremble, thou earth, at the presence of the Lord,
> At the presence of the God of Jacob,
> Who turned the rock into a pool of water,
> The flint into a fountain of waters. (1–8)

So it is obvious that the Passover was more than a solemn dinner; it was a joyous feast celebrating the wonderful victory God had wrought to free His people from bondage to the Egyptians. It was not only a memorial to not being killed; it was a celebration of being set free to live!

Sometimes we turn the Lord's Supper into the same solemn, somber feast I had mistaken the Passover for. We huddle soberly and focus on the horrible suffering Christ went through on our behalf. We literally bow under the burden of guilt, knowing it was our sins for which He died. The Lord's Supper thereby becomes a sad, almost depressing reminder of the monumental sacrifice our Lord made for us when we did not deserve it—not even a little.

Wait a second! The Lord's Supper was built out of the Passover feast. That's what Christ and His apostles were eating when He instituted the new feast. *Christ* was declared to be *our Passover* in 1 Corinthians 5. Our feast ought to resemble their celebration, should it not? Just like the ancient Hebrews, we were enslaved to a horrible enemy—in our case sin. Just like them, the gates of Sheol had hold of us. As we were being overwhelmed, God sent His Son to work an awesome salvation. Instead of being freed from slavery, we have been freed from sin and the paralyzing fear of death. The author of Hebrews calls God's efforts on our part a "great salvation" (Heb 2.3), and Paul revels in our victory over death:

> For this corruptible must put on incorruption, and this mortal must put on immortality. But when this corruptible shall have put on incorruption, and this mortal shall have put on immortality, then shall come to pass the saying that is written, Death is swallowed up in victory. O death, where is thy victory? O death, where is thy sting? The sting of death is sin, and the power of sin is the law, but thanks be to God, who gives us the victory through our Lord Jesus Christ. (1 Cor 15.53–57)

Isn't it obvious that our Passover feast should be a jubilant celebration, just as the shadow feast of the Old Law was? Our God, through His great love for us, had mercy on us, sacrificed His Son for us, and defeated all our enemies. We stand clean from the filth of our sin due to the magnitude of this victory. As the psalmist boasts in 118.6, "Jehovah is on my side, I will not fear. What can man do to me?" Or Paul in Romans 8.31: "If God is for us, who can be against us?"

While there is a place for mourning the atrocity of Christ's death and realizing the magnitude of our sin, that cannot be the end-all of our Passover. Instead of *only* mourning our old ways of life that made Christ's sacrifice necessary, let us also rejoice and celebrate the new life we are privileged to live because God won so great a victory.

A Disreputable and Scandalous Meal

Patrick N. Halbrook

When we share a meal with others, we convey a significant message about the relationship between ourselves and the others around our table. This was especially true in Jesus' day, when it was very important for "respectable" people to choose carefully those with whom they would eat.

If someone wanted to be a good Jew, he would never have considered sitting down to eat with a Gentile. A Gentile not only ate foods that were deemed unclean and condemned by God, but the Gentile *himself* was unclean. Dining with a Gentile would have been like sitting down to eat with a filthy dog.

Another person to avoid was someone from a different economic class. Now while the poor certainly would not have turned down an invitation to attend a banquet at a rich man's house, the chances of receiving such an invitation were highly unlikely. That rich man down the street would not have wanted the poor at his banquet. Remember Jesus' story of the rich man and Lazarus? The rich man "feasted sumptuously every day" while Lazarus sat at this man's gate, wanting nothing more than to dig through the trash can and eat discarded scraps (Luke 16.20–21 ESV). The thought of inviting Lazarus to dinner probably never crossed this rich man's mind. And why should it? Lazarus dressed himself in rags, was covered with sores, and carried little with him besides a foul stench. There was no way a respectable member of Judea's upper-class would want someone like this at his table.

A third person to avoid was someone publicly recognized as a sinner. Keeping company with—or even speaking to—prostitutes, drunkards, and thieving tax collectors could destroy a good Jew's reputation. Never mind their current spiritual state—what mattered was that they had already tarnished their lives by committing despicable sins, and a good Jew would want to stay as far away from them as possible. Eating with them would send the message that one was just like these sinners and approved of their wicked, ungodly lives.

For these reasons, a good first-century Jew would have found the practices of Jesus of Nazareth and His followers to be shocking and scandalous. Though Jesus seemed like a righteous man, He and His followers regularly spent time with these sinners. He even ate with them: "And as Jesus reclined at table in the house, behold, many tax collectors and sinners came and were reclining with Jesus and His disciples. And when the Pharisees saw this, they said to His disciples, 'Why does your teacher eat with tax collectors and sinners?'" (Matt 9.10–11).

Not only did Jesus eat with sinners, He also taught that the rich should start inviting poor people to their banquets:

> When you give a dinner or a banquet, do not invite your friends or your brothers or your relatives or rich neighbors, lest they also invite you in return and you be repaid. But when you give a feast, invite the poor, the crippled, the lame, the blind, and you will be blessed, because they cannot repay you. You will be repaid at the resurrection of the just. (Luke 14.12–14)

But perhaps even more reprehensible than either of these practices was that Jesus' followers ate with Gentiles. After Peter baptized the Gentile Cornelius, allowing him to become a Christian without making him become a Jew first, Peter stayed in Cornelius' house for several days and ate with him and his family. When Peter returned to Jerusalem, many—even among the Christians— could not understand why he had done this. But he explained to them that God had made the Gentiles clean, and they were never again to be considered inferior to Jews (Acts 11.1–18).

By promoting the idea that it was permissible, even noble, to eat with sinners, the poor, and Gentiles, Christians broke social taboos, violated religious traditions, and ruined their own reputations. But Jesus and His followers understood something their critics did not. They understood that "the LORD sees not as man sees: man looks on the outward appearance, but the LORD looks on the heart" (1 Sam 16.7). For them, the unity of God's people could not be based on artificial social distinctions, but on Christ and Christ alone. As Paul wrote, "There is neither Jew nor Greek, there is neither slave nor free, there is neither male nor female, for you are all one in Christ Jesus" (Gal 3.28 NKJV), and, "Here there is not Greek and Jew, circumcised and uncircumcised, barbarian, Scythian, slave, free; but Christ is all, and in all" (Col 3.11 ESV).

The good news of Jesus Christ is that through Him we may be reconciled to both God and to our fellow man. One of the ways we proclaim this truth to the world is by partaking of the Lord's Supper in community with the church. There is a reason the Lord's Supper is not to be observed when we are alone, during our personal devotional times. Christ instituted His memorial service as a meal because when we eat and drink together, we are recognizing that Christ has broken down all ethnic distinctions, economic inequalities—all that divides us from each other—and He has invited to His banquet even sinners—a caste which, as it turns out, excludes not one of us.

When the Corinthian Christians struggled with unity, their divisive and arrogant attitudes manifested themselves when the church would not eat the Lord's Supper together. "For in eating," Paul described, "each one goes ahead with his own meal. One goes hungry, another gets drunk" (1 Cor 11.21). Some of the Christians (perhaps the wealthier ones) were arriving earlier and indulging themselves without waiting for the rest of Christ's body to show up. But a Lord's Supper eaten in a divided church is not the Lord's Supper at all (v 20). Paul had many other criticisms of the Corinthians, but their fundamental misunderstanding of the Lord's Supper and consequent failure to use it as an opportunity to declare their unity in Christ was among the most serious problems.

Our willingness to eat and drink together should express and testify to the way Christ has reconciled us together. Though we were once estranged from God and at enmity with each other, Christ has healed these broken relationships. Jew, Gentile; rich, poor; righteous man or repentant sinner—Christ accepts us regardless of these labels, and He calls us to accept each other as well. Like our first-century brothers and sisters, we need not get caught up in or concern ourselves with social respectability. Instead, we may take joy and comfort in proclaiming publicly that our God is not a God of favoritism but a God of mercy, forgiveness, and love.

In Anticipation of the Final Victory

Martin Pickup

When Paul recounts the establishment of the Lord's Supper, he makes the following statement: "For as often as you eat this bread and drink the cup, you proclaim the Lord's death *until He comes*" (1 Cor 11.26 NASB). Christians today have no trouble understanding that the Lord's Supper commemorates the past event of Jesus' death on the cross, but we may not realize that this memorial meal also looks ahead to the future victory celebration with Christ at the end of the age.

The Passover and Future Deliverance from Bondage

Jesus established the Lord's Supper on the occasion of the Passover, a Jewish feast that was itself a commemorative meal that looked forward as well as backward. The Passover reminded Jews of Israel's past deliverance from Egyptian bondage, yet it also came to signify God's promise of future deliverance from spiritual bondage at the consummation of the heavenly kingdom. The historical restoration of a remnant of Israel after 70 years of Babylonian captivity had not completely ended the people's state of exile. Most Jews were unable to return to the Promised Land, and the displaced condition of these Diaspora Jews among the nations symbolized the spiritual enslavement to sin and death that all of God's people still endured. But the Old Testament prophets declared that this state of bondage would end with the advent of the Messiah and that there would be a victorious celebration after every enemy was defeated and a complete restoration occurred (Jer 23.3–8; Isa 61.1–3).

Using figurative language, the prophets described this end-time celebration as a victory banquet. Isaiah declared,

> The Lord of hosts will prepare a lavish banquet for all peoples
>   on this mountain;
> A banquet of aged wine, choice pieces with marrow,
> And refined, aged wine.
> And on this mountain He will swallow up the covering which
>   is over all peoples,
> Even the veil which is stretched over all nations.
> He will swallow up death for all time,
> And the Lord God will wipe tears away from all faces,
> And He will remove the reproach of His people from all the earth.
> (Isa 25.6–8; *cf.* 65.13–18; Amos 9.11–15)

As a result of such prophecies, Jews looked forward to the time of joyful feasting in the fully consummated kingdom of God. The sect who produced the Dead Sea Scrolls regularly ate communal meals designed to call to mind this future feast.[1] The writings of a variety of Jewish groups speak of it as occurring after the last enemy is defeated, the dead are raised, and the full return from exile is complete.[2] Presiding over the victory banquet will be the Messiah.[3]

Jesus himself spoke of this celebration of triumph over sin and death, saying, "Many will come from east and west, and recline at the table with Abraham, Isaac and Jacob in the kingdom of heaven" (Matt 8.11). It is described in Revelation 19:9 as the marriage supper of the Lamb, the occasion when Christ will finally be united with His betrothed bride, the Church (*cf.* Matt 22.1–14; 25.10). It is "the period of restoration of all things about which God spoke by the mouth of His holy prophets" (Acts 3.21).

On one occasion during Jesus' earthly ministry, as He ate dinner in the home of a Pharisee, a fellow dinner guest exclaimed, "Blessed is everyone who will eat bread in the kingdom of God" (Luke 14.15). Jesus used the incident as an opportunity to teach a parable about who would be granted a place at the victory banquet at the consummation of the kingdom (vv 16–24). The guest's remark illustrates how easily any meal setting could prompt Jewish minds to think of the end-time feast. The Passover meal especially evoked such thoughts (Luke 22.15–16). It was a meal designed by God to point His people to His role in delivering them from bondage—both in the past and in the future.

Jesus' Words at the Last Supper

With this background in mind, it is not surprising to see that when Jesus gathered His disciples together at the Last Supper—a Passover meal no less—the occasion naturally prompted thoughts of the future consummation of the kingdom. In the interim, though, Jesus was departing to heaven, and His disciples would be separated from Him until He returned at the end of the age. So He said to them, "I have earnestly desired to eat this Passover with you before I suffer; for I say to you, *I shall never again eat it until it is fulfilled in the kingdom of God*" (Luke 22.15–16). As He administered the Lord's Supper, Jesus said of the cup, "This is My blood of the covenant, which is poured out for many for forgiveness of sins. But I say to you, *I will not drink of this fruit of the vine from now on until that day when I drink it new with you in My Father's kingdom*" (Matt 26.28–29; *cf.* Luke 22.17–18).

People commonly understand Jesus to have meant that He is with us in spirit each Sunday as we partake of communion. So interpreted, His words are then used to refute the premillennial notion that the Church is not to be identified with the kingdom. But though premillennialism is a false doctrine, and though there is a sense in which Jesus is indeed present with us as we partake of the Lord's Supper (*cf.* Matt 28.20), I do not believe that is what Jesus meant by the above statements. Several times during the Last Supper, Jesus told His disciples that He was about to leave them (Luke 22.22; John 13.33)—a point He had made repeatedly throughout the latter months of His ministry (Matt 16.21). In this context, therefore, and with all of the implications that a Passover meal evoked for Jews, it seems evident that when Jesus said to His disciples that He would not eat the Passover and drink of the fruit of the vine until He ate and drank anew with them in the kingdom, He meant that He would be absent from

His disciples until the time of His second coming, and then He would feast with them in the consummated kingdom. The great end-time banquet that the Old Testament prophets foretold and that Passover adumbrated is, therefore, what the Lord's Supper points us to. At that time we will be reunited with Jesus and enjoy the glorious victory feast.

As we partake of the Lord's Supper each Sunday, our Lord is in heaven and we are on earth, with the battle against the enemies of God raging about us. But we need to realize that our risen Lord has already dealt the fatal blow to sin and death, and ultimate victory awaits us on that resurrection day. The memorial meal that we eat each week is a foreshadowing of the victory banquet we will enjoy with our Lord when He returns in triumph and we are together with Him forever in heaven. So as we partake of the Supper, let us truly proclaim the Lord's death until He comes. Come quickly, Lord Jesus!

Part Two

Seeing Jesus through the Bible

The Lord Will Provide
Genesis 22 and the Lord's Supper

Matt Harber

The roots of the Lord's Supper stretch far back into the Old Testament. But perhaps this is not the best way to state the connection; maybe it is better to say that the Lord's Supper itself encapsulates and completes the message of the Old Testament. In order to do justice to the implications of this memorial feast, Christians must appreciate how all Scripture anticipates the sacrificial death of Christ. Once we understand (as the New Testament writers did) that the Law and the Prophets were ultimately about Jesus, we should begin to see the story of Jesus on every page of the Old Testament—not through some forced, allegorical hermeneutic, but through what many writers have termed a "salvation-historical" reading of the Bible. In other words, the individual stories, events and characters of the Old Testament were really components of a much greater story: the working out of God's plan for a people in need of redemption. Although God's people often enjoyed deliverance, vindication and restoration throughout their history, we remain acutely aware as we read these stories that such times of deliverance and blessing were temporary at best and ultimately imperfect. The Lord's Supper, on the other hand, powerfully shows us the true climax to these stories: Jesus Himself, the uniquely-qualified savior, righteous sufferer, and supreme sacrifice. Many aspects of God's salvation that were only dimly visible in Israel's history are gloriously manifested in the cross of Christ.

One particularly poignant example of this principle is the binding of Isaac, as recorded in Genesis 22.1–19. In this chapter, Abraham faces an incredible test of faith as God commands him, without explanation, to offer his son Isaac as a burnt offering on Mount Moriah. Abraham obediently follows these instructions, going so far as to take the knife in his hand before the Lord's angel steps in and spares Isaac, providing a ram for the sacrifice. This story is fascinating both in its similarity to and its divergence from the crucifixion narrative of the gospels. Several clear points of connection exist between the two stories, but there are also fundamental differences that challenge our understanding of the Genesis account.

This ancient story has intrigued and troubled its readers for centuries with its apparent theological and ethical difficulties. How, for example, could God have expected Abraham to practice human sacrifice? Why was Abraham commanded to destroy the child of promise? Was it capricious on God's part to order such an agonizing test of faith when He presumably knew the outcome? Is Genesis 22 a portrait of an unsympathetic Creator? Few of these questions have easy or obvious answers, especially in the story's immediate context. Ultimately, as we will see, the sacrifice of Christ provides the most satisfying explanations to the harrowing trial Abraham endured.

> Now it came about after these things, that God tested Abraham, and said to him, "Abraham!" And he said, "Here I am." He said, "Take now your son, your only son, whom you love, Isaac, and go to the land of Moriah, and offer him there as a burnt offering on one of the mountains of which I will tell you." (Gen 22.1–2 NASB)

The narrator prefaces the account by stating that "God tested Abraham" (v 1). Like Job, Abraham was challenged to accept the loss of a child without explanation, trusting that God's will was being accomplished through his suffering. As with Job, the majority of Abraham's trial occurred amid deafening silence from heaven. The three-day journey to Moriah must have been torturous as Abraham walked beside Isaac with the wood and the knife (v 6), mentally weighing his dreadful commission to sacrifice Isaac against the seemingly irreconcilable promise of a great nation (Gen 17.1–8; 21.12). Why did God not appear to make sense of this senselessness?

It is unimaginable what Abraham must have felt as Isaac innocently asked where they would obtain the sacrifice. His fatherly perspective is relentlessly emphasized by the tenfold repetition of the word *son* in the narrative.[1] The only answer this father was able to give his son was "God will provide" (v 8), although the identity of the sacrifice was no doubt clear to him: his beloved child. How could God ask such a thing of a father?

Ultimately, of course, Abraham passed the test in spite of the tremendous pressures working against his obedience, and Isaac submitted to his father even when Abraham's intentions became clear. After God halted the sacrifice, commended Abraham's faith, and presented a substitute sacrifice in exchange for Isaac's life, Abraham repeated his earlier statement to Isaac by naming the place "The-Lord-Will-Provide" (v 14), certainly a more confident declaration of trust than that in verse 8. At the conclusion of the episode, God reiterated His promises to Abraham in light of his obedience (vv 15–18).

Despite the "happy ending" to this story, however, several questions persist, although they can be summed up in the following question: was God right to make Abraham sacrifice his beloved son as a test of faith? The lesson Abraham learned from this experience was that "the Lord will provide"—but is this a satisfying answer for those who seek to learn from Abraham's trial? Indeed, this was the explanation with which other righteous sufferers of the Old Testament—such as Job and Habakkuk—had to content themselves. Although God appeared in this story (and throughout the Old Testament) as a gracious and merciful God who provides for and delivers His people, His offering did not appear to be on par with Abraham's. God provided a ram; Abraham had to provide "his own son, his only son" (*cf.* v 2). Therefore, it might seem as though God were requiring more from Abraham than might be reasonably expected—even more than what God had offered of Himself, some might argue. Abraham and Israel's Yahweh was righteous, holy, generous, loving, but not sacrificial in the truest sense of the word. Was this test a reasonable request by God, or an absurd one?[2]

Frankly, such a challenge could prove difficult to refute from the pages of the Old Testament—not because of some innate character flaw of God, but because the true depths of God's character were only progressively revealed through the course of the Bible. As we enter the New Testament, we can observe some important qualities of God—perhaps the most important—as revealed in Jesus. Jesus, as the Son of God, lays aside His divine privileges (Phil 2.5–8), becomes a servant (John 13.13–15), obediently suffers (Heb 5.8), and ultimately offers His own blood as a substitute sacrifice for mankind (Heb 9.11–14). The idea of a crucified, sacrificial God proved unexpected and startling—even absurd—to many in the first century:

> But we preach Christ crucified, to Jews a stumbling block and to Gentiles foolishness, but to those who are the called, both Jews and Greeks, Christ the power of God and the wisdom of God. Because the foolishness of God is wiser than men, and the weakness of God is stronger than men. (1 Cor 1.23–25)

According to Paul, then, this seemingly foolish requirement which God imposed upon Himself—the selfless offering of His own Son—was a demonstration of His divine wisdom and purpose. What appeared from man's perspective as a failed mission was actually a climactic moment of salvation history. Simply put, God knew what He was doing when He offered up Jesus.

It is with these points in mind that we should revisit Genesis 22. The story of Jesus' ordeal subtly changes our perspective on Abraham's ordeal, and we are drawn to the similarities between the two:

- As Abraham's obedience was tested through suffering (22.1), so was Christ's (Heb 5.8)
- God commended Abraham for not withholding "your son, your only son" (22.2, 12) and used similar language when referring to Jesus (Matt 3.17; John 3.16; Rom 8.32)

- According to 2 Chronicles 3.1, Moriah became the location of the first temple (a place of sacrifice) and was thus the approximate location of Jesus' crucifixion as well
- Abraham laid the wood upon Isaac to carry (22.6), "like a condemned man, carrying his own cross"[3]
- Isaac was referred to as a sacrificial *lamb* (22.8) a title often applied to Jesus (*e.g.,* John 1.29)
- Isaac was bound and stretched out to be killed, like Jesus (22.9, *cf.* Matt 27.2, 35, *etc.)*
- God provided a substitute sacrifice for Isaac (22.10), as Christ offered Himself for us (Rom 5.8)

This list is sufficient to show the extent to which Jesus relived the experience of Abraham. Indeed, Jesus assumed the roles of multiple characters in Genesis 22: Abraham as righteous sufferer, Isaac as innocent victim, the ram as sacrificial substitute. The point of this comparison is not to allegorize Abraham's story, but to demonstrate that when God demanded such a radical act of obedient faith from Abraham, He was not demanding anything that He Himself would be unwilling to give. God's sacrifice went even further than Abraham's, in fact, in that He allowed His own Son to die. We see not a portrait of a callous Creator, but a sympathetic and loving Father.

It is not always clear why God does what He does or why He demands what He demands. What *is* clear is that the motive behind even His most difficult and "absurd" commandments is the salvation of His people: "God was well-pleased through the foolishness of the message preached to save those who believe" (1 Cor 1.21b). Abraham was saved by believing and obeying God's message in spite of its apparent senselessness, understanding that somehow the Lord would provide (*cf.* Rom 4). Christ, however, completes our understanding of this story by revealing that God was commanding Abraham not to do something absurd, but something God-like: to sacrifice, to give fully of himself. The death of Jesus enriches our understanding of God as a God who was willing to offer us the most precious of gifts in order to draw closer to us. Through his willingness to offer Isaac, Abraham drew closer to his God by becoming more like Him and His Son. His test of faith resulted not in heartache and anguish, but in blessing: "In your seed all the nations of the earth shall be blessed, because you have obeyed My voice" (Gen 22.18). Even this blessing looks forward to Jesus as prefigured in Abraham, the seed of Abraham who blesses the world through His obedient death.

The name *Moriah* likely means "land of vision/provision,"[4] and thus plays an important thematic role in Genesis 22, where Abraham wrestles with the question of God's ability to provide. The Lord's Supper, as a memorial of Christ's death, reminds us not only that the Lord *will* provide, as Abraham declared, but that the Lord *has* provided. In a sense, we who have the benefit of hindsight have an advantage over Abraham, in that we have no need to wonder about God's ability to empathize during our times of testing: "For since He Himself was tempted in that which He has suffered, He is able to come to the aid of those who are tempted" (Heb 2.18). If we are tempted to view our trials as absurd, we need only remember the ultimate "absurdity": the cross of Christ.

It is probable that we will face doubt and uncertainty over the details of God's plan, yet because of Christ we can be confident of God's loving purpose. We can joyfully participate in the Lord's memorial feast—lifting up our eyes to Moriah, as Abraham did—in the full assurance that the Lord has provided the greatest gift of all: our salvation.

A Look Through God's Eyes
1 Chronicles 21

Edwin L. Crozier

We all know sin is bad. Yet I am not convinced I always see sin the way God sees sin, all sin, any sin. To me, at times, sin is merely a mistake. At times, I see it as a character flaw; at other times, a problem. I know it is wrong. I don't really want to sin, but most of the time I just don't think about it. I'll offer my prayers, ask for forgiveness and be done with it.

However, in those times of admitted spiritual weakness, passages such as 2 Samuel 24 and 1 Chronicles 21 show my perspective to be inadequate. It opens my eyes to see through God's. The account of David's census, the ensuing plague and the sacrifice at Araunah's/Ornan's threshing floor brings me back to reality. The world's weak view of sin is not reality. Rather, it is Satan's attempt to get us to gloss over our violations of God's great will. Sin is far more than inappropriate behavior. Sin is far more than a social *faux pas*. Sin is far more than slipping up or making a mistake. Sin is a devastating division between us and God. Sin is dreadful wickedness, vile evil and horrendous presumption.

I don't know about you, but I have read Romans 3.10–18 and Ephesians 2.1–3 and thought to myself, 'Come on, now. I wasn't *that* bad.' Sadly, I often get the meaning of these passages backward. I act as if these passages mean I am only a sinner when I am as bad as they say. That was not God's intent. His point was that I was that bad because I sinned. This is how God saw me when I was in sin. I was by nature a child of wrath. I was following the course of the world. I was following the prince of darkness, Satan. I was unrighteous and worthless. My throat was an open grave. My mouth was full of the venom of asps, curses and bitterness. In my paths were ruin and misery. I did not see myself that way, but God did.

Consider David's sin in 1 Chronicles 21.1. What did he do that was so bad? He sent Joab out to number Israel. Frankly, I don't get it. After all, in my home country, we take a census every couple of years. What could possibly be so bad about this census in Israel? We could, no doubt, waste our time speculating exactly why God did not want His people counted. We might even come up with some really good reasons, but in doing so we may miss the point. The issue is not *why* God did not want this done; the issue is *that* God did not want this done. *He* gets to define sin. He is God.

Further, we can quibble about how David was supposed to know. I see this as an issue of lawlessness, a lack of authority. God had not asked for the census; David should not have done it. Some may see a different reason. What I do know for sure is that Joab knew it was wrong (1 Chron 21.30), which means David should have known. Yet he proceeded anyway. He probably felt the same way about it that I do. 'What could be so wrong with this numbering? Even if it is a sin, it is not a very big one. It won't matter.'

But it did matter. It mattered to God. He takes sin—every sin—seriously.

Because of David's sin, God struck Israel. It was as if God was saying to David, 'You think the number of Israelite warriors is important? I'll show you what can happen to your Israelite warriors.' He gave David three choices—three years of famine, three months of devastation by the nations around him or three days of the sword of the Lord. David chose the sword of the Lord. He hoped God would be merciful. Pestilence came upon Israel and 70,000 men fell (1 Chron 21.14). The census had found 1,570,000 men in Israel and Judah combined (1 Chron 21.5); in one fell swoop, God wiped out nearly four-and-a-half percent of Israel's warriors. Look through God's eyes in this story. This is how He sees sin. This is how vile our disobedience is to Him. This is the cost of our sins. This is what we deserve because we sin.

God could have gone even further with this punishment, but David was right to place himself in God's hands. As Ezekiel 18.23 explains, God has no pleasure in the death of the wicked. How much less did He take pleasure in the deaths of these men when David was the one who had actually sinned (1 Chron 21.17)? God Himself, therefore, provided the means by which David could stay the punishment for his sin. In 1 Chronicles 21.18, the angel of the Lord told the prophet Gad what David could do to stay the punishment. David did not figure it out on his own. David did not make a guess. God's messenger told David what to do. What an amazing God David served!

David was told to go to the threshing floor of Ornan the Jebusite, a foreigner who had remained in David's city even after David had defeated the Jebusites (1 Chron 11.4–9), and raise up an altar to the Lord. When David arrived, Ornan and his sons were hidden; they had seen the angel of the Lord coming, and mistakenly believed they could hide from the sword of the Lord. When David told Ornan the plan, Ornan was willing to give away his threshing floor and the necessary sacrifices. How important his life and the lives of his sons were to him. Perhaps he had other land. Perhaps he had other threshing floors. If so, the text does not say. Thus it appears that Ornan was willing to give away his livelihood to preserve his life. David, however, would have none of that. "I will not take for the LORD what is yours, nor offer burnt offerings that cost me nothing" (1 Chron 21.24, ESV). The sin was David's, and the sacrifice would be David's.

David built an altar. He sacrificed the offerings. He called on the Lord. The Lord responded with fire from heaven. Often, fire from heaven meant judgment. God rained fire from heaven on to Sodom and Gomorrah (Gen 19.24). He judged Egypt before Moses with fire from heaven (Exod 9.23). He consumed Nadab and Abihu with fire (Lev 10.2). But here, God's fire meant acceptance and approval as it would mean for Solomon and the temple that would be built on this very spot (2 Chron 7.1), as it would mean for Elijah on Mt. Carmel in his contest with the prophets of Baal (1 Kings 18.38). God had seen David's sacrifice and answered.

What most intrigues me about this story is how David responded to God's answer. David did not wipe the sweat from his brow and act as if it was all over. Rather, having seen how devastating his sin was, when the punishment was abated, he could do nothing but turn to the Lord in thanksgiving. He did not cease his sacrifices because the punishment was removed. Rather, he sacrificed all the more (1 Chron 21.28). More than just offering sacrifices at that time, this new altar became his place of sacrifice, instead of the tabernacle in Gibeon. Further, this would be the resting place of the tabernacle and the ark when it came to Jerusalem. This would be the place for God's name, God's house and God's sacrifices for the rest of Judah's history (1 Chron 22.1).

That, however, was David. He is dead and gone. The ark and tabernacle he moved are lost. The temple his son built was destroyed. The city for God's name was defeated. Why should I be bothered by this incident? Because David is me. I am David. I haven't numbered Israel, but I have sinned. We all have. We have lusted, lied, cheated, gossiped, slandered, coveted, become drunk, committed immorality, stolen, killed, and on and on and on. If you are like me, you can easily gloss over your sins because you haven't been as bad as some people. The reality for me, however, is that I have done far worse than numbering Israel. If numbering Israel was so bad, so devastatingly evil, where does that put me?

The sword of the Lord may not be coming for me, for us, within three days of pestilence. But it is coming. The wages of our sin is death (Rom 3.23). The soul who sins will die (Ezek 18.20). We may not see the dreadful nature of our failures, but God certainly does. His wrath is unbearable. We do not want to fall into His living hands (Heb 10.31). It is a certain and terrifying prospect. It is what we deserve no matter what Satan whispers into our ears.

Yet as God provided David with the solution to his sin, He has provided us with one as well. In our case, He has gone even further. While David had to pay for his sacrifice and build his own altar, God has provided the altar and the sacrifice for us, so that they cost us nothing. While David's sacrifice came after his repentance, God provided our sacrifice when we were still sinners and enemies (Rom 5.6–8). I am in awe of God's mercy toward me and humbled by His grace. Considering the cost of David's sins, how could God simply wipe mine away—and do so by paying the cost with His Son's life instead of mine? Yet that is the extent of His love for us.

We gather on the first day of the week to celebrate this forgiveness. As we partake of the memorial Jesus established, we should remember the vileness of our sins, the power of His love and the forgiveness coming from His sacrifice. However, this must not merely be a reminder of God's past events. It should be a catalyst for our future lives. As David did not merely offer his sin sacrifice and then quit, we should not merely partake of the Supper and then move on with our lives. Rather, we must let this reminder pave the path of our conduct. As David continued to sacrifice to God, we must sacrifice to God. It is true that our sin sacrifice has cost us nothing. We have received the free gift of life from God. However, at the same time, in the face of God's great gift, we must be willing to pay the ultimate cost. As Jesus sacrificed Himself for us, we must sacrifice ourselves for Him. Paul said we are to be living sacrifices (Rom 12.1). We must not merely remember Jesus' sacrifice on Sundays, but offer ourselves as a sacrifice every day. Paul also said he crucified himself with Jesus, allowing Jesus to live through him by faith in Him (Gal 2.20). We must not merely remember Jesus' crucifixion on the first day of the week, but crucify ourselves with Him every day of the week. We must take up our cross and follow Him (Luke 14.27). No, we will not build another altar. We will not build a temple to house God. Instead, we must become the temple of God. We are God's house, sacrificing ourselves daily in His honor because He sacrificed Himself for our forgiveness.

When we partake of the Lord's Supper, let us see ourselves through God's eyes so we can truly remember what Jesus has done for us and motivate ourselves to live for Him.

The Hill

Keith Ward

An old man and a boy climbed up the hill. He was hardly a boy; at the least in his late teens, as he was hefty enough to carry sufficient wood to burn a sacrificial animal. The old man was obviously brooding, for his son had to break in to ask, "Where is the sacrifice?" Out of the conundrum that had troubled his mind for days—'How could the son of promise be the sacrifice?'—he spoke, "God will provide the lamb." The willing Isaac, the upraised knife, the angel speaking, the ram caught in the thicket....

About a thousand years later, a king stood on the same hill bargaining for a packed-down piece of dirt, the threshing floor of Ornan (2 Sam 24; 1 Chron 21). David had sinned by numbering the people, and God had sent a plague that killed thousands. When David interceded and offered himself in the place of the people, to die for them, God commanded David to buy that threshing floor and to build an altar there. David obeyed, offering burnt offerings and peace offerings, and the plague—the punishment for sin—was averted. Later, Solomon built the temple on that spot, not far from, or maybe, providentially, exactly where Abraham's and David's altars stood.

Another thousand years later, outside the gates of the temple on that same mountain, the Lamb of God hung on a strange altar. The Jews never solved Abraham's conundrum, yet inadvertently fulfilled God's plan. The child of promise became the perfect sacrifice. In agony, suspended between earth and heaven, He cried out, "My God, My God, why hast thou forsaken me?" This time, there could be no angel to stop the Father's hand: "He was cut off out of the land of the living for the transgression of my people to whom the stroke was due" (Isa 53.8 ASV).

To spare the people the consequences of their sins, He offered himself. He was sacrificed as a burnt offering so that the wrath of God might be appeased.

Now that geographical mountain has passed into insignificance, for we are "come to Mount Zion… the heavenly Jerusalem… the church of the firstborn… to Jesus the mediator of a new covenant and to the blood" (Heb 12.22–24).

We climb the mountain with our hands empty. We bring nothing but ourselves, because God has provided the sacrifice. In the Lord's Supper, the bread is the means by which we remember the life given for us. The cup brings us to our knees in memory of the "soul poured out unto death," that we might live, forgiven.

Supper with Betrayers

Jady S. Copeland

The story of Joseph son of Jacob contains some of the clearest fore-shadowing of the Christ in all the Old Testament. Consider the following parallels between Joseph and Jesus: both were punished for crimes they did not commit; both were punished by men who knew better—or should have (can't we see Pilate in Potiphar?); both were raised from "the pit" and made rulers of nations; not only rulers, both were saviors who brought life and food to all the world (doesn't the image of pilgrims flowing into Egypt for Joseph's grain remind us of Isaiah 2, or Joseph's handing out bread remind us of John 6?). Joseph and Jesus were prophets, the beloved sons, rejected by their families, forced to be separated from their fathers. Joseph, in the ranks of Moses, David, and Jeremiah, stands out as a bright reflection of the Light in the time before Christ was fully revealed.

One incident near the end of Joseph's Genesis narrative begs for careful comparison. In Genesis 43 it is the time of the famine, and Joseph's brothers have already been to Egypt once. Though Jacob urges them to return for more food, the sons of Israel refuse to go, reminding their father that the journey would be futile without Benjamin. It is only after Judah offers his pledge of safety that Benjamin is given permission to go. Now all the brothers (minus Simeon who is still in Egypt) head to Egypt for food. Even with Benjamin, the brothers remain fearful of the ruler's reaction to seeing them again. After all, the last time they were in Egypt they hadn't paid for their food.

When he sees them, and sees Benjamin with them, Joseph tells his steward to prepare a meal for him and his brothers. (As an Egyptian, he won't actually be able to eat with them, but he'll sit close enough to enjoy their company.) Again, the brothers are fearful, but the steward tells them not to worry. Simeon is brought out, their feet are washed, and they sit down as a family (more or less) to eat a meal of meat, bread, and wine.

It's impossible to know exactly why Joseph planned this meal. Certainly he still had trickery planned for his brothers, such as seating them according to birth order at the dinner table or putting the cup in Benjamin's sack. (In Joseph's trickery, it seems that at best, he is simply making sure that his father will come to Egypt; at worst he's treating his brothers to a little taste of the anguish he himself has suffered at their hands.) But here at the dinner table, after the shock of the seating arrangement, it is a time of merriment: "Portions were taken to them from Joseph's table, but Benjamin's portion was five times as much as any of theirs. And they drank and were merry with him" (Gen 43.34 ESV).

I believe we see a foreshadowing of the Last Supper of Jesus and His disciples in this meal Joseph has with his brothers. There are common details in the two events: there are twelve present (and confused), the twelve have their feet washed, and they eat bread and wine with the most powerful person in the world. There's even something to be said of a parallel between Joseph's favorite, Benjamin—the only brother who had not betrayed him—and Jesus' favorite, John—who is the only one of the twelve, as far as we know, at the cross. Both Benjamin and John receive obvious favor from the host of the feast.

It's not hard to see these similarities between Joseph's meal and Jesus' Last Supper, and, God be praised, we find that this picture of Jesus in the Old Testament is helpful. This type of Jesus in Genesis actually helps us to see Jesus better in the Gospels. The similarities are no gimmick; Joseph's meal is an aid to help us better understand what is going on in the Lord's Supper.

First, note that in both meals the twelve are present. Joseph eats with all of his brothers, the whole of the sons of Israel, while

Jesus eats with the New Israel, His twelve. In the Genesis narrative, Joseph's brothers are finally reunited—and all the children of Israel, for one of the only times in their troubled history, are at peace with one another. At Jesus' table, the New Israel is united in communion with Christ. Joseph brings perfect peace and unity to his troubled family; Christ brings His own brothers into perfect peace and fellowship with Him.

Perhaps it would be better to say near-perfect peace. Yes, Joseph has reunited the sons of Israel in a meal of joyful fellowship, but they are still a family with problems. They have yet to be reconciled fully to their brother, whom they betrayed, and their father, to whom they have lied. And it's not hard to see that Jesus' twelve disciples are not as unified or at peace with each other as they should be. Even during the Last Supper, during the Passover meal, they are still vying for first place in the Lord's kingdom (Luke 22.24). So near the end of Jesus' ministry, there is dissension among the New Israel. And if we are honest, it's not hard to see that Jesus' disciples are still not as unified or at peace with each other as they should be. We still have spats; we still bicker and vie for superiority in the Kingdom; we still are working to overcome the hurt feelings of past sins and betrayals. But at the table we come and find communion with the Lord. At the table we are reminded of His body and how we are a part of it. At the table, the Host's brothers are reunited.

A deeper look at Joseph's story helps us to appreciate better another aspect of the Last Supper. When we read Genesis 43, it doesn't surprise us much that Joseph is not allowed to eat at the same table with his brothers. They sit before him, in his presence, and they interact with him, but the ruler of the land was not to sit with foreigners, peasants, or shepherds (*cf.* Gen 46.34). Joseph, we remember, was second in the whole kingdom, perhaps in the world! He was the man with power to give food or not to give, to bind and to loose, as all the earth was coming to Egypt in their poverty (Gen 41.57). Of course he wouldn't sit with foreigners. Nobody sat with Joseph!

Then we see the Lord, the Son of God, descending from Heaven and living as a foreigner among His people. He walks with them and eats with them, and by the time we have read enough of the gospel story to reach the Last Supper, we forget that He is Immanuel. Joseph's story helps remind us how inappropriate it is that the Lord of the whole earth is eating with peasants. If the King of Egypt can't sit with the sons of Abraham, why should the King of Kings?

Joseph's distance from his brothers similarly highlights the strangeness of Jesus' washing His disciples' feet. Genesis 43.24 doesn't make clear if Joseph's brothers washed their own feet before the meal or a servant of Joseph did the washing for them. Having your feet washed was normal before a meal. How strange would it have been if Joseph had taken off his royal garments and costly robes to don a towel and wash his brothers' feet! That wouldn't be at all appropriate. I doubt the thought even crossed Joseph's mind. Yet Jesus, the rabbi, their host, the Master of the world, humbles himself to do the work of the lowliest servant. Joseph helps remind us how strange and shocking it is to have a Lord who is the greatest of all—and the servant of all.

Perhaps the greatest contrast between the two stories of Joseph's meal and Jesus' meal is seen in Jesus' greater grace. Yes, Joseph shows a great deal of kindness to his brothers, but Jesus' kindness is shown, in contrast, to be limitless.

Joseph's kindness is apparent in his dealings with his brothers. To appreciate this kindness, it is important to remember exactly what Joseph's brothers have done to him before their dinner together and their subsequent reunion. The ones Joseph dines with—Simeon, Dan, Zebulon, Judah, and the rest—are not merely his brothers; they are his betrayers! They are the ones who sold him into slavery. They are those who, for 20 shekels of silver, delivered him into Egyptian bondage. How does Joseph, the "lord of all Egypt," treat his betrayers? We know from the rest of the story that he reacts with kindness and gentleness. He has forgiven them their trespasses, even before they know who he is. Yes, he has had over twenty years to move past the sorrow of betrayal, but they have not been twenty years of ease: Egypt has been the land of his affliction (Gen 41.52). By the grace of God, Joseph acts with grace toward his brothers. His forgiveness is complete. Even after his father's death, Joseph weeps at his brothers' fear that he has planned some hidden, final retribution (50.17).

Though we marvel at Joseph's lovingkindness, Jesus' love towards His disciples is the more amazing. He speaks kindly and patiently to them, even though He knows what weakness is hidden in their hearts. They say they love Him and would never betray Him; Jesus knows better. But our Lord, knowing what terrible isolation He will feel when they all flee from Him, is still supremely merciful. Jesus is a merciful host even to Peter, who will be guilty not only of abandoning Him, as will the other disciples, but also of openly denying Him. Jesus knows they will hurt Him, but He invites them to His table anyway.

Joseph was surely comforted by the repentance and change of heart he was able to see in his brothers. Judah, who had led his brothers in selling Joseph into slavery (Gen 37.26–27) and who was now the leader of the family (*cf.* 43.8–10), was clearly a changed man. He had given himself as a pledge of Benjamin's safety (43.9) and would later be the one to beg Joseph not to keep their youngest brother as his slave (44.18).

Jesus had no such repentance to comfort Him. Jesus' own Judah—Judas—was in the process of selling Jesus to the Pharisees when his Master washed his feet. Yet Jesus still patiently served him. John's gospel emphasizes this when it points out Jesus' willingness to wash even the feet of His betrayer:

> During supper, when the devil had already put it into the heart of Judas Iscariot, Simon's son, to betray him, Jesus, knowing that the Father had given all things into his hands... rose from supper. He laid aside his outer garments, and taking a towel, tied it around his waist. Then he poured water into a basin and began to wash the disciples' feet. (John 13.2–5)

Why was Jesus willing to serve and comfort those who He knew were about to abandon Him? Because He loved them. That's why He does the same to us. When we come to the Lord's Table on Sunday, doesn't Jesus know where our souls are weak and to the point of breaking? Doesn't He know where we have made provision for the flesh so that we might later fall into temptation? Doesn't He know where we think we are strong, although we afterward sin? Of course He does. He knows we will betray Him—maybe even later in the day—though, of course, we protest we never will. But He prays that our faith may not fail and that when we have turned again, we will strengthen our brothers (*cf.* Luke 22.32). And He still invites us to His table.

When we first become Christians, we come to the Lord like Joseph's brothers. We come with guilt, knowing that we are the ones responsible for tearing the beloved Son from the side of the Father. We are members of a broken family, yearning to be reunited with the King, our dear brother who went before into Egyptian bondage to save us. We are reunited, with the hope that our greatest sin lies behind us.

Later, we come to the table like Jesus' twelve. We come with Christ's blessing, even though we are weak and frail. He serves us, even as we fall short of the glory of God. He humbly washes us, even as we nourish pride in our hearts. We boldly state that we will never deny Him. God help us not to! Still we know, as we reflect on our lives, that we have, in our past, betrayed our Lord. Yet He continues to serve and invite us. We, His betrayers, are welcome at His table.

Jesus the Great King

Kelly Cook

"I will put enmity between you and the woman, and between your offspring and her offspring; he shall bruise your head, and you shall bruise his heel." (Gen 3.15 ESV)

As we eat the Lord's Supper, we celebrate and remember what the Lord gave and what He accomplished on that great day of His cross. Yet as we eat and remember, we remember more than just His work on that one great day. We remember all of His loving work that shaped human history to prepare us for Jesus' work on the cross, and we remember our great need for Him.

The Bible, in simple terms, is a recounting of God's work throughout human history to reunite Himself with us, His children who have rejected Him. In the garden He begins to tell us, at least in general terms, how He will do that. Someone, He says, will *crush* the head of our greatest enemy, who deceives us into breaking away from God. From that point on, the Lord begins to work His great plan to bring that someone and to reunite us to Himself. Generation after generation, no man was able to crush that enemy.

Throughout the Old Testament the Lord is constantly showing us that no man—even His own devoted servants—was able to crush our enemy and to reunite us with Him. Consider that no one—whether prior to the flood (including Noah) or after (including the patriarchs, Moses or Joshua—and certainly not the judges!), or even the godly prophets and priests—was able to accomplish what we most need. It is an impressive list of men who failed.

For the moment, let's think just about the failure of the kings of Judah and Israel. Beginning with Saul, the first king, no king of Judah or Israel ever proved to be the promised someone of Genesis 3. First, consider that no king was ever really pure in heart or life. King after king sins and fails God and nation. Even all the best kings, whether David or Hezekiah, had their failures and moral lapses; David's sins are well known, and Hezekiah's pride and self-focus at the time of the Babylonians' visit leaves us aching for a king who will not fail the Lord God and His purposes.

Second, no king faithfully and dutifully served God's people. Case in point: Solomon. Solomon started well by asking for wisdom to serve God and God's people. His request was selfless and noble—a foretaste of God's great king. Nevertheless, sometime well before the end of Solomon's reign the tail began to wag the dog. The king no longer existed to serve God's people; the nation existed to serve, support, furnish and supply the king and His enormous family and court (1 Kings 4.27–28; 12.4). Solomon's self-focus became, it seems, the norm among leaders of God's people. There were moments when some kings were set on serving God and His people, but by and large, the monarchy was a history of serving self. By the time of Ezekiel—and later Jesus—the shepherds of Israel, including their kings, were corrupt, using their position not for service but for self (Ezek 34.2; Matt 23.1–7).

Finally, the most obvious failure of the kings is that not one of the kings ever truly united Israel. Even before the nation was divided, Saul, David and Solomon all had trouble holding onto God's people and uniting the nation (1 Sam 10.7; 2 Sam 20.1–2; 1 Kings 12.4). Later, after the nation's division (which continued longer than the nation had been one), no king ever made any significant progress reuniting God's people. King after king ruled without success and without a hope of undoing the division. Perhaps the closest the nations come to unity was through the horrible arrangement of marriages masterminded by Jezebel (2 Kings 8.16–18). In fact, when we read the books of history, it never occurs to us to expect the reunion of the nations. The children of Israel were a great people, but they were, it seems, irrevocably divided.

The books of history (and, really, all the Old Testament) leave us hungering for a greater king. God, in His own divine way, was preparing His people for a King who is to yet come. The shock was that when Jesus the great King came, He was so much more than anticipated.

Christ certainly accomplished God's promise from the garden when He *crushed* our enemy. Unlike the kings of Judah and Israel, Jesus was and is morally pure. Likewise, He selflessly served God and God's people. From His humble birth through His selfless life to His painful death, He lived to serve the Lord and His nation.

His accomplishments, however, did not stop there. Jesus accomplished our reuniting with God and with one another. He restored what seemed to have been forever lost between all of us and God. Jesus reversed all the effects of our enemy's work *and more*. Jesus did not just send us back to the garden, but He sent us, hand in hand with one another, to God's very house—an astonishing reunion.

For the moment, think of His reuniting work among men on earth. Judah and Israel were irrevocably divided, politically and emotionally. By Jesus' day, relations between the Jews and Samaritans could not have been worse. As we know from our own day, local ethnic prejudices and anger are those which burn hottest. Yet even before His death, Jesus began to show His power and ability to reunite Jew and Samaritan. In John 4 and later in Acts 8, Jesus accomplished what those of His generation never considered possible or even desirable. Through Jesus, the great king, Jew and Samaritan were reunited and made one. Who would have thought that any of these warring and bitter cousins would come to love, serve and respect each other? Yet Jesus accomplished just that!

Although we are shocked that Jew and Samaritan could live in peace and unity, Jesus further stuns us by making Jew and Gentile brothers. Jesus' work was not limited to some small corner of the world; His accomplishments were global, a point God makes clear in Ephesians 2.12–22. There Paul shares his appreciation for the reuniting work of Jesus: Who would have thought Jew and Gentile could become brothers who would love, live and die together? Such a reuniting is a living example of Jesus' words in Mark 3.35: "My brothers and sisters are those who do the will of God." To everyone's surprise, Jew and Gentile became brother and sister—family—bound together for eternity. Jesus alone accomplished the reunion of all mankind.

As impressive as Jesus' reuniting work was in the local and national prejudices of times past, He did not end His work there. Jesus works in the same way today in you and me. He accomplishes the same uniting work in present relationships among His disciples.

First, consider what a marvel it is that individuals of all skin colors, backgrounds, and education are united through His work. Through Him we all know the beauty and wonder of our union with brothers or sisters with whom we would otherwise have absolutely nothing in common. In our own day, where else is such a uniting of mankind possible or lasting?

Second, consider His uniting work among us, even when we find ourselves working against His uniting purposes. Jesus knew His own twelve's inclination to fight and divide—not over love of Him and His words but over love of self. Think of what Luke tells us they were discussing at the Last Supper: "A dispute also arose among them, as to which of them was to be regarded as the greatest" (Luke 22.24). It is frightening that we have the capacity to be so self-absorbed and divisive, even during the most solemn moments that should take our focus off ourselves. Nevertheless, through Him have we not all known the beauty and wonder of forgiveness and reunification with a brother against whom we have sinned and with whom we have been at war? Only through Jesus' work is such a reunification accomplished! Deep wounds typically take a long time to heal, but it is not time that heals wounds among His people. It is Jesus and our devotion to Him that heals—and heals quickly—wounds and divisions.

It is right for us to marvel at His reuniting work throughout both human history and in our own lives, but we must not forget that His accomplishments took great strength and work. Why should we ever think that our participation in His reuniting work will cost us little? While Matthew 18.15–17 speaks to the process of how we deal with one another when we sin against one another, does it not also give us an example of the determination and length to which we should go to retrieve one another and to be reunited with one another? Jesus says it plainly: We can't be one with Him if we won't be one with one another (1 John 4.20–21). As disciples we must be willing to give ourselves to Jesus' reuniting work if we are going to be reunited with Him. His words make clear our share in His reuniting work: "So if you are offering your gift at the altar and there remember that your brother has something against you, leave your gift there before the altar and go. First be reconciled to your brother, and then come and offer your gift" (Matt 5.23–24). Seeking a reunion with a brother is not easy, but then neither was Jesus' work of reuniting us with the Lord God.

The breadth and depth of Jesus' work leaves us astonished. Jesus crushed our enemy and accomplished what no man ever even thought of doing: reuniting us with God. As the great King, He was not only pure, but He also selflessly served all men and, in doing so, brought us together as one family in God. Is not Jesus' reuniting work wonderfully represented in the Supper we share with Him and with others in the kingdom? Nowhere is our reuniting with God and our brother more clear and sweet. When we eat we are reminded of God's work throughout all of human history to bring about our reuniting with Him. While eating we are reminded that no one other than Jesus was able to crush our enemy and to accomplish our reunion with God. We are truly the closest to Him and to being at home with Him, at least in this life, as together we eat His Supper.

As we eat, we are reminded that He has reunited us with each other. Not just feuding Judah, Israel and Samaria—His work was and is throughout all nations. Beginning with Jew and Gentile, Jesus made all men who are His to be at peace with one another. And though we have sinned against and failed one another, through His perfect work we can be forgiven and reunited with Him—and with each other. As we eat, we may sit side by side with a brother or sister with whom we have absolutely nothing in common outside of Him. And we may sit next to a brother with whom we have, only moments before, been at odds or at war, but by His grace we have been made one again.

As we eat, we are astonished at His work, its scope, and its results in each of our lives. In 1 Corinthians, God uses Paul to remind us that as we eat, we are at peace with God and bound together with each other: "Because there is one bread, we who are many are one body, for we all partake of the one bread" (1 Cor 10.17; *cf.* 11.18, 33–34). What a marvel! And what a great moment as we all eat together in His presence, in His unity, each of us at that moment reflecting on Him and the marvel of our re-union with Him and all those around us. Where else on this earth do we experience such peace and unity? Surely for us His Supper is a taste of the great reuniting we will know with God and with all His people in Heaven forever.

Psalm 113

Lucas Ward

Praise ye Jehovah.
Praise, O ye servants of Jehovah,
Praise the name of Jehovah.
Blessed be the name of Jehovah
From this time forth and for evermore.
From the rising of the sun unto the going down of the same Jehovah's
name is to be praised. (Psa 113.1–3 ASV)

Psalm 113 begins the Hallel, six Psalms sung during the Great
Feasts. According to Delitzsch, Psalms 113 and 114 were sung
before the Passover feast and Psalms 115 through 118 were sung
afterward.[1] So it is likely that our Lord sang this Psalm with His
disciples before eating the Last Supper. What would this Psalm
have meant to Him? What can we learn about our Lord's attitude
toward His sacrifice as our Passover by studying this Psalm?

"Jehovah is high above all nations, and his glory above the heavens. Who is like unto Jehovah our God that hath his seat on
high?" (vv 4–5 ASV).

These verses would have reminded Jesus of what He gave up:
being with Jehovah on high, above all, comparable to none. Jesus
had been there. Jesus was *God* (John 1.1–4). His thoughts as He
sang this phrase could have run to, 'I really miss that,' or 'Is this
really worth the sacrifices I have made?' At every Passover of His
life, our Lord had been forcefully reminded of what He had given
up to complete His mission.

"[Jehovah] humbleth himself to behold the things that are in heaven and in the earth" (v 6).

These verses would not have eased Jesus' burden. God on high humbles Himself to notice us. The implication is also that His notice means His help. So God lowered Himself to help His people. Singing this, Christ could easily have thought, 'Have I ever humbled myself! Look at me!' Indeed, look at the Being declared God, who then became flesh (John 1.14). The Great Jehovah God, creator and upholder of all, gives up His equality with God to become flesh, to be a creature, to be a man (*cf.* Phil 2.5–8).

At this point in the singing of the Psalm, our Lord may have wondered, 'Do I really want to go through with this? Look at how much this is costing me!' If our Lord ever had these thoughts, verses 7–9 would have reminded Him of why He came: "He raiseth up the poor out of the dust, and lifteth up the needy from the dunghill; that he may set him with princes, even with the princes of his people. He maketh the barren woman to keep house, and to be a joyful mother of children."

These people—His people—who loved Him and tried to serve Him, were in trouble. We, the people of God, had been caught up in serious problems that overwhelmed us. We were not just physically enslaved to a wicked Pharaoh. It was sin that had entangled us. Just as God had humbled Himself to notice the enslaved Hebrews in Egypt, just as He had raised them from the dust, from out of the dunghill, to make them princes, so God again noticed our troubles and humbled Himself to help. Christ was here to raise us from the putridity of our sin. We, as poor sinners, were to be exalted and set with heavenly princes. We, as a people, were barren and unfruitful, sinful as we were, but He would make us fruitful—like a "joyful mother."

This Psalm, as it was sung every year at Passover, may have reminded our Lord of what He had given up to be here—but it would also have reinforced His resolve by pointing out the desperate circumstances of His people. Psalm 113 surely reminded Jesus how much we needed Him—and how much He could help.

The Lord went from the Last Supper to Gethsemane, where the enormity of what was about to happen hit Him full force. The anguish of Jesus' impending sacrifice weighed upon Him and filled Him with dread. He began to beg the Father, "Let this cup pass." Then He found the resolve—the strength to go on.

It was surely the providence of God that, only a short time before, our Lord had sung a song reminding Him yet again of how much we, His people, need Him and of how greatly His sacrifice would transform His people.

This Cup

Gary Fisher

"And in the same way He took the cup after they had eaten, saying, 'This cup which is poured out for you is the new covenant
in My blood'" (Luke 22.20 NASB). Paul repeated this teaching
of the Lord: "In the same way He took the cup also after supper,
saying, 'This cup is the new covenant in My blood; do this, as often as you drink it, in remembrance of Me'" (1 Cor 11.25). Jesus'
use of the phrase *this cup* should give us pause. Where have we
heard that phrase before?

When Jesus was praying in the garden, He begged the Lord,
"My Father, if it is possible, let this cup pass from Me; yet not as
I will, but as You will" (Matt 26.39; *cf.* Mark 14.36; Luke 22.42).
What did Jesus mean when He asked that the cup be taken away
from Him? Jesus told Peter, "Put the sword into the sheath; the
cup which the Father has given Me, shall I not drink it?" (John
18.11). And when they requested special seats of honor in Jesus'
kingdom, He spoke with James and John about drinking His cup
(Matt 20.22–23; Mark 10.38–39). So, what cup was Jesus going
to drink?

The expression *this cup* was frequently used in the Old Testament: "For thus the Lord, the God of Israel, says to me, 'Take
this cup of the wine of wrath from My hand and cause all the
nations to whom I send you to drink it'" (Jer 25.15). This is a
figurative expression that communicates the idea of God's anger
and judgment in terms of a venomous potion that is drunk by

the victim to his own demise. In this context, the cup of God's wrath would cause the nations to stagger and go mad (Jer 25.16) and to "vomit, fall and rise no more" (Jer 25.27). It was a cup Jeremiah was to give to all the nations on the face of the earth. In Jeremiah, then, the idea of drinking this cup was the idea of receiving the punishment, the wrath, of God.

God often used the concept of drinking a cup to symbolize a nation's receiving His wrath and punishment. Consider Isaiah 51.17–23, where the "cup of His anger" is called the "chalice of reeling." There, this cup is taken from Jerusalem and put into the hand of "your tormentors." Ezekiel 23.31–34 speaks of a cup "which is deep and wide," first drunk by Samaria and then by Judah. It is a "cup of horror and desolation" that fills the one drinking it "with drunkenness and sorrow." Habakkuk speaks of the "cup in the Lord's right hand" that fills "with disgrace" (Hab 2.15–16). Asaph writes, "For a cup is in the hand of the Lord, and the wine foams; it is well mixed, and He pours out of this; surely all the wicked of the earth must drain and drink down its dregs" (Psa 75.8). Consider this announcement:

> If anyone worships the beast and his image, and receives a mark on his forehead or on his hand, he also will drink of the wine of the wrath of God, which is mixed in full strength in the cup of His anger; and he will be tormented with fire and brimstone in the presence of the holy angels and in the presence of the Lamb. (Rev 14.9–10)

The list continues: Job 21.20; Jeremiah 49.12; Lamentations 4.21; Zechariah 12.2. In sum, drinking the cup is a standard prophetic image to express the idea of receiving God's punishment, His just wrath.

When Jesus spoke of drinking the cup, He used an expression well known to students of Scripture. He spoke of drinking God's wrath, of being the object of God's punishment. The cup Jesus would drink was more than just enduring the scourging, the nailing onto the cross, and the asphyxiating death. He was also going to be the object of God's anger.

Why would God do this to Jesus? Jesus never sinned. He did

not deserve God's punishment. Of anyone who has ever lived, He was the one in whom God was well pleased. Why was the object of God's absolute pleasure to be the recipient of God's fierce wrath?

Consider another prophetic image: Isaiah described the Lord's care for His people in terms of a man carefully providing for a vineyard that he hoped would produce good grapes (Isa 5.1–7). The man spared no expense nor effort in giving the best of everything to his esteemed vineyard. He hoped for delicious grapes. The vineyard, however, produced only worthless ones. The vineyard represented God's people who should have produced the fruit of righteousness and justice, but instead were filled with violence and deceit. Therefore the Lord warned,

> I will lay it waste;
> It will not be pruned or hoed,
> But briars and thorns will come up.
> I will also charge the clouds to rain no rain on it.
> For the vineyard of the LORD of hosts is the house of Israel
> And the men of Judah His delightful plant.
> Thus He looked for justice, but behold, bloodshed;
> For righteousness, but behold, a cry of distress. (Isa 5.6–7)

Later, however, Isaiah spoke of the vineyard God was keeping, watering constantly and protecting (Isa 27.2–6). God said about this vineyard, His people, "I have no wrath" (Isa 27.4). What caused God's wrath to cease? Isaiah wrote also, "I will give thanks to You, O LORD; for although You were angry with me, Your anger is turned away, and You comfort me" (Isa 12.1). Why did God turn His anger away?

The reason God's anger ceased is because Jesus drank the cup of God's wrath. God whipped Jesus in our place. The cup of wrath that our sins richly deserved was quaffed by the Lord Himself. Consider these familiar words:

> Surely our griefs He Himself bore,
> And our sorrows He carried;
> Yet we ourselves esteemed Him stricken,
> Smitten of God, and afflicted.
> But He was pierced through for our transgressions,

He was crushed for our iniquities;
The chastening for our well-being fell upon Him,
And by His scourging we are healed.
All of us like sheep have gone astray,
Each of us has turned to his own way;
But the Lord has caused the iniquity of us all
To fall on Him. (Isa 53.4–6)

God has not punished us for our sins; instead, He took the punishment upon Himself. *He* suffered the wrath our sins deserved.

The depth of Jesus' sacrifice of Himself for us is unfathomable. He not only suffered great physical anguish, but He suffered God's wrath, God's punishment, in our place. We will never have to experience this wrath since Jesus took it upon Himself for us. As we drink *this cup* we remember *this cup* that Jesus dreaded so much to drink. And we remember that He suffered the punishment merited by our sins.

We Who Have Burdened Him
Isaiah 43.22–26

Andy Cantrell

The Bible contains 66 books; Isaiah has 66 chapters. The Old Testament has 39 books which explain God's holiness, righteousness, and justice and the judgments against a people who failed to understand Him; Isaiah's first 39 chapters are thematically the same as the Old Testament record. Failures of holiness, righteousness, and justice brought judgment on a people who revolted against the God who raised them (see Isa 1.2–3). The New Testament has 27 books which explore themes like God's compassion, comfort, mercy, and grace by revealing the Servant through whom these were manifested; Isaiah's last 27 chapters parallel that record. From the opening words of chapter 40—"Comfort, O comfort My people"—to the prophetic revealing of the Servant who would be the source of that comfort, Isaiah's writings are remarkably similar to the grand story recorded for us from Matthew to Revelation. Isaiah is the Bible in miniature form. I hesitate to attribute such to either providence or coincidence but I am confident enough to call it exceptional.

My purpose in this observation is to provide a context for the Scripture on which I've chosen to focus. It is found in the section of Isaiah concerning God's comfort, mercy and grace. It is Isaiah 43.22–26:

> Yet you have not called on Me, O Jacob;
> But you have become weary of Me, O Israel.

You have not brought to Me the sheep of your burnt offerings,
Nor have you honored Me with your sacrifices.
I have not burdened you with offerings,
Nor wearied you with incense.
You have bought Me not sweet cane with money,
Nor have you filled Me with the fat of your sacrifices;
Rather you have burdened Me with your sins,
You have wearied Me with your iniquities.
I, even I, am the one who wipes out your transgressions for
   My own sake,
And I will not remember your sins.
Put Me in remembrance. (NASB)

God had a charge against His people: they had failed Him. They had grown weary of God and, as a result, had ceased calling on Him. For no good reason, they had failed to sacrifice.

God had not made it too hard on them. He had not burdened them by asking too much from those whom He had bought, honored, filled, and blessed. All He requested was reciprocation. He found none. He had not burdened them, but they had burdened Him with their sins. He had given them no cause for weariness; rather, they had wearied Him with their iniquities. What is God to do with such unfair, disrespectful and unjust people?

I'd say destroy them. When my love is spurned, I grow angry. When I've wearied myself to love others only to have them ignore my sacrifices, I give up (at best) or seek vengeance (at worst). Not God. He is patient and merciful. He may discipline and send His children into bondage in foreign places, but He does not abandon them there or leave them without hope of reconciliation. Hear Him: "I, even I, am the one who wipes out your transgressions for My own sake, and I will not remember your sins" (v 25). What a promise! What a God, who suffers so much at our hands, yet continues to give!

Notice what God asks of them: "Put Me in remembrance" (v 26). There is more in the following verses, but this request is the essence. What a grand appeal! Is there anything more important to remember? But shouldn't they remember His gifts, His provisions, His deliverance, His patience, His constancy, His power, and His sustenance? Yes, but in remembering *Him* they will remember all that He is and has done. Remembering events, and gifts, and laws, and blessings is only valuable when the Giver is clearly honored. It was entirely possible, and common, to remember laws of sacrifice, a day of Passover, a feast of booths, yet forget the God who provided the meat, supplied the atoning blood, and sustained the wanderer in the wilderness. It is still common today.

It would be difficult to miss the similarities between this great passage and the tremendous themes of the Lord's Supper. When we assemble around the table there is much we need to remember, but simply one central memory will suffice. "Do this in remembrance of Me," Jesus said (Luke 22.19). And oh, what remembering Him will accomplish!

Remembering Him will remind us of our failures. The same failures Isaiah charged Israel with—the failure to call, to endure, to sacrifice, and to honor—are also our own. When we see His burden, we will recall that it is not God who has burdened us but we who have burdened Him with our sins. When we meditate on His suffering, we will remember that it is not God who wearies us but we who have wearied Him with our iniquities. "Surely He has borne our griefs, and carried our sorrows; yet we esteemed Him stricken, smitten by God, and afflicted. But He was wounded for our transgressions, He was bruised for our iniquities" (Isa 53.4–5 NKJV). We are to blame for His burden.

When we come to the table we must also recognize what God accomplished through bearing our burden and being wearied by our sin. Once again, remembering Jesus is the key. "Without shedding of blood there is no forgiveness" (Heb 9.22 NASB). Unless His body breaks and bleeds we have no hope. But if it does, then what God says through Isaiah is right: "I, even I, am the one who wipes out your transgressions for My own sake, and I will not remember your sins." Such power I do not understand. How can He erase all the wrong I've done? But more than that, what ability Jehovah has to forget! And perhaps greater still, what love is this that will both erase and forget the sins of the one who is the very cause of the burden He had to bear? Only a holy, benevolent and sovereign God can possess such power.

I must confess that I struggle at the table. Sometimes the weight of guilt for the burden I caused Him overwhelms my thoughts, clouding the gratitude due Him. On the other hand, at times the tremendous joy for the burden He bore obscures the reverent regret which is appropriate for such a memorial. I believe this beautiful passage in Isaiah 43 can bring balance to my struggle. For in it, both I and God are rightly portrayed. I am the burden bringer, He the burden bearer. I am the wearying, He is the wearied. I am the sinner, He the forgiver. I forget Him, He forgets my sin. I come empty-handed, He fulfills the sacrifice.

The Suffering Savior of Isaiah 53

Sewell Hall

Written approximately 700 years before Christ, Isaiah's report of his prophetic vision must have seemed, even to him, almost incredible. He begins it with the words: "Who has believed what he has heard from us?" (v 1 ESV).

In the preceding paragraph Isaiah had introduced God's servant who would act wisely, be high, lifted up, and exalted (52.13). Yet many would be astonished because "his appearance was so marred, beyond human semblance, and his form beyond that of the children of mankind" (52.14). Isaiah, however, expressed confidence that in the future "kings shall shut their mouths because of him; for that which has not been told them they see, and that which they have not heard they understand" (52.15).

Isaiah's Incredible Vision of God's Servant

An incredible manifestation. "For he grew up before him like a young plant, and like a root out of dry ground; he had no form or majesty that we should look at him, and no beauty that we should desire him" (v 2).

An incredible reception. "He was despised and rejected by men; a man of sorrows, and acquainted with grief; as one from whom men hide their faces he was despised, and we esteemed him not" (v 3).

An incredible substitution. "Surely he has borne our griefs and carried our sorrows; yet we esteemed him stricken, smitten by God, and afflicted. But he was wounded for our transgressions; he was crushed for our iniquities; upon him was the chastisement that brought us peace, and with his stripes we are healed" (vv 4–5).

An incredible imputation. "All we like sheep have gone astray; we have turned every one to his own way; and the Lord has laid on him the iniquity of us all" (v 6).

An incredible submission. "He was oppressed and he was afflicted, yet he opened not his mouth; like a lamb that is led to the slaughter, and like a sheep that before its shearers is silent, so he opened not his mouth" (v 7).

An incredible sacrifice. "By oppression and judgment he was taken away; and as for his generation, who considered that he was cut off out of the land of the living, stricken for the transgression of my people? And he made his grave with the wicked and with a rich man in his death, although he had done no violence, and there was no deceit in his mouth" (vv 8–9).

An incredible sequel. "Yet it was the will of the Lord to crush him. He has put him to grief; when his soul makes an offering for sin, he shall see his offspring; he shall prolong his days; the will of the Lord shall prosper in his hand. Out of the anguish of his soul he shall see and be satisfied; by his knowledge shall the righteous one, my servant, make many to be accounted righteous, and he shall bear their iniquities" (vv 10–11).

An incredible blessing. "Therefore, I will divide him a portion with the many, and he shall divide the spoil with the strong, because he poured out his soul to death and was numbered with the transgressors; yet he bore the sin of many and makes intercession for the transgressors" (v 12).

The Mystery

What could such a vision mean? Possibly, Isaiah himself did not know. The apostle Peter wrote, "Concerning this salvation, the prophets who prophesied about the grace that was to be yours searched and inquired carefully, inquiring what person or time the Spirit of Christ in them was indicating when he predicted the sufferings of Christ and the subsequent glories" (1 Pet 1.10–11).

Peter may well have had in mind this prophecy of Isaiah, for he quotes from it extensively in this epistle.

What Isaiah had anticipated concerning the uncovering of the mystery, Peter affirms had occurred in his own day. "It was revealed to them that they were serving not themselves but you, in the things that have now been announced to you through those who preached the good news to you by the Holy Spirit sent from heaven, things into which angels long to look" (1.12).

The Incredible Becomes Credible

One of those who preached the good news "by the Holy Spirit sent from heaven" was Philip "the evangelist," a word that means "teller of good news" (Acts 21.8). On the road from Jerusalem to Gaza he encountered an Ethiopian eunuch who was reading this very portion of Isaiah (Acts 8.26–33). It was still a mystery to the Ethiopian because he had not yet heard the good news. "Then Philip opened his mouth, and beginning with this Scripture he told him the good news about Jesus" (Acts 8.35).

What had seemed almost inexplicable to the prophet, and still defies explanation by those who have not accepted the good news, was entirely credible when the Ethiopian heard the story of Jesus. In His birth, humanity, rejection by His countrymen, His trial, Pilate's acknowledgment of His innocence, His vicarious death, resurrection, coronation, and priestly intercession Jesus had lived out perfectly the vision of Isaiah.

Jesus "himself bore our sins in his body on the tree, that we might die to sin and live to righteousness. By his wounds you have been healed" (1 Pet 2.24).

I Will Allure Her

David McClister

"I will allure her, bring her into the wilderness. …I will give her… the Valley of Achor as a door of hope." (Hos 2.14–15 NASB)

Hosea preached during a time of moral laxity in the early days of the northern kingdom. A combination of conditions had made the kingdom of Jeroboam II prosperous, and with that prosperity the people ignored their relationship with God. Many, it seems, had attributed the good times to Baal, not to God. In that context the prophet with an unfaithful wife preached—and lived out—his message to Israel: like Gomer, the nation has been unfaithful to her husband, but her husband wants her back.

In chapter 2—the chapter that summarizes Hosea's message—the prophet looked far into the future when God would be reunited with a faithful Israel. The sins of the past would be punished, and a new situation would come.

God promised that He would bring His bride into the wilderness. Every Jew knew that the wilderness was the place where the God-Israel relationship, the covenant, originally had been forged. To go back to the wilderness was to go back to the beginning. This time would be different, however. Instead of betrothing Himself to a bride who followed her sensual desire to illicit relationships with others, God would now have a faithful wife. God would allure her, and she would find herself forever attracted to Him. It is not insignificant in this regard that when John the Baptist appeared on the scene, he preached in the wilderness.

With John, the new Israel was being called to the wilderness, to a new beginning.

In that situation of a renewed covenant, God said that He would give Israel the valley of Achor as a door of hope. The valley of Achor was the scene of one of the most egregious crimes against God in all the Old Testament. When Israel first entered into the land of Canaan, in fulfillment of God's promise, they came to the city of Jericho. Now God had demanded of His people that the first of everything they had belonged to Him (*cf.* Exod 13 and 23). Since Jericho was the first city they would take in the conquest of the land, its spoils belonged to God. However, Achan, with the help of his family, stole loot from Jericho during the siege and hid it under his tent. The matter was discovered easily enough, and Achan and his family were executed at a place called Achor (Josh 7).

Achor was a blemish in what was an otherwise optimistic time. Under faithful Joshua the Israelites had every prospect of conquering the land that held tremendous blessings. Their successes in Transjordan had demonstrated that God would be with them against their enemies. Israel would indeed know the abundance of God's generosity in that land, but they had to wait for a moment, as it were. The spoils of the first city were for God, not for them; their portion would come afterward. But Achan did not want to wait. He took God's share and paid the price for his greed. Once his sin was punished, the nation could resume its work of pressing on into the fullness of the promised land.

How could this story, which the people of that day probably would rather have forgotten, serve as "a door of hope" in a new relationship with God? As embarrassing as it was, Achor was a good thing. Achan represented the attitude that could ruin everything. He was a man who trusted in what he saw in front of him instead of trusting in the promise of God. He allowed his fleshly desires, his greed, and his selfishness to dictate his actions. He was a fleshly man in the midst of what was supposed to be a holy people, a man who walked by sight in the midst of a people walking by faith. With Achan gone, the nation could press on and enter into the fullness of blessing that God had promised to them. In its own strange way, then, the death of this one man actually made the further blessing of Israel possible.

So in the Messianic age, God would make the new relationship between Himself and Israel possible by the death of one man, a man who bore the guilt of sin and died for it so that the rest of God's people might go on to greater blessing. Jesus took the role of Achan, but not because He Himself had lived a fleshly life or because He had robbed God. We were the ones who did that.

As a gift, God gave us the valley of Achor, the death of a man in our place, so that we might press on to the fullness of God's blessing. In the cross of Jesus the words of Hosea are fulfilled. The hill of Calvary is the valley of Achor, and the death of a condemned man is the door of hope for us all.

The Suffering Savior in Zechariah

Gary Fisher

The prophets give great insight into Jesus. Well-known texts like the servant songs in Isaiah (chapter 53, for example) and the covenant passage in Jeremiah (chapter 31) give many details about the Lord and His work. The prophets themselves did not always understand exactly what their writing meant (1 Pet 1.10–12), but we who are the recipients of their promised blessings can discern much by studying prophetic texts.

Zechariah is one of the least-studied prophets, but he gives tremendously helpful insights into the work of Christ. Since the book of Zechariah was written after the return from captivity, he does not see, as many earlier prophets did, a double fulfillment in the redemption from Babylon and in the redemption from sin. While the book of Zechariah may contain foreshadowing of the events of the intertestamental period or the work of Zechariah himself, Zechariah contains strikingly clear visions of Jesus and His work. His book easily divides itself into three sections: a series of eight visions (1–6), question and answers about fasting (7–8), and a series of highly apocalyptic prophecies (9–14).

Consider the glimpses of Jesus in the earlier parts of the book. 1. In 2.8–13 there is one—the Lord—who is sent to dwell in their midst. 2. In 3.1–5 clean clothes are put on the filthy high priest, Joshua, to symbolize purification from sin. No explanation of how this is accomplished is given in the context, but we understand from the New Testament that this cleansing comes through the atonement Jesus provides. 3. In chapter 4, Jesus is symbolized by two olive trees (king and priest) that provide constant oil to light the lampstands (the people of God). 4. In 6.9–15, we find one of the most striking predictions of the book: a person named Branch will build the temple of the Lord and unite priesthood and kingship in one office. 5. In chapter 8, the great blessings of God come through a Jew (see especially 8.23).

These prophecies of Jesus, scattered through the first eight chapters, provide the Christian with unusual but helpful perspectives on Jesus' roles: Immanuel, Sanctifier, King, Priest, Son of Abraham. Much of the rest of the book, however, sheds light on another important function of our Lord—Suffering Savior.

The Suffering Savior

Consider the Suffering Savior in Zechariah 9–14. First, in 9.9 the King is portrayed as "humble, and mounted on a donkey, even on a colt, the foal of a donkey." This shows Jesus' meekness. He did not ride into the capital city on a steed, a black stallion, nor a white charger. He rode in on the offspring of a donkey! From birth to death, Jesus humbled Himself and lived a lowly life. The words of a hymn by C.E. Couchman come to mind:

> God incarnate, can it be?
> Ponder now the mystery:
> He, the Fount of Eternal Life,
> Must drink the cup of mortality.
> Immanuel, God with us.

> Shepherds wonder at the scene:
> Swaddling robes for Deity;
> Heaven's throne now a bed of straw
> Within these borrowed stable walls.
> Immanuel, God with us.

> God Creator, now created,
> Lord of all in infancy.
> Hands that lighted the evening stars
> Reach out for comfort in Mary's arms
> Immanuel, God with us.[1]

Second, in 11.4–14 Zechariah himself prefigures the Savior. God sends Zechariah with a mission to rescue the doomed flock of His people. Their previous shepherds had only exploited the sheep for their own gain. So Zechariah takes over and begins to provide good shepherding. The people reject Zechariah's efforts, however, and he resigns from the job. He asks the people either to give him his severance pay or just to forget it. But they do neither; instead, they give him an insultingly pitiful sum, which really only serves to demonstrate their disdain. A mere thirty shekels of silver! Zechariah orders the money thrown to the potter to show how disgusting it is to be insulted like that.

Do you see the parallels? God sent Jesus to be the Good Shepherd. He did everything to bless the people, but they turned on Him, rejected Him and sold Him for a mere pittance, which was then used to buy a potter's field. Jesus—like Zechariah, but to a much greater degree—experienced deeply the hurt and pain of rejection.

Third, in 12.10 the Redeemer is pierced, a term which probably is used to sum up His horrifying crucifixion. Terms like *pierced* do not have to be fulfilled literally to be valid (see Psalm 22.16 also), but God draws greater attention to them as Jesus' flesh was literally perforated by the nails in His hands and feet. Jesus' soul was cut by the defection of the disciples and the ridicule of the multitude. His scalp was broken by the crown of thorns. His back was deeply lacerated by the jagged bits of bone, metal and glass attached to the scourgers' whips. For hours, just to breathe, Jesus had to push against the nails that penetrated His extremities. It is not hard to see Jesus as the fulfillment of Zechariah; He is the One whom they pierced.

Finally, in 13.7 we see God striking the Shepherd—the one whom He had sent—with His sword. Jesus' death was according to God's predetermined will (Acts 2.23). The awfulness of this truth is overwhelming. He did not take His horrible cup of wrath away from the lips of Jesus. Yes, Judas betrayed Jesus, the Jews delivered Him to the authorities, and the Romans nailed Him onto the cross; nevertheless, in reality, Jesus died by God's will and decision. This is staggering: God executed His wrath on His only Son.

Our Response

How are we to respond to this vivid picture of Jesus in Zechariah? In 12.10–13.6, Zechariah offers four steps to responding properly to the Suffering Servant. First, we are to *look on* the One who is pierced (12.10). This look involves both turning to Him and trusting in Him. Considering all the anguish that Jesus suffered for us, we should meditate on Him and then seek His will in everything. We are doing this very thing in the Lord's Supper. We are to look on the one we have pierced.

Looking on Him will produce the second step: intense mourning (12.10–14). Zechariah describes it as mourning as for a firstborn son—an only son—like the annual mourning for the death of Josiah. He is describing here some of the most poignant grief that exists. Proverbially, it is harder to bury a child than a parent, and worse yet, a firstborn or only child. Our sins—and the price that had to be paid for them—should make us grieve to the very limits of human sorrow.

In Zechariah 12, the mourners include the royal families of David and Nathan (*cf.* 1 Chron 14.4) and the priestly families of Levi and Shimei (*cf.* Num 3.18; 1 Chron 6.17). It is individual mourning, each family to itself, and not a case of mass psychology or ritual. Each individual must genuinely repent of and deeply grieve for his own sin. When we partake of the Supper, we should feel anguish by what our sin cost our Lord.

Third, we must take advantage of the fountain opened for sin and impurity (13.1). The fountain here is a symbol of the pardon and cleansing God offers. Though sorrow is essential, no amount of weeping can cleanse our sins. Only God, through the sacrifice of Jesus, can do that. When we eat the bread and drink the cup, we are thinking of the abundant forgiveness the Lord's opened fountain provides.

Finally, there must be a radically changed life. In Zechariah's prophecy, the besetting sins of Israel's past—idolatry and false prophecy—are totally eliminated (13.2–6). The people's commitment to righteousness is so strong that parents even execute their own wicked children (*cf.* Deut 13; Luke 12.51–53). Just as our sorrow for what we have done must rival the sorrow that we might feel if we were to lose our firstborn child, our commitment to the Lord must be such that we are willing to make any sacrifice to serve Him, even if that means our own children.

When we turn to the Lord from our sins, zeal for the truth must override human relationships. No one wants to admit idolatry. We would prefer even to be thought of as wounded by 'friends,' rather than to be seen having idolatrous markings on our bodies (Zech 13.4–6). When we now contemplate the Lord's death, we resolve more fully to break with our own besetting sin and give ourselves as a living sacrifice to God, regardless of the cost.

These are the reactions to the Lord's death that we should bring to His table. Zechariah helps us see Jesus, what He did for us, and most of all, what our commitment to Him should entail. Zechariah shows us not only how to mourn for our sins, but how to turn to Christ's fountain for forgiveness.

At the Lord's Supper, we focus on the One whom *we* have pierced. We look on the one who was wounded for our transgressions (Isa 53.5), whom God struck for our sins. Such love—such willingness to suffer for us—should drive us from our sins into repentance and humble obedience. Perhaps Isaac Watts says it best:

When I survey the wondrous cross
On which the Prince on glory died,
My richest gain I count but loss,
And pour contempt on all my pride.

Jesus Christ and Jacob's Ladder

Doy Moyer

Jesus found Philip. Then Philip found Nathanael, who was reluctant to believe in Jesus until after Jesus demonstrated that He had seen Nathanael under a fig tree. Nathanael replied, "Rabbi, you are the Son of God! You are the King of Israel!" Jesus then told Nathanael that he would see "greater things" (John 1.43–50, ESV). What could he possibly see that was greater?

"Truly, truly, I say to you, you will see heaven opened, and the angels of God ascending and descending on the Son of Man" (John 1.51).

This statement by Jesus has puzzled many readers. To help solve this puzzle, we first note that the idea of the heavens being opened carries with it the concept of God conferring blessings. Psalm 78.23–24 shows this: "Yet he commanded the skies above and opened the doors of heaven, and he rained down on them manna to eat and gave them the grain of heaven." God took care of the children of Israel in the wilderness by opening the "doors of heaven" and raining down manna for their sustenance. He blessed them by opening up the heavens.

We find a parallel, of course, to Jesus as the bread of life who came down out of heaven (John 6). He is the "true bread from heaven" (v 32), and by coming to Him and partaking of Him we gain the life that He promises: "This is the bread that comes down from heaven, so that one may eat of it and not die. I am the living bread that came down from heaven. If anyone eats this bread, he will live forever. And the bread that I will give for the life of the world is my flesh" (John 6.50–51). In this sense, then, God has opened the doors of heaven to provide life for us through our partaking of Jesus—not just in partaking of the Lord's Supper, but by imbibing Jesus and His teachings throughout all of life. The blessings that God provides through sending Jesus are even greater than what Jesus had told Nathanael about seeing him under the fig tree.

As a second point, consider the "Son of Man" language. This phrase was commonly used by Jesus as a self-reference. While we recognize that it conveys a basic recognition of Jesus' humanity, the phrase itself is a Messianic title. Jesus' use of the phrase calls people to recognize the Son of Man as the Messiah pictured in Daniel 7.13–14, in which the son of man figure is presented before the Ancient of Days to receive "dominion and glory and a kingdom, that all peoples, nations, and languages should serve him." The emphasis is that Jesus, though come in the flesh, is of heavenly origin, has divine authority, and will reign forever. Thus, through the universal reign of the Son of Man, we are blessed by God: "Do not labor for the food that perishes, but for the food that endures to eternal life, which the Son of Man will give to you. For on him God the Father has set his seal" (John 6.27).

Still, how are we to take John 1.51? We haven't explained "the angels of God ascending and descending on the Son of Man." The only time in Jesus' life on earth when the heavens were said to have been opened was at His baptism (Matt 3.13–17). After he came up from the water, the heavens were opened and the Spirit of God descended and rested on Him. Then the voice came from heaven: "This is my beloved Son, with whom I am well pleased." We could also point to the heavens' being opened in connection with Jesus when Stephen, as he was about to die, saw Jesus, "the Son of Man," standing at the right hand of God (Acts 7.56). But neither of these passages explains John 1.51, and we find no other event in Jesus' life coinciding with angels ascending and descending upon Him like this. We are left with one viable alternative: Jacob's vision in Genesis 28.10–22 is the key.

Jacob was on his way from Beersheba to Haran, a place well north of Palestine. He came to a city, rested, and had a vision. A ladder was set on the earth and reached into heaven. He saw angels ascending and descending on this ladder. The Lord stood above it and spoke, reaffirming the promises that were made to Abraham. Thus the heavens were opened for Jacob and God conferred His blessings. When Jacob awoke, he was afraid and said, "How awesome is this place! This is none other than the house of God, and this is the gate of heaven" (v 17). This place came to be called Bethel ("house of God"), and here Jacob affirmed his covenant with God.

As we note the key components of this vision, we can perhaps see the import of Jesus' statement in John 1. The ladder reaching from earth to heaven clearly depicts access to God. As the heavens are opened to confer blessings, the ladder is used in both directions. God's messengers both descend and ascend this ladder. God sends His message to earth, and His message invites us back to heaven. Yet God is ever in control. These are His messengers, and He controls the access as well as the blessings.

The covenant context of Genesis 28 is also significant. God renewed the Abrahamic covenant here with Jacob, including the critical promise, "In you and your offspring shall all the families of the earth be blessed" (v 14). Indeed the greatest blessing conferred by God out of heaven is this seed promise. This is the promise Peter points to:

> You are the sons of the prophets and of the covenant that God made with your fathers, saying to Abraham, "And in your offspring shall all the families of the earth be blessed." God, having raised up his servant, sent him to you first, to bless you by turning every one of you from your wickedness. (Acts 3.25–26)

In other words, the great blessing here is forgiveness of sins.

How can we have this great blessing? We cannot simply reach up into heaven. No, but God has opened up the heavens by sending Jesus for this very purpose. By means of Jesus' death on the cross, the shedding of His blood, God has opened the heavens in the greatest sense (see Heb 9.11–14).

So why did Jesus use the language of Genesis 28 to describe to Nathanael the "greater things"? Because it shows that Jesus is the ultimate answer to Jacob's vision. He is the fulfillment of the promise. He is the true access to heaven itself. He is that ladder that reaches from earth to heaven and the means by which God bestows the greatest blessing of forgiveness, so that fellowship can be restored with His creation and we can all share in the glory of heaven. Through the death and resurrection of Jesus, God has indeed opened the heavens in the most profound way and allows us to participate in the seed promise of Abraham. The blood of the cross has opened heaven.

Jacob's response to the vision is significant. He set up a stone as a pillar, called the place Bethel, and recognized the place as the "gate of heaven." For us, God has set Jesus as the cornerstone upon which we are built as living stones in the spiritual house of God (1 Pet 2). When we look at the cross, and as we partake of the body and blood of the Lord, let us see in this memorial the gate of heaven which God has lovingly opened on our behalf.

John 2

Water to Wine

David McClister

Jesus' first miracle was done at a wedding feast in a little back-woods village, and in such a way that most of the people there did not even know that a miracle had happened. When we reflect upon the humble nature of Jesus and the kingdom He came to establish, it is fitting that the world's first glimpse of the miracle-working power of the Messiah should be in a place of no special significance. We should also immediately note that Jesus' ministry both began and ended using the symbolism of wine. At the beginning of His ministry He turned water into wine, and at the end of His ministry He sat at another feast with His disciples and told them that the cup which they drank, filled with fruit of the vine, symbolized the blood of His death. Two feasts. One joyous, the other ominously sad. Are they related? Can the miracle at Cana help us think about the Lord's Supper?

First, it is easy, I think, to get the wrong impression about the circumstances under which Jesus worked this miracle. Some have read the account in John 2 as if Jesus did not want to work a miracle that day, but was somehow coaxed into it by Mary. However, it is hard to believe such a scenario. Jesus was always in control of His ministry. If He had judged that it was inap-propriate to work a miracle there, on that day, Mary could not have changed His mind. It is better, I think, if we see Mary's words as suggesting that Jesus do something publicly—open and spectacular—that would announce to everyone at the feast, and in the village, that the long-awaited Messiah had arrived with all His power. Such a display, however, was not the impression Jesus wished to create. As insightful as Mary may have been into the true identity of her son, hers was not the way the Messiah or the kingdom would come.

There was, however, something quite appropriate about this occasion that no doubt factored heavily in Jesus' actions. The prophets had often spoken about the Messianic age in the imageries of both wine and weddings. Joel said,

> The LORD will answer and say to His people, "Behold, I am going to send you grain, new wine and oil, and you will be satisfied in full with them; and I will never again make you a reproach among the nations. …The threshing floors will be full of grain, and the vats will overflow with the new wine and oil." (2.19, 24 NASB)

Isaiah described the Messianic age as a banquet (a feast) in which God served the best of everything, including wine: "The LORD of hosts will prepare a lavish banquet for all peoples on this mountain; a banquet of aged wine, choice pieces with marrow, and refined, aged wine" (25.6). Isaiah also spoke of the Messianic age in terms of a wedding:

> It will no longer be said to you, "Forsaken," nor to your land will it any longer be said, "Desolate"; but you will be called, "My delight is in her," and your land, "Married"; for the LORD delights in you, and to Him your land will be married. For as a young man marries a virgin, so your sons will marry you; and as the bridegroom rejoices over the bride, so your God will rejoice over you. (Isa 62.4–5)

Wine and weddings were themselves symbols of the good things of life, and God used them as images and symbols of the goodness of the Messianic age. This point is important. To see these prophetic pictures in a literal or physical way is to miss the point of them altogether, and would in fact be a serious misunderstanding of them. It is not that the Messianic age would literally be a time of wine and weddings. The Messianic age would be *like* wine and weddings in that it would be a time to enjoy the best things God gives to man. As in the parables Jesus taught, physical things point to spiritual things.

When Jesus turned the water into *wine* at a *wedding feast* in Cana, we must see this as a calculated action on Jesus' part, intended to convey the fullness of the imagery that was at hand on that day. By performing this miracle, Jesus was announcing that the Messianic age, the time that would be like wine and weddings, had begun. The Messianic feast was here, the wedding of God and His people was to happen, and they would all enjoy the sweet wine of God's goodness in the greatest possible way. Although Jesus did not make a formal, verbal announcement that day, His miracle proclaimed what was going on. Anyone who knew the words of the prophets would have seen immediately the true significance of this miracle.

Weddings were not the only place in Jewish culture that had a positive association with wine. The Jews had also added wine to the items of the Passover meal. Exactly when this practice began is unknown, but the rabbis associated the four cups of wine drunk at the Passover with the four statements of redemption in Exodus 6.6–7. That is, the rabbis made a connection between the blessing of God's redemption and the symbolic quality of wine to represent blessing. To them, it seemed natural to remember the blessing of redemption at the exodus with wine at the Passover. Furthermore, all of this was part of a feast that, perhaps more than any other Jewish rite, anticipated the Messianic age. The idea is clear: the wine that had been added to the Passover meal not only symbolized Israel's past rescue from Egypt, but also symbolized and anticipated the ultimate redemption that was to come in the Messianic age.

A cup of wine, however, could also be a biblical image for the wrath of God. The dark-red color of grape juice naturally resembled blood, and God used the image of wine in scenes of judgment: "I have trodden the wine trough alone, and from the peoples there was no man with Me. I also trod them in My anger and trampled them in My wrath; and their lifeblood is sprinkled on My garments, and I stained all My raiment" (Isa 63.3), and, "For thus the LORD, the God of Israel, says to me, 'Take this cup of the wine of wrath from My hand and cause all the nations to whom I send you to drink it. They will drink and stagger and go mad because of the sword that I will send among them'" (Jer 25.15–16). So it is not surprising that Jesus spoke of His death using this same imagery. He once asked His disciples, "'Are you able to drink the cup that I am about to drink?' They said to Him, 'We are able.' He said to them, 'My cup you shall drink'" (Matt 20.22–23), and at the Last Supper: "And when He had taken a cup and given thanks, He gave it to them, saying, 'Drink from it, all of you; for this is My blood of the covenant, which is poured out for many for forgiveness of sins'" (Matt 26.27–28).

At the Last Supper, Jesus exchanged the joyous symbolism of wine that had come to be part of the Passover with the ominous symbolism of wine associated with the judgment of God. The wine of God's goodness in the Messianic age turned out to be the wine of God's judgment on sin. The joyous Messianic feast would be served with the "wine" of God's condemnation of human sin.

It is fitting, when we partake of the fruit of the vine in the Lord's Supper, that we understand that it has roots in imagery that communicated both the blessing of God and the wrath of God. Both were joined in perfect union in the Messiah's death: "By his bruises we are healed." In the same One, and in the same act, we comprehend both the condemnation and salvation of God. The wrath of God that Jesus endured for us has produced the great blessing of eternal redemption, and the blessing could come only through the suffering for man's sins. The Messianic time of wine and wedding has come, and with the same cup we appropriate the wine of God's wrath and the wine of God's blessing.

The Serpent, the Son, and Deliverance
Numbers 21 and the Cross

Ethan R. Longhenry

"And as Moses lifted up the serpent in the wilderness, so must the Son of Man be lifted up." (John 3.14 ESV)

We can only imagine the increasing level of confusion experienced by Nicodemus as he sat and listened to Jesus on that Judean evening. Jesus taught Nicodemus many spiritual truths that were difficult for him to understand, but the lesson of verse 14 was perhaps particularly difficult. Nicodemus surely understood the story to which Jesus referred, yet the application mystified him. Of what did Jesus speak?

Jesus' Referent: Moses and the Serpent

If we are to understand Jesus' application, we must first understand Jesus' referent. Jesus speaks of Moses lifting up a serpent in the wilderness, and we find the narrative of that event in Numbers 21.4–9:

> From Mount Hor they set out by the way to the Red Sea, to go around the land of Edom. And the people became impatient on the way.
>
> And the people spoke against God and against Moses, "Why have you brought us up out of Egypt to die in the wilderness? For there is no food and no water, and we loathe this worthless food."
>
> Then the LORD sent fiery serpents among the people, and they bit the people, so that many people of Israel died.

And the people came to Moses and said, "We have sinned, for we have spoken against the LORD and against you. Pray to the LORD, that he take away the serpents from us." So Moses prayed for the people.

And the LORD said to Moses, "Make a fiery serpent and set it on a pole, and everyone who is bitten, when he sees it, shall live." So Moses made a bronze serpent and set it on a pole. And if a serpent bit anyone, he would look at the bronze serpent and live.

In this story, the Israelites sin by not respecting the gifts given to them by God, and God punishes them with serpents. To deliver them from the serpents, God commands Moses to create a likeness of the serpents; the people must look up at the image of the serpent to be healed. Deliverance from death thus comes by God's power to those who look upon the image of the serpent.

Jesus *Lifted Up* on the Cross

Jesus indicates in John 3.14 that just as Moses lifted up the serpent in the wilderness, so also the Son of Man must be lifted up. What Nicodemus may not have understood in John 3 is rather clear to us: as Moses lifted up the serpent, Jesus will be lifted up on the cross.

Jesus knows full well the fate that will befall Him; He begins to describe the fate awaiting Him in Jerusalem to the disciples in Matthew 16.21, and as He institutes the Lord's Supper in Matthew 26.26–28, He describes the cup as "the blood of the covenant, which is poured out for many for the forgiveness of sins" (Matt 16.28). As the "Lamb of God who takes away the sin of the world" (John 1.29), Jesus teaches Nicodemus the sober truth about His own fate.

The parallel goes beyond the simple act of being lifted up. Not only is Jesus lifted up as Moses lifted up the serpent, but the result is also deliverance. Jesus had no need to die for His own sin or for any infraction that He committed, for in Him there was no sin, neither was there any deceit in His mouth (*cf.* Isa 53.9; 1 Pet 2.20–22; Heb 4.15; 7.27). He was lifted up for our transgressions, so that we could have the remission of sin in His blood, and have restored association with God (Isa 53.5; Matt 26.28; 1 John 1.1–7). As it is written,

> And I will pour out on the house of David and the inhabitants of Jerusalem a spirit of grace and pleas for mercy, so that, when they look on me, on him whom they have pierced, they shall mourn for him, as one mourns for an only child, and weep bitterly over him, as one weeps over a firstborn. (Zech 12.10)

We understand that this prophecy is directly fulfilled by the Roman soldiers who pierce the side of Jesus with a spear to verify His death (John 19.37), yet we must also internalize the prophecy for ourselves. We have pierced God by our sin, for He went to the cross on our behalf for our transgression (Isa 53.5; Rom 5.6–8). We must look upon Christ on the cross, the One whom we have pierced, and we should mourn for our sin and its terrible consequences. If we look upon Him in obedient faith, we gain our deliverance. Just as the Israelites looked to the image of the serpent to be healed of their wounds, so we must look to Jesus on the cross if we desire to be healed of our iniquities.

Jesus *Lifted Up* in the Resurrection

Jesus is not only lifted up on the cross. If it were so, His death would be worthless, and we would still be lost in our sins (1 Cor 15.12–18). On the third day, however, the first day of the week, Jesus was again lifted up—in the resurrection (John 20).

Jesus is no less aware of His coming resurrection than He was of His impending death on the cross (Matt 16.21; 26.29). In John 2.13–22, as Jesus cleanses the temple in Jerusalem, He says, "Destroy this temple, and in three days I will raise it up" (John 2.19). While everyone thought He spoke of the temple, Jesus' disciples would later remember the event and understand that He spoke of the "temple of His body" (v 21); they then understood Him to be speaking of His resurrection. No doubt Nicodemus, reflecting upon his dialogue with Jesus as recorded in John 3 after everything had taken place, would also recognize that Jesus spoke of His death and His resurrection in John 3.14.

Still, how does Jesus' being lifted up in the resurrection have anything to do with Moses lifting up the serpent? The connection may not be immediately apparent, but we can understand it if we look at the events in Numbers 21.4–9 as the type of the reality seen in the resurrection. God plagues the sinful Israelites with serpents; to deliver them from death, God commands Moses to make an image of the serpent. In this event, looking upon the image of the thing that kills brings life.

The serpent also represents a much deeper level of mortality. We remember in Genesis 3 how the serpent beguiled Eve into eating of the fruit of the tree of the knowledge of good and evil (Gen 3.1–6), incurring sin and death for mankind. But God did not leave man without promise: "I will put enmity between you and the woman, and between your offspring and her offspring; he shall bruise your head, and you shall bruise his heel" (Gen 3.15).

While men have been bitten by snakes and have in turn killed snakes for millennia, we understand that God is speaking primarily of the conflict between man and Satan who is represented by the serpent (*cf.* Rev 12.9). Through sin, Satan has successfully bruised the heel of all men and women, and we all are under the sentence of sin and death because of it (Rom 3.5–23). Jesus was the one who was able to bruise Satan's head by conquering both sin and death, dying on the cross for the remission of sin and being raised to life again on the third day (Rom 5.12–18; 1 Cor 15.21–22). Jesus gained the victory, and we are able to be victors in Him, as it is written:

> When the perishable puts on the imperishable, and the mortal puts on immortality, then shall come to pass the saying that is written:
> "Death is swallowed up in victory."
> "O death, where is your victory?
> O death, where is your sting?"
> The sting of death is sin, and the power of sin is the law. But thanks be to God, who gives us the victory through our Lord Jesus Christ. (1 Cor 15.54–57; *cf.* Rom 16.20)

Moses' lifting the serpent in the wilderness represents the type: the Israelites were bitten by snakes; by looking upon the image of a snake they were healed. This points us to the resurrection of Jesus and our own victory: we have been bitten by sin, and by looking to Jesus who was made to be sin (2 Cor 5.21) and then lifted up in the resurrection, we have the victory over death, beginning in our baptism and ending in our resurrection on the final day (Rom 6.3–7; 1 Cor 15; 1 Pet 1.3–9).

Conclusion
The bronze serpent that Moses created, also called Nehushtan, is found again in 2 Kings 18.4. It had remained with the Ark and the Tabernacle (and later the Temple) for about 700 years. Then Hezekiah, king of Judah, had it destroyed. It had become an object of worship: "for until those days the people of Israel had made offerings to it" (2 Kings 18.4).

The end of Nehushtan provides us with a sober reminder: it is very easy for humans to begin to worship the object of deliverance and not the God who provided the power behind the object. In our own day we find many who venerate the cross and even the emblems of the Lord's Supper, doing much the same as their Israelite forebears.

Nevertheless, God intended that His people never forget what He accomplished on the cross and in the resurrection. To that end, Jesus established the Lord's Supper, the bread and fruit of the vine representing His body and blood, and Christians observe that memorial on the first day of the week, the day upon which He was raised from the dead (Matt 26.26–28; Matt 28.1ff; Acts 20.7). The Lord's Supper was never designed to focus on the bread, the fruit of the vine, or the first day of the week, but to provide Christians with a concrete reminder of what was done on their behalf and the victory achieved by God's power. The Lord's Supper provides us the opportunity to look upon Jesus, both on the cross and in His resurrection. We have the opportunity to look upon Him whom we have pierced with our sins and grieve for them and for the suffering Jesus experienced because of them. Our partaking on the first day of the week provides us the reminder that Jesus was raised and that we are under His lordship and await His return (Matt 28.18; 1 Cor 11.23–26). As the Israelites looked up to Nehushtan and received temporary deliverance from death, let us take the opportunity provided us in the Lord's Supper to look up with eyes of faith to Jesus, that we may receive eternal life (John 3.15).

The Rock of Living Water
Exodus 17 and John 4

Ethan R. Longhenry

And all drank the same spiritual drink. For they drank from the spiritual Rock that followed them, and the Rock was Christ. (1 Cor 10.4)

The situation in Corinth was dire. Paul knew that the brethren needed to understand the consequences of disobeying God, so he turned to the story of Israel's exodus and wanderings in the desert to illustrate God's reactions to sin. To make his point clear, Paul wrote of the exodus and the wanderings of Israel through allegory. In so doing, Paul presented a wonderful way to understand those events in Christian terms—and also to understand our own walk with Christ in terms of Israel's exodus and wanderings.

One such aspect of Israel's wanderings is illustrated in 1 Corinthians 10.4: Israel's drinking from the *spiritual Rock*. This Rock *followed* them, and the *Rock was Christ!* Paul says much here that requires spiritual insight and understanding.

Israel and the Rock
When Paul speaks about Israel drinking from a rock, he refers to Exodus 17.1–7:

All the congregation of the people of Israel moved on from the wilderness of Sin by stages, according to the commandment of the Lord, and camped at Rephidim, but there was no water for the people to drink.

Therefore the people quarreled with Moses and said, "Give us water to drink."

And Moses said to them, "Why do you quarrel with me? Why do you test the LORD?"

But the people thirsted there for water, and the people grumbled against Moses and said, "Why did you bring us up out of Egypt, to kill us and our children and our livestock with thirst?"

So Moses cried to the LORD, "What shall I do with this people? They are almost ready to stone me."

And the LORD said to Moses, "Pass on before the people, taking with you some of the elders of Israel, and take in your hand the staff with which you struck the Nile, and go. Behold, I will stand before you there on the rock at Horeb, and you shall strike the rock, and water shall come out of it, and the people will drink."

And Moses did so, in the sight of the elders of Israel. And he called the name of the place Massah and Meribah, because of the quarreling of the people of Israel, and because they tested the LORD by saying, "Is the LORD among us or not?" (ESV)

Moses later strikes another rock to provide water for Israel, although he was commanded merely to speak to it (Num 20.2–12).

When we read of Israel's wanderings in the wilderness, we must not think of wildernesses with which we are familiar, with trees and birds and the like. The wilderness in which Israel wandered was desert, quite inhospitable, and on its own insufficient to sustain Israel's numbers. While Israel wandered in the wilderness, they were entirely dependent on God for food and water; He always provided for them.

We understand from Exodus 16.2–5 that manna, the food with which God sustained Israel, fell like dew from the heavens. The water in Exodus 17.1–7, however, comes from striking a rock, an object not normally known for retaining water. Why did God intend for Moses to provide water for Israel through a rock? And how does Moses' striking the rock that provides water correlate with Christ's being a rock? We must understand that the rock of water in Exodus 17.1–7 represents a type of which Jesus is the substance, as the Gospel of John makes clear.

Jesus and Living Water

John recorded for us, in John 4.4–26, an interaction between Jesus and a woman of Samaria that introduces us to the concept of *living water*. Jesus sits at a well and requests water of this woman, and when she asks Him why He would make such a request from a Samaritan, He responds by indicating that if she knew who He really was, she would ask for and receive living water (John 4.4–10). In the following exchanges it becomes clear that Jesus speaks spiritually while the Samaritan woman thinks physically. She would love to need no longer to drink water and carry it home from the well—but Jesus is not speaking of physical water. He indicates that the water He offers becomes a spring that wells up within a man to eternal life (John 4.14). While the Samaritan woman ends up believing in Jesus as the Messiah, it is not clear whether she ever understands His meaning.

Jesus later proclaims a similar message in the Temple: "On the last day of the feast, the great day, Jesus stood up and cried out, 'If anyone thirsts, let him come to me and drink. Whoever believes in me, as the Scripture has said, "Out of his heart will flow rivers of living water"'" (John 7.37–38).

From this proclamation we may better understand what Jesus meant by *living water*. Jesus is the source of eternal life for all who believe in Him, and the living water represents the Word, the way of salvation, which Jesus manifested in the world (John 1.1, 14). God's message of salvation and eternal life in the Son refreshes the believer who then has no need for refreshment from another. Such is the living water provided by Jesus, also attested in Revelation 22.17: "The Spirit and the Bride say, 'Come.' And let the one who hears say, 'Come.' And let the one who is thirsty come; let the one who desires take the water of life without price."

The idea of Christ as a rock is presented in other Scriptures. Jesus is the *chief cornerstone* that is rejected by builders but accepted by God, as prophesied in Psalm 118.22–23. Jesus also is the foundation of the faith, as Paul establishes in 1 Corinthians 3.11; likewise, the confession that He is the Christ is the rock upon which Christ builds His church (Matt 16.18). We see that the New Testament presents Jesus both as the source of *living water* and also as the *Rock*, the foundation of our faith.

Conclusion

We gain understanding of Paul's meaning in 1 Corinthians 10.4 by conflating all the imagery described above. The New Testament speaks of Jesus as a rock and as a source of living water, and the Old Testament speaks of Israel being sustained by water provided by God through the striking of a rock. Thanks to Paul's blending of the two, we may understand Jesus as the Rock, struck to provide living water leading to eternal life for those who believe.

Paul's concept directly applies most clearly to the Lord's Supper and our observance of this memorial of Christ's death. The Scriptures speak of Jesus being struck for our sins (Isa 53.4–5; 1 Pet 2.21–25). John provides the description of Jesus being pierced while on the cross, with blood and water pouring forth (John 19.34). While this is consistent with medical understanding of the result of death by crucifixion, it also represents an insightful mix of powerful imagery: the blood of atonement and the water of eternal life coming out of our Savior on the cross.

> So Jesus said to them, "Truly, truly, I say to you, unless you eat the flesh of the Son of Man and drink his blood, you have no life in you. Whoever feeds on my flesh and drinks my blood has eternal life, and I will raise him up on the last day. For my flesh is true food, and my blood is true drink. Whoever feeds on my flesh and drinks my blood abides in me, and I in him." (John 6.53–56)

Although Jesus does not speak directly of the Lord's Supper while speaking to the Jews, His words certainly evoke it. When we observe the Lord's Supper, let us reflect on the Rock that was struck for our sins, and how we are able to drink the living water, flowing from Him, that leads to eternal life.

If I Am Lifted Up from the Earth

David McClister

"And if I am lifted up from the earth, I will draw all men to myself." (John 12.32)[1]

What did Jesus mean when He spoke of being "lifted up"? The question is appropriate if for no other reason than because it appears that none of His contemporaries understood what this expression meant, even though Jesus apparently spoke of it fairly often. In John 12, Jesus' respondents seem to have thought that Jesus was speaking of leaving the earth. They said, "We have heard out of the Law that the Messiah will remain forever, so how do you say that the Son of Man must be lifted up?" (v 34). *Lifted up* was obviously the opposite of *remain forever*, in their way of thinking. A Messiah who came and then left was not what the Jews were expecting or hoping for. Exactly what passage from the Hebrew Bible they had in mind is hard to say, although a good guess may be Psalm 89.4, 36, which speaks of the seed of David (v 51 the anointed, or the Messiah) as enduring forever, and His throne as established forever.

We must also realize that these respondents' reference to the Scriptures reveals more about their own theologically- and politically-charged reading of the Scriptures than it does about the true meaning or message of the Scriptures themselves. It is not hard to see that what these people had gathered from the Scriptures was a scenario of a Messiah who came to earth, established the kingdom of God for the Jews, and then stayed among them to ensure that things never went wrong again. In many ways, it would be a kind of utopia. How could all of this happen, however, if the Messiah did not stay?

That Jesus was speaking of His ascension is often still the first thought that runs through people's minds when they read John 12.32 today. As it turns out, this is only partially correct. The fact is that there were three things that constituted Jesus' being *lifted up*. First, Jesus understood that His return to the Father (John 13.3; 16.28) involved going the route of the cross. "I have a baptism with which to be baptized, and how tormented I am until it is accomplished" (Luke 12.50). "Unless a grain of wheat falls into the earth and dies, it remains alone, but if it dies, it bears much fruit" (John 12.24). The way to glory led through the suffering of the crucifixion; the benefit *(fruit)* for the world would come only through His death. The first thing that Jesus had to do, then, was to be lifted up on the cross. This is exactly what He meant in John 3.14, when He said, "Just as Moses lifted up the serpent in the wilderness, so it is necessary for the Son of Man to be lifted up." Moses lifted a serpent on a pole, off the ground, as an object of faith for the relief of the suffering which had been caused by the Israelites' faithlessness. Jesus pointed to that incident and identified it as a type of Himself, specifically of His crucifixion. The first *lifting up* that Jesus would experience would be that of the cross.

Second, Jesus would have to be lifted up, or raised up, from the dead. The cross would result in His death, so another *lifting up* was necessary. In the resurrection the Father not only restored life to the body of Jesus, but defeated the power of death so that Jesus, having died for the sins of all, could return to the presence of the Father from whom He came. In the resurrection God was continuing a process in which He was exalting His Son and bringing Him back to Himself forever.

Third, Jesus' ascension completed His return to the Father. God, having lifted Jesus up on the cross and having lifted Him up out of the grave, then lifted Jesus from the earth to heaven to sit at His right hand and reign according to the promise made in

Psalms 2 and 110. The historical account appears at the end of Luke and the beginning of Acts. The men who saw the ascension then went around preaching that they were witnesses of it, and proclaiming on the basis of their eyewitness experience that Jesus had ascended to the Father as triumphant Lord.

Of these three meanings, being lifted up on the cross was, arguably, the most crucial one. There would be no resurrection if Jesus refused to go to the cross, nor would there be an exaltation to glory if His mission failed. The plan of God centered around the death of Jesus, plain and simple. That *lifting up* was the one that would set the others in motion. Without it the plan stalled and failed. First and foremost, then, when Jesus spoke of being *lifted up*, He was referring to His death on the cross. This is especially clear in passages such as John 8.28, where Jesus said, "When *you* lift up the Son of Man, then you will know that I am He." The lifting up of the Messiah would be something that people did to Jesus. That could be true only of the crucifixion, which the Jews did by the hands of the Romans (Acts 2.23).

How the Messiah would enter into His reign was not at all what the Jews expected. Instead of some show of physical force that left dead Romans everywhere, Jesus would enter His reign by being lifted up on the cross. That is, instead of coming to kill Romans, Jesus came to be killed by the Romans. His death at their hands would accomplish the plan of God that the Son should die for the sins of the world. Once that goal was accomplished, God would lift Him up again, this time out of the grave, and then, once it was clear to the disciples that God had really done both of these things before their eyes, God would lift Him up for the last time and bring Him back to heaven from which He had been sent. Furthermore, true to Jewish expectation, the Messiah would indeed remain forever. *Where* He would remain, however, was not what they expected. Instead of setting up some earthly kingdom and remaining on earth forever, Jesus remains in heaven.

We should note that Jesus said that His being lifted up would draw men to Himself. However, when Jesus spoke of people coming to Him, it was always with the understanding that He is the way to God. "No one comes to the Father except through me" (John 14.6). "I am the door. If anyone enters through Me, he will be saved" (John 10.9). "Everyone who hears and learns from the Father comes to Me" (John 6.45). Jesus always saw His work as gathering the people of God to bring them to the Father (John 17.6). This enables us to see not only the meaning of Jesus' words, but also the significance of their referent. The reason the plan of God involved the death of His Son is that "God so loved the world that He gave His only-begotten Son" (John 3.16). The ultimate desire of God is for people to come to Him willingly and deliberately. In accordance with this desire, it is the intention of God to draw people to Himself, to touch them in such a way that they will be moved to come to Him. While He could do this by some supernatural means that no one could resist, such a method would not result in people's coming to God of their own free will. Instead, God draws people by the power of His divine, sacrificial love. Nor must we think that Jesus was simply some passive agent in all of this. He loved us just as much as the Father loved us. He fulfilled His part in the plan of God not because it was forced upon Him, but because He loves us too (Gal 2.20). The image of Jesus lifted up on a Roman cross proclaims, at heaven's fullest volume, the love of both God and Jesus for all people. In that awful scene of blood and pain, both God and Jesus were demonstrating Their love for us.

When we look at the Jesus who was lifted up from the earth on a Roman cross, our hearts should be touched by the overwhelming display of divine love we see there, and that should in turn provoke within us a desire to go to the Father who loves us so much. To use the biblical phrase, we should feel ourselves drawn to the One whose love for us is unconquerable. In the cross, then, Jesus was drawing all of us, by the power of divine love, to Himself, and through Himself to God.

The Departure of Judas

Nathan Ward

Then after he had taken the morsel, Satan entered into him. Jesus said to him, "What you are going to do, do quickly." ...So, after receiving the morsel of bread, he immediately went out. (John 13.27, 30 ESV)

While three of the four gospels record Jesus' prediction that one of His apostles would betray Him, John's Gospel is the only one that mentions the departure of Judas from the twelve. And in reading this, we learn the precise moment Judas left—between two other key events. It is also significant that Jesus was in control of Judas' departure. *He* sent Judas out when *He* was ready for him to leave. The timing of his departure teaches us important lessons about Jesus' ministry and being in communion with him.[1]

First, Judas' departure was *after Jesus had washed his feet.* Jesus, knowing that Judas would betray him, knelt down before Judas to do the work of the lowest servant. Why? For the same reason He gave Peter: "If I do not wash you, you have no share with me" (13.8).

The lesson is that Jesus' cleansing is for everyone. His work of service was for all mankind. He invites all to be washed. What's more: no one is beyond salvation! There is no one whose sins are so reprobate that Christ cannot provide cleansing.

A further application is seen in Jesus' command for His disciples to wash one another's feet. No one is too evil to be the recipient of our service, if it is needed.

Second, Judas' departure was *before Jesus instituted the Lord's Supper.* Jesus was not going to establish the memorial of His death and hope of His second coming with Satan and Judas in the room. Though Jesus had just proved that He is willing to accept anyone to be washed, one must actually be washed to be in fellowship with Him.

The lesson is that while Jesus' invitation is for all, not just anyone can be in communion with Him. The one who will not receive cleansing remains unclean.

While we cannot see the hearts of men as Jesus could, He does expect us to examine our own hearts before coming into communion with Him (1 Cor 11.28–29). If our hearts are filled with Satan, we need not partake of His feast.

Even the vilest of acts teaches great lessons. Such is true with the treachery of Judas. By including Judas in the foot-washing but excluding him from the Lord's Supper, Jesus teaches us a very important lesson: He can cleanse anyone, but those who are not clean cannot share in His fellowship. His washing is for all without distinction, but not all without exception.

The Lord's Supper and Jesus' Priestly Prayer

Jerold Redding

It should go without saying that an essential aspect of our participating acceptably in the Lord's Supper is unity—fellowship among disciples who share the supper and fellowship with the Lord at whose table the supper is offered. We are His guests; He is the host, the object of and meaning behind it all. How we understand—and thus participate in—that fellowship is, therefore, of the utmost importance. John 17 provides us with valuable insight into the concept of unity and fellowship because it gives us a glimpse into the mind of Christ on these matters.

Before we get to John 17, we will begin by examining the concept of fellowship that involves eating together, both in the customs of New Testament times and in the Lord's Supper. We will then examine the concept of fellowship as Jesus prayed for it in John 17.

Sharing a meal was an important part of fellowship in my grandfather's day. If visitors arrived unexpectedly, they *had to* be invited to stay for the next meal. Such invitations were offered automatically, without thought of whether there were necessary provisions in the house. I've heard stories of how my grandmother had to scramble, on short notice, to find enough food and then prepare it for unexpected guests. But it had to be done. It would have been insulting to their guests if a meal had not been offered, and nearly as offensive for the guests to refuse without good reason.

Eating together, even in our modern culture, provides an opportunity of intimacy rarely found elsewhere. It is at a table where pleasantries are exchanged, hearts opened and feelings shared. At the table we get to know and bond with one another. Such invitations, offered and accepted, are often considered an honor for both host and guest.

But eating together had an even greater significance in ancient times. It was almost a pledge of allegiance. A few passages illustrate the point. Jesus' enemies levied this charge against Him: "This man receives sinners and eats with them" (Luke 15.2 ESV), and they called Him "a friend of tax collectors and sinners" (Luke 7.34). Sharing a table was equated with friendship, acceptance and approval. Jesus instructed that an unrepentant offender, after all efforts at restoration had been exhausted and refused, was to be treated "as a Gentile and a tax collector" (Matt 18.17). In other words, disciples were to have no further social intercourse with him. Paul says this very thing: "I am writing to you not to associate with anyone who bears the name of brother if he is guilty of sexual immorality or greed, or is an idolater, reviler, drunkard, or swindler—not even to eat with such a one" (1 Cor 5.11).

Peter considered restrictions such as these to be common knowledge. Peter told Cornelius, "You yourselves know how unlawful it is for a Jew to associate with or to visit anyone of another nation" (Acts 10.28). Note that when the brethren in Jerusalem heard what Peter had done, they accused him, saying, "You went to uncircumcised men and ate with them" (Acts 11.3).

This idea of close fellowship at the table is seen even in the Old Testament. In Psalm 41.9 David paints a graphic picture: "Even my close friend in whom I trusted, who ate my bread, has lifted his heel against me." The phrase "lifted his heel against me" is equivalent to (what we might say) 'he kicked me.' David, it seems, is trying to show how close this person had been to him before the betrayal: *he had even eaten bread with me!* After eating at David's table, this person's treachery amounts to the worst kind of betrayal. Likewise, Judas' betrayal is even greater, since he had shared the fellowship of Christ at His table. Jesus surely saw Judas' betrayal in the same light, and thus applied David's psalm to him (John 13.18).

With these thoughts in mind, let's turn to the Lord's Supper, which is a sharing of a meal at the Lord's Table. Fellowship here is paramount from the very first. At the Last Supper, in the upper room, Jesus explains to His disciples, "I have earnestly desired to eat this Passover with you before I suffer" (Luke 22.15). *Earnestly desired*—literally, *with desire I have desired* (ASV)—is a common Hebraic way to express intense desire. Jesus, in His final hours, *yearned* for the fellowship of His closest disciples—*table* fellowship.

It is, of course, at this Passover meal that Jesus institutes the Lord's Supper. The synoptic gospels report that Jesus, as He shares the fruit of the vine, says that He will not take it again until the kingdom comes when He will take it anew (Luke 22.18; Mark 14.25). Matthew's account is the most complete. "I will not drink again of this fruit of the vine until that day when I drink it new *with you* in my Father's kingdom" (Matt 26.29 ESV). Jesus, then, was desirous not only of the fellowship of that last meal with His beloved disciples, but also of sharing it with them again *after* His death.

Furthermore, Jesus, breaking the bread, instructed them to "do this in remembrance of me" (Luke 22.19). Memories of a dear departed one easily fill our minds as we engage in some special event that this precious loved one found especially meaningful or pleasurable. So it is to be at the Lord's Supper as we share a table and remember the intimate fellowship he shared with His disciples.

The necessity of our fellowship with one another in the Lord's Supper is highlighted in 1 Corinthians 11. Paul's words are sharp and scathing: "I praise you not, that ye come together not for the better but for the worse. ...When therefore ye assemble yourselves together, it is not possible to eat the Lord's Supper" (11.17, 20 ASV). The problem was that divisions and factions exist within the church and even at the table (vv 18–19). It may have been a supper, but it certainly was not the Lord's. Do you suppose for one moment that this is the kind of supper Jesus had in mind for us? Or that He would want to take part in such a thing? *It is not possible,* Paul says bluntly.

Proceeding from these verses to the end of the chapter, Paul describes the divisions among the Corinthian brethren. Regardless of how one interprets some of these verses, the issue does not seem to be doctrine, but fellowship. It is not that they had a false teaching that Paul needed to correct, but a false understanding of what the Lord's Supper meant for their association with one another. Their problems centered mainly on their lack of consideration for one another. They were basically uncaring and self-centered. The members were called to examine and judge themselves. One brings guilt and judgment on himself by partaking "in an unworthy manner" and "without discerning the body" (vv 27, 29 ESV).

Over time, I have thought about *discerning the body* in different ways, and a variety of interpretations have been suggested by various expositors. But in this context, I lean more and more toward thinking that the body that must be discerned here is the assembly. Failing to recognize the unity and fellowship of the body of Christ—either by fracturing the church's brotherhood with divisions or even by harboring selfish attitudes—surely brings guilt and judgment on ourselves. It makes assembling together a thing "not for the better but for the worse" (v 17). How do we take the supper as a memorial to the Lord and honor His memory while we are in a state of discord with His other disciples? Paul settles the question: *It is not possible.*

In any case—regardless of how one interprets these verses—it seems impossible to miss this point: unity and fellowship are prime elements and basic requirements for partaking of the Lord's Supper acceptably. It was so when Jesus instituted the meal. It was so in Paul's day. It is so now.

With this understanding of the fellowship involved in Lord's Supper, we may now ask: what is the nature of that fellowship? This question leads us to John 17, in which Jesus prays for and describes the kind of fellowship He envisions for His disciples. To say that John 17 is rich in meaning is true, but a gross understatement. A variety of jewels can be mined here, but the contents of this chapter can be drawn together under one heading: fellowship. Since fellowship is such an important part of the Lord's Supper, a study of this passage will certainly enhance our appreciation of the Lord's Supper.

Chapters 13–16 form the backdrop of our text. Throughout these chapters, Jesus' primary concern is for His apostles, who have little concept of what is occurring and how it will affect them. These chapters contain Jesus' efforts to teach, warn and encourage them to prepare them for what is to come. These chapters—five chapters covering only one evening—relate the private communication between Jesus and His twelve disciples.

The events of chapters 13 and 14 take place in the privacy of a borrowed upper room where Jesus and His little band share a Passover meal. It is during this meal that the Lord's Supper is instituted. The discussion among the apostles about which of them will be greatest in the coming kingdom (see Luke 22.24) reveals the depth of their misunderstanding. Thus Jesus provides an object lesson on servitude by washing their feet (John 13.1–17). During the meal Jesus shocks them by announcing that one of them will betray Him (John 13.18ff). Jesus continues through chapter 14 to teach the disciples and prepare them for His imminent departure.

At the end of that chapter, Jesus says, "Rise, let us go from here" (14.31). Both Matthew and Mark tell us that "when they had sung a hymn, they went out to the Mount of Olives" (Matt 26.30; Mark 14.26). Thus the party leaves the upper room and begins to make its way toward the Mount of Olives and Gethsemane, where the Lord will be betrayed and arrested.

The Passover was an evening meal, and—allowing time for all these events—it must have been nearly midnight when they left the upper room. In the quiet stillness of the late night, they wound their way through the dark deserted streets of Jerusalem toward the gates leading to the Mount of Olives. This allowed sufficient time for Jesus' teaching that is recorded in chapters 15 and 16, where Jesus continued to prepare His disciples for His demise. This little band of men walked along, perhaps pausing at times as Jesus emphasized some point, or as in chapter 17, when "he lifted up his eyes to heaven" (v 1) and prayed to His Father.

Chapter 17 records one of Jesus' last prayers, His longest recorded prayer. Since it is not a model for teaching the disciples to pray but rather His own personal prayer, it has been called the "real" Lord's Prayer. Jesus' supplication is generally referred to as His high priestly prayer because He intercedes for His disciples. Others have called it a prayer of consecration. All these labels are apt.

This chapter contains, for all practical purposes, the dying words of Jesus, for He knew His earthly life was at an end—as His words "Father, the hour has come" (17.1) indicate. Even in our times, we tend to give special consideration to the last words of a dying man. During His last hours on earth, what was going through Jesus' mind? What concerned Him? For what did He pray? These questions are answered in this chapter. It furnishes insight into the mind of our Lord during His final hours. We must consider intensely profound what was foremost on His mind and that for which He prayed. His prayer in John 17 is His final entreaty to God on behalf of His disciples—His disciples, I say, including us. The significance of these words cannot be overemphasized.

This prayer does not mention the Lord's Supper but has a great deal to say about fellowship. Jesus expresses His desire for fellowship from every possible angle. He prays for oneness among His disciples. The unity He prays for is modeled after—and even repeatedly spoken of as being—the same kind of relationship that exists between the Father and the Son. In a sense, the passage defines *fellowship*. The concept of fellowship in this prayer will, therefore, impact our understanding of the Lord's Supper, itself an act of fellowship.

The following is a simplified outline of Jesus' prayer:
1–5: Jesus prays for Himself and His relationship with the Father.
6–19: Jesus prays specifically for His apostles.
20–26: Jesus prays for His disciples in general.

Space will not allow a complete analysis of John 17. Furthermore, there is little difference between the desires Jesus expresses for His apostles and those He expresses for all disciples, especially regarding the matter of fellowship. Therefore, for our purposes, this essay will consider them as one.

One of the noticeable features of prayer is the interplay among the parties—the shared relationships. A relationship exists between the Father and the Son that is mutual and reciprocal. All the disciples' relationships, both with one another and with the Father and Son, are described in the same terms. The result is a three-way fellowship: Father, Son, and disciples. We will consider this fellowship under the headings of glory, love, joy, and oneness.

Glory

In verse 1, Jesus asks the Father to glorify Him: "Father, the hour has come; glorify your Son." He asks for glory, not merely to selfishly bask in it, but to glorify the Father, adding, "that the Son may glorify you." Of course, the way to glorify God is to obey Him. Jesus' opening words are about His death, the ultimate example of obedience.

The request for mutual glory is expressed more fully in verses 4–5: "I glorified you on earth, having accomplished the work that you gave me to do. Father, glorify me in your own presence with the glory that I had with you before the world existed." Jesus, who has glorified the Father in His obedience *on earth*, asks to be glorified *in heaven* ("in your own presence," v 5) and to dwell in the shared glory that He had shared with the Father from eternity.

Later, when Jesus prays specifically for His immediate disciples, He says, "I am not praying for the world but for those whom you have given me. ...I am glorified in them" (17.9–10). In the context of the divine persons' shared glory, the thought of disciples' being able to glorify the Lord is an arresting thought. Glory is given and received, fully shared with the Father, the Son, and the disciples. It is a grand picture of fellowship.

The concept of sharing and mutual benefit continues in verses 6–8:

> I have manifested your name to the people whom you gave me
> out of the world. Yours they were, and you gave them to me, and
> they have kept your word. Now they know that everything that
> you have given me is from you. For I have given them the words
> that you gave me, and they have received them and have come
> to know in truth that I came from you; and they have believed
> that you sent me.

Notice the interplay here. All parties here are drawn together with
common objectives and, while each may have separate functions,
they are intimately entwined.

- What the Father has done: He has sent the Son, given Him
  His words and given Him His people.
- What the Son has done: He has manifested the Father's name to
  them, given them His words, and made it known that the Father
  sent Him and that everything He has is from the Father.
- What the disciples have done: They have received, believed and
  kept the Father's words.

All parties are drawn together in a common fellowship. Compare
this with verses 2–3, where Jesus says of the Father, "You have giv-
en him [the Son] authority over all flesh, to give eternal life to all
whom you have given him. And this is eternal life, that they know
you the only true God, and Jesus Christ whom you have sent."

The Father gives authority over everyone to the Son; the Son
uses that power to benefit them by giving eternal life through
knowledge of the Father. Nothing is for self. It is always for the
other. Glory is shared. Authority is used for mutual benefit. All
function together for the good of the other. What fellowship!

Love

In verse 23, Jesus makes a distinction between the world, for
which He is not praying (at the moment), and the disciples. His
desire, however, is for the world to understand that the Father
loves the disciples. That same love, Jesus says in the following
verse, the Father had for the Son "before the foundation of the
world." Furthermore, He prays that "the love with which you
have loved me may be in them" (v 26). The request is that the love

which the Father has always poured out on the Son might be in the disciples.

Did you ever wonder what God did through eternal ages before creation? This passage offers a little insight into the Godhead: The Father and the Son loved each other! (v 24) This love is not merely emotional love, but love as revealed in Scripture. Love, by its nature, is not solitary but is active and outgoing. Such love as defined in 1 Corinthians 13, Matthew 5, and elsewhere, seeks the benefit of the other, seeks to please the other. The very essence of God *is* love (1 John 4.8, 16). God, in loving the Son before the creation, was simply being Himself. By loving us, as He does now, He is being Himself. (By contrast, when we love we are not being our natural selves; rather, we are being like God.) Once again, we have described a fellowship that is almost beyond our imagination. Love is flowing freely, being exchanged among all parties.

Joy

"But now I am coming to you, and these things I speak in the world, that they may have my joy fulfilled in themselves" (John 17.13).

"These things I have spoken to you, that my joy may be in you, and that your joy may be full" (John 15.11).

It is not surprising to find Jesus desiring to share His joy as He does the glory and love of the Father. What He now asks is that this joy (mind you, that same joy, *His* joy*)* be in His disciples, that it be *fulfilled* in them. Think about it. Each party—Father, Son and His disciples—giving joy to the other.

Oneness

This brings us to the final heading. I have called it oneness, but it could also be called fellowship or unity (it matters little what we call it as long as we practice it). All of our considerations up to this point—glory, love, joy—could be drawn together under this one heading. All of the parties, Father, Son, disciples, are envisioned in one grand fellowship. Consider these verses from John 17:

And I am no longer in the world, but they are in the world, and I am coming to you. Holy Father, keep them in your name, which you have given me, *that they may be one, even as we are one.* (v 11)

That they may all be one, just as you, Father, are in me, and I in you, that they also may be in us, so that the world may believe that you have sent me. The glory that you have given me I have given to them, *that they may be one even as we are one, I in them and you in me, that they may become perfectly one,* so that the world may know that you sent me and loved them even as you loved me. (vv 21–23)

I made known to them your name, and I will continue to make it known, *that the love with which you have loved me may be in them, and I in them.* (v 26)

What is described here is a unity and fellowship, not merely among brethren, but with the divine persons. And not merely *like* Them, but *in* Them. Permit me to put it this way: it goes beyond *one*ness; it describes *in*-ness. It is one grand fellowship in which glory, love, and joy are freely shared (allow me to say it again) *with one another and also with the Father and the Son.*

Jesus has described the kind of fellowship—of oneness—that characterizes the relationship He has with His heavenly Father. He then opens the doors of that fellowship and invites us to come in and share fully in it. This is the fellowship Jesus desired and prayed for. It's not a theory but a reality. It should leave us breathless!

Now, with all of this in mind, imagine sitting down to eat a meal with people in such fellowship. But we need not imagine, for we do exactly that each Lord's Day: it is called the Lord's Supper. We all, together, on His day, at His table, remember Him—all of us in one fellowship. At least, that is what it is supposed to be. The Corinthians failed to fulfill the Lord's desire for fellowship, making the Lord's Supper impossible for them. In our day, do we fail? May it not be so!

We do not merely eat the Lord's Supper, we eat it *together.* It is a fellowship meal. We see it as a spiritual meal, yes, but we are sharing the experience with one another. Our Lord longed to share one last meal with His disciples. We should desire to be in the presence of one another as well. In remembering Him during this supper, we should recall how He desired that fellowship. His actions and words, His thoughts—indeed, His priestly prayer—focused on His disciples' being in perfect fellowship.

Fellowship may be a term so overworked these days that it loses some of its force. We often use that word so that it means not much more than acceptance. Thus being "in fellowship" with a person or a group may simply mean that we approve of their religious activities or positions. While using "fellowship" that way may not be wrong, it hardly covers the scope of the New Testament concept.

The Lord's Supper is a meal of fellowship. Jesus' prayer in John 17 clarifies the nature of this fellowship. The Lord's Supper, then, is a time for us to come together in the intimate sharing the table provides. It is time to open our hearts, time to forgive, time to bond together, time to remember the glory, love and joy that we share. And to remember that we share all this with one another— *and with the Lord.*

How can we remember Him while holding to broken relationships and divisive attitudes toward each other? We can't. How will Jesus, in any sense, be a participant in such an affair? He won't. How are we His disciples if we violate His desire expressed so fervently in His final prayer? We aren't.

The Lord's Supper reminds us of what the Lord wanted so very much—unity—by allowing us to remember and participate in the fellowship that He fervently prayed for. The desire of His heart—His dying wish—was for this to be so.

Please, Lord, help us to make it so!

Jesus in Gethsemane

Melvin D. Curry

Jesus went to the garden of Gethsemane to pray, and He knew what awaited Him. He must die for the sins of the world. The words He spoke when He instituted the memorial of His death still echoed: "This is My blood of the new covenant, which is shed for many for the remission of sins" (Matt 26.28 NKJV). An understanding of the agony He experienced in prayer as He anticipated His death should help us participate more meaningfully in the Lord's Supper.

Gethsemane: Jesus' Emotional Anticipation of the Cross
Peter, James, and John entered the garden with Jesus, and He told them, "Sit here while I go and pray over there" (Matt 26.36). Two passionate statements express the Lord's emotions before He begins to pray.

The first statement contains two feelings that He held within Himself: "He began to be sorrowful and deeply distressed" (v 37). The term "sorrowful" *(lypeo)* means *be sad,* or *grieve;* it expresses His anticipation of death. And "deeply distressed" *(ademoneo)* suggests a word picture in itself. It literally conveys the idea of *not [being] at home,* but figuratively suggests the discomfort anyone feels under stressful circumstances, namely, being *uncomfortable, troubled,* even *anxious.*

The second statement is spoken expressly to the disciples: "My soul is exceedingly sorrowful, even to death" (v 38; Mark 14.34). The expression "exceedingly sorrowful" *(perilypos)* is an intensified form of the first term. It means *very sad, deeply grieved*. The preposition *peri*, which is attached to the verb, conveys the notion of being *encompassed with (grief)*. Most of us have heard a similar utterance of sorrow by someone who stands at the coffin of a loved one.

Gethsemane: Jesus' Willing Anticipation of the Cross

Matthew records that Jesus actually prayed three separate times, returning after each prayer to the place where the disciples waited, before He went a little distance from them to pray again. The Lord assumed more than one posture in prayer. Luke says that He "knelt down" (22.41); Mark suggests that He "fell on the ground" (14.35), and Matthew is even more vivid, saying that Jesus "fell on His face, and prayed" (26.39). There was nothing casual about these prayers offered to God.

Two prayers are summarized in Matthew's account; the third is mentioned without elaboration. The first time Jesus prayed, saying, "O My Father, if it is possible, let this cup pass from Me; nevertheless, not as I will, but as You will" (Matt 26.39). The construction of the conditional sentence leaves no doubt that the Lord fully believed in God's power to deliver Him from death: "If it is possible—and it is!" Yet Jesus' whole life among humans was a selfless expression of love; He did not come to earth to have His own way: "I have come down from heaven, not to do My own will, but the will of Him who sent Me" (John 6.38). And the Father expressed compassion toward the Lord's dilemma: "an angel appeared to Him from heaven, strengthening Him" (Luke 22.43).

Gethsemane: Jesus' Purposeful Anticipation of the Cross

Because He shared with us in "flesh and blood" (Heb 2.14), Jesus recoiled at the prospect of death and all that would accompany it. Surely when our Lord spoke of "this cup," He had reference to the experience (cup) of suffering, which He had already told the disciples they would share with Him (Matt 20.22–23).

But the Lord knew that He must die if He was to effect God's gracious offer of salvation to mankind. His death would be necessary to destroy the devil, "who had the power of death, and to release those who through fear of death were all their lifetime subject to bondage" (Heb 2.15). The Father had purposed from eternity that the cross would be the painful means of redemption, the way by which He could answer the demands of both justice and mercy (Rom 3.24–26). And we can but stand in awe of His grace.

The second prayer of our Lord in the garden of Gethsemene expressed Jesus' resignation: "O My Father, if this cup cannot pass away from Me unless I drink it, Your will be done" (Matt 26.42). Perhaps Luke has in mind this prayer or the next when he writes, "And being in agony, He prayed more earnestly. Then His sweat became like great drops of blood falling down to the ground" (22.44). These words describe an almost unimaginable intensity as Jesus anticipates the suffering He must endure for us.

Gethsemane: The Disciples' Intense Sorrow

And what did Jesus find when He returned after each prayer to the spot where He had left Peter, James, and John? He found them sleeping, because their willingness to watch had given way to the weakness of the flesh (Matt 26.38). And if we only read Matthew's account, we may be far too hard on the disciples. Luke's clarification, therefore, is necessary to round out the picture: "He found them sleeping from sorrow" (22.45).

I hope that we share their emotion when we partake of the Lord's Supper and our minds drift back to Gethsemane. Such sorrow, moreover, should only increase our gratitude for Christ's willingness to go to the cross, but our tears will be tears of joy because we know our Savior lives.

A Friendship Forged in Blood

Mark Moseley

But they kept on insisting, saying, "He stirs up the people, teaching all over Judea, starting from Galilee even as far as this place." When Pilate heard it, he asked whether the man was a Galilean. And when he learned that He belonged to Herod's jurisdiction, he sent Him to Herod, who himself also was in Jerusalem at that time. Now Herod was very glad when he saw Jesus; for he had wanted to see Him for a long time, because he had been hearing about Him and was hoping to see some sign performed by Him. And he questioned Him at some length; but He answered him nothing. And the chief priests and the scribes were standing there, accusing Him vehemently. And Herod with his soldiers, after treating Him with contempt and mocking Him, dressed Him in a gorgeous robe and sent Him back to Pilate. **Now Herod and Pilate became friends with one another that very day; for before they had been enemies with each other.** (Luke 23.5–12 NASB)

After the death of Herod the Great (the Herod who was ruling at the time of Christ's birth), Emperor Augustus divided the territory he ruled among Herod's three sons—Herod Antipas, Philip and Archelaus. Herod Antipas ruled over Galilee and Perea. Archelaus was appointed ruler over the regions of Judea, Idumea and Samaria. In AD 6, Archelaus was deemed incompetent by Augustus and was replaced by a prefect or governor. Pilate was the fifth governor of the area, appointed by Emperor Tiberius.

That little bit of background is sufficient for us to appreciate why Pilate and Herod were "enemies." Herod's family had long controlled the area. They were Idumeans who were (pseudo-)converts to Judaism and controlled the religious ruling party and the office of the high priest. Pilate was the leader of the Roman occupying force. He controlled the Roman military militia. He was responsible for the collection of taxes and the keeping of order. Naturally, there were often conflicts between the Jewish and Roman leadership.

In short, Pilate and Herod were political rivals.

Of course, there were many reasons why Pilate sought to absolve himself of the responsibility of deciding the case of Jesus. I'm sure that Pilate's actions were motivated more by selfish reasons than a desire to placate Herod. Nevertheless, his effort to avoid his own destiny with Jesus caused him to acknowledge the jurisdiction of Herod. By sending Jesus to Herod, Pilate showed deference to Herod's jurisdiction.

After Herod examined Jesus, he sent him back to Pilate. Herod too, no doubt, was motivated by his own selfish motives. 'It's not my problem to solve.' He mocked Jesus and sent the Christ back to Pilate—now deferring to Pilate's authority. Ultimately, Pilate declared, "I find no guilt in this man!" and yet permitted the Jewish rulers to act under his authority in putting Jesus to death.

And from that day, that awful day, that day when His judgment was taken away as foretold by the prophet Isaiah, Herod and Pilate became friends!

Perhaps they both now recognized they were "brothers under the skin." They formed a friendship forged in blood. They shared a common lust for power; a common disdain for truth and its Author; a common willingness to allow justice to give way to political expediency. More than that, they shared a common decision about Jesus, the Christ. They rejected Him as their King. They were accomplices to His crucifixion. They were instruments of the Evil One, willing collaborators in the greatest crime of humanity.

Those who join together to partake of the "communion" also share and declare a common decision about Jesus. While we, too, collaborated with evil to bring about the necessity of the cross, ultimately, we surrendered to its power. We declare Jesus to be Lord of lords and King of kings! And by that acknowledgment we are bound as brethren—even if we were formerly enemies. The walls of separation are broken down. A friendship, a fellowship, *a family* forged by blood.

Barabbas

Wilson Adams

Although Barabbas never takes center stage, he plays a major role in the drama of darkness surrounding the death of Jesus. Having been condemned to die, he is undoubtedly aware that three executions have been planned for the day and that one of those crosses is probably reserved for him. He hears the jailer approach with an entourage of soldiers. His clammy hands wipe beads of perspiration from his brow as he contemplates the agony of crucifixion. He hopes death will come quickly. He hears the rattling of keys and sees the huge iron door begin to open. What happens next is absolutely unbelievable....

The Custom
No one knows how the custom began (Matt 27.15). Perhaps as a gesture of political courtesy, the Romans capitalized on the Jewish custom of Passover by "passing over" one convicted. No doubt, the custom was a thorn in the side of Pilate, the anti-Semitic and brutal governor of Judea. On this occasion, however, he welcomed it with a sigh of relief.

First, Pilate was frustrated. He knew the charge against the Nazarene was petty—the result of jealousy from the Jewish leaders (v 8). He also knew that if he did not cooperate with their demands, the Jews would cause continued unrest and political grief for one already warned to keep the peace or else.

Second, Pilate faced a judicial dilemma. What little conscience he had left had already dictated a verdict: "Not guilty!"

The crowd, however, would not hear of it. They smelled blood and would settle for nothing less.

That is when Pilate was struck with a thought of brilliance: *Barabbas!* Barabbas was the perfect solution to a judicial mess. Of all the prisoners incarcerated, Barabbas was the most notorious. Pilate would offer a prisoner exchange that would do two things— set free the innocent Nazarene and shut up the Jewish Sanhedrin (and send them home). Confident of his plan, Pilate pitched the idea to the people (vv 16–17). It was then he learned that he had miscalculated the power of religious hatred (v 20).

His Name

Barabbas was not his given name. *Bar* means *son of* ("Blessed are you, Simon Barjona"—literally "Simon son of Jonah." Simon was his *given* name; Barjona was his *received* name). Our *received* name is our last name. Our *given* name is our first name. *Bar-Abbas,* his received name, means *son of the father.* But what was his *given* name?—His *first* name?

Some manuscripts of this passage list the given name of Barabbas as Yeshua—which is the same as Jesus. The name Jesus was common and it is quite possible that Pilate makes a play on their names: "Whom shall I release—*Yeshua* Barabbas or *Yeshua* the Christ?" Pilate smiled. He had them.

His Location

Not far from the judgment seat of Pilate—an elevated courtyard outside the fortress of Antonia (which served as a prison, headquarters for Roman soldiers, and even housing for visiting dignitaries such as Pilate)—sat the terrorist Barabbas. The exact distance between The Pavement (John 19.13) and his holding cell is unknown, but it is not impossible that Barabbas, although unable to hear the lone voice of Pilate, could hear the chants of the mob—growing larger and louder by the moment. And what did he hear?

"Barabbas... Barabbas... Give us Barabbas... Crucify! Crucify! Let him be crucified! ...Let his blood be upon us!"

It's not difficult to conclude what Barabbas may have thought from hearing this half of the dialogue. He had heard the chanting: this was a lynching party, a crucifixion party. It matters not how hardened he was; any man would cringe at the brutality of Roman crucifixion. He could hear them coming. He knew this was the end. Whatever goes through the mind of the condemned the moment the door is opened and he is led away to the chamber, the chair, the cross—would have occupied the thoughts of Barabbas. It was over.

His Release

"Barabbas," said the soldier, "This is your lucky day! Believe it or not, they hate someone else more than you."

He was supposed to die that day. There were, after all, three crosses—one reserved for him. Instead, Barabbas walked into the sunshine of that Friday morning a free man. Another had taken his place.

The force of impact from this scene is directed not at the notorious Barabbas but on the notorious you and me. We deserved to die. We are murderers with hatred in our hearts. We have committed insurrection against the King of kings. We are thieves and liars and guilty of many other crimes against God and man. *All have sinned.* As with Barabbas, someone else has taken our place.

Maybe you sit in a dungeon of unconfessed, unforgiven sin. You live with a guilty conscience, imprisoned to a painful past. The *best news* of the ages is this: you can be freed from sin. Because Jesus took what He did not deserve, you can go someplace you do not deserve. In the words of Mrs. Frank Beck:

> There was One who was willing to die in my stead,
> That a soul so unworthy might live.

The Triumph of the Cross

Ralph Walker

But thanks be to God, Who made us His captives and leads us along in Christ's triumphal procession. Now wherever we go He uses us to tell others about the Lord and to spread the Good News like a sweet perfume. (2 Cor 2.14 NLT)

As a small boy, he was told repeatedly that when he grew up he would be a god.[1] But his divinity came sooner than anyone expected. His father died and he inherited a throne, a kingdom that spanned the known world and his country's brand of divinity. His first acts were bloody ones—he murdered his mother and his younger brother. He was seventeen years old, and it was 54 years after the birth of Jesus. His name was Nero.

Nero needed a *triumph* to finalize his deity. Triumphs were Roman parades for notable citizens.

Triumphs were of two kinds. The most common (though there was nothing common about a triumph) honored the military victories of a general who had defeated a foreign enemy; squelching internal enemies like slave uprisings didn't count. To be rewarded with a triumph, the general had to have been responsible for the deaths of at least 5,000 enemy troops. He was honored when he returned his army to Rome for retirement.

The other kind of triumph celebrated the ascendancy of a new emperor to divine status. In presenting himself before the gods, the emperor was also begging Jupiter (Rome's patron god) to continue blessing his city and citizens. There was no other ceremony in pagan history in which god and man stood so close to each other.

What knowledge we have of triumphs comes from written reports as well as monuments and relief sculptures of these events.

In a triumph, the first act of the day was performed by the elite troops of the emperor—his Praetorian guard—who would appear before him to dress him for the procession. He would be clothed in a purple robe (reserved for royalty and the rich because of the expense of extracting that color dye from crustacean shells) and usually a laurel crown of gold. The emperor's face was painted bright red to represent vitality (blood = life). The soldiers would bow and declare their allegiance: "Hail, Caesar/Lord."

The procession lined up outside the city. Heralds would announce the entrance of the triumphator. At the front of the procession would usually be found condemned enemies, slaves, bearers of placards with his titles, sometimes even maps of his realm—all to proclaim his accomplishments and power. The emperor came near the end of the procession, led rather than leading the procession. His mode of travel was usually a chariot, sometimes a horse, sometimes a palanquin.

A key role was played by a bull or bulls in the triumph.

Thomas Schmidt says that a white bull was crowned and draped in ceremonial garments very like the emperor's. This animal represented the gods.

Reliefs of triumphs show this bull walking alongside the triumphator. And always a step behind is an accompanying official, called a lictor, carrying a double-bladed axe for the eventual execution of the bull.

Triumphs ended at a historical spot, the Temple of Jupiter Capitolinus, perched on the crest of the Capitoline Hill. Dionysius of Halicarnassus records a legend that when the foundation of the temple of Jupiter was being laid, a human skull was found buried there:

> The soothsayer, accordingly, finding it impossible for him either
> to impose upon the men or to appropriate the omen, said to them:
> "Romans, tell your fellow citizens it is ordered by fate that the

place in which you found the head shall be the head of all Italy." Since that time the place is called the Capitoline hill from the head that was found there; for the Romans call heads *capita*.[2]

At the Capitoline Hill the sacrifice of the bull took place. The triumphator took a cup of wine presented to him and poured it out on the head of the bull and the altar nearby. As the bull was sacrificed, its life was symbolically passed to the emperor, who became god in its place. The bull died; the emperor lived. One god died and another took his place.

In depictions of triumphs, the emperors were then presented to the masses with two officials who stood, one on the right and one on the left. Even today, the President of the United States addresses Congress with the Vice President and Speaker of the House on his right and left. This evidently symbolized the uniting of power into one leader, as generals or senators were often asked to "back up" the emperor.

At this point the people took up a chant: "Triumph! The god appears!" This signaled the end of the triumph and the beginning of a long celebration by the citizens.

This symbolic parade was known to many people, even those outside Rome, having occurred over 500 times in Rome's history. It is almost certain that the writers of the New Testament knew about triumphs. Paul surely did, since he spoke of one in 2 Corinthians 2.[3]

What is intriguing to me is that the events surrounding the death of Christ parallel this tradition too closely for the similarity to be a coincidence. Look at God's triumph for His Son, as depicted in Mark's gospel, chapter 15.

In verses 15–18, it is the Praetorian guard which renders mocking allegiance to Jesus, cloaking Him in purple and plaiting a crown for His head, then declaring Him King.

In verses 19–20, Jesus, His face surely a crimson mask, is led out to His death (just as the Emperor was led in the triumph).

Verse 21 tells us that an unwilling servant was added to the parade organized for Jesus. This Simon carried the sign of Jesus' life—the cross—in the procession to the place of execution. Notice also the reversal of the parade route. Emperors began outside the city and finished in the heart of Rome. Hebrews tells us that Jesus went outside the gate to end His triumph (13.12).

Verse 22 provides another parallel. Both triumphators ended their processions at the place of the skull: Capitoline Hill for the King of the Romans, Golgotha for the King of the Jews.

Verses 23–26 speak of the inscription Jesus bore and the cup of wine He refused. Then the text tells us the sacrifice occurred. In this instance, Jesus is Himself the lamb, the sacrificial animal that is deity dying.

Verses 27–28 parallel the appearance of the divine one with the two others appearing on either side of Him. In this case, Jesus identifies Himself more with the common, the sinners, the outcasts than with power and politics and prestige.

Verses 37 and 39 reveal the declaration of a herald. The centurion heralds not a man declared to be a god, but God who had been a man.

And the cry is picked up by disciples and believers throughout the ages and across the globe. Truly, this is the Son of God! We declare it every time we participate in the Supper, our celebration of His death and life. We proclaim the good news that Jesus died for us and that He lives for us. God died; God lives. Praise God.

Jesus, Keep Me near the Cross
The People at the Crucifixion

Jason Hardin

The Thieves: Can a Demon Open the Eyes of the Blind?

"Truly, truly, I say to you, I am the door of the sheep. All who came before me are thieves and robbers, but the sheep did not listen to them. I am the door. If anyone enters by me, he will be saved and will go in and out and find pasture. The thief comes only to steal and kill and destroy. I came that they may have life and have it abundantly. I am the good shepherd. The good shepherd lays down his life for the sheep." (John 10.7–11 ESV)

The gospels are full of the accounts of wandering sheep making their way into the fold of the Good Shepherd. Nicodemus came by night. Lepers came seeking a miracle. A centurion came on behalf of his paralyzed servant. Disciples of John came with questions. Peter came on the waves of Galilee. A father brought his epileptic son. Jairus brought a plea for his dying daughter. Martha came with news of Lazarus' death. A woman brought an alabaster flask filled with costly ointment. Each, in his own way, was seeking what only the Good Shepherd could provide: abundant life.

Others also came to the Good Shepherd, but in search of something different. Pharisees came, defending their traditions. Scribes came, demanding a sign. Sadducees came, seeking to trap Him with difficult questions. Great crowds sought Him out, not because of His message, but for a meal. Judas came with the kiss of betrayal. A mob came to Gethsemane with swords and clubs. Each, in his own way, rejected the pasture that the Good Shepherd offered.

And so Jesus promised,

> I have other sheep that are not of this fold. I must bring them also, and they will listen to my voice. So there will be one flock, one shepherd. For this reason the Father loves me, because I lay down my life that I may take it up again. No one takes it from me, but I lay it down of my own accord. I have authority to lay it down, and I have authority to take it up again. This charge I have received from my Father. (John 10.16–18)

The reaction of Jesus' audience?

> There was again a division among the Jews because of these words. Many of them said, "He has a demon, and is insane; why listen to him?" Others said, "These are not the words of one who is oppressed by a demon. Can a demon open the eyes of the blind?" (vv 19–21)

Such division and disagreement over Jesus' identity flourished throughout His ministry. From His hometown synagogue, to a boat on the freshly calmed Sea of Galilee, to the halls of the Temple itself, men and women were forced to ask, "Who is this Jesus?" Even on the day of His death, the dispute continued.

"Two others, who were criminals, were led away to be put to death with him. And when they came to the place that is called The Skull, there they crucified him, and the criminals, one on his right and one on his left" (Luke 23.32–33). How ironic that Jesus was placed squarely in the middle of what would grow to be opposing opinions.

Both criminals saw the charge against this one dying on the center cross: "This is Jesus, the King of the Jews" (Matt 27.37). Both criminals heard the Good Shepherd's heartfelt cry, "Father, forgive them, for they know not what they do" (Luke 23.34). And once again, there was division.

"One of the criminals who were hanged railed at him, saying, 'Are you not the Christ? Save yourself and us!'" (Luke 23.39). If you are indeed the Good Shepherd of Israel, why not come down from the cross? While you are at it, why not save your fellow sufferers? And if not, this criminal was content to hurl abuse at the imposter. 'Perhaps this Jesus has a demon,' he might have said. 'Maybe he is insane. Why should I listen to him?' This first criminal stands in a long line of those who rejected the message and methods of the Good Shepherd.

But on the other side hung a second criminal. "The other rebuked him, saying, 'Do you not fear God, since you are under the same sentence of condemnation? And we indeed justly, for we are receiving the due reward for our deeds; but this man has done nothing wrong'" (Luke 23.40–41). After all, what sort of man prays for those who have driven nails in His hands and feet and continue to mock His every agonizing move? 'Why listen to him? These are not the words of one who is oppressed by a demon. Can a demon open the eyes of the blind?'

This second criminal also stands in a long line—the line of those whose blinded eyes have been opened, whose hardened hearts have been melted. Here is one more sheep that struggles to enter the Good Shepherd's fold of safety before death's door finally closes. His plea? "Jesus, remember me when you come into your kingdom" (Luke 23.42).

How will Jesus respond? To welcome Nicodemus is one thing—he is influential and educated. To accept Jairus is to accept a ruler of the synagogue. Receiving a centurion could certainly have its privileges. Peter, while a little rough around the edges, has great potential. Even the healed leper presents Jesus with an opportunity to confirm His power.

But a criminal? *This* criminal? What does he have to offer? What possible benefit can be derived? He is at death's doorstep. Why *wouldn't* he beg?

As the Good Shepherd struggles to lift the head that has been pierced by thorns, how will He respond? As He opens the eyes that have swelled from the beatings of those who rejected Him, what will He say? As He opens the mouth that has been silent before His accusers, how will He answer?

The Good Shepherd has not forgotten His promise—"If anyone enters by me, He will be saved and will go in and out and find pasture." He believes, He lives, and He dies by His own words.

> What man of you, having a hundred sheep, if he has lost one of them, does not leave the ninety-nine in the open country, and go after the one that is lost, until he finds it? And when he has found it, he lays it on his shoulders, rejoicing. And when he comes home, he calls together his friends and his neighbors, saying to them, "Rejoice with me, for I have found my sheep that was lost." Just so, I tell you, there will be more joy in heaven over one sinner who repents than over ninety-nine righteous persons who need no repentance. (Luke 15.4–7)

How does Jesus respond to the lowly criminal? "Truly, I say to you, today you will be with me in Paradise" (Luke 23.43).

This criminal is much more than a hypothetical case study of the beginning and end of the covenants. He was an image-bearer of God. The dust of his body may have returned to the earth, but his spirit has returned to the God who gave it. The joyful cries of the angels echoed throughout the throne room of heaven over this one sheep who was willing to come back into the arms of the Good Shepherd.

There are many things we can learn from that most famous of criminals. So many elements of God's amazing plan to redeem mankind either came to an end or were inaugurated with the death of the Good Shepherd. However, let us never lose sight of this simple, straightforward truth: a forgiven criminal continues to rejoice with joy inexpressible in Paradise.

Was he unworthy? Absolutely. But so are we.

Did he deserve death for his crimes? Certainly. But so do we.

What could possibly qualify him to enjoy a place at the table of the King? Only the amazing grace of his Creator and the atoning blood of Jesus! But are we not also helpless and lost without the undeserved favor and atonement of God?

Let us always remember the price that was paid so that we might find our own place beside forgiven thieves and sinners at the table of the Lord.

For while we were still weak, at the right time Christ died for the ungodly. For one will scarcely die for a righteous person—though perhaps for a good person one would dare even to die—but God shows his love for us in that while we were still sinners, Christ died for us. Since, therefore, we have now been justified by his blood, much more shall we be saved by him from the wrath of God. For if while we were enemies we were reconciled to God by the death of his Son, much more, now that we are reconciled, shall we be saved by his life. More than that, we also rejoice in God through our Lord Jesus Christ, through whom we have now received reconciliation. (Rom 5.6–11)

Mary: The Piercing of a Mother's Own Soul

What would it be like to sit down with Mary, the mother of Jesus, and just listen to her stories? Can you imagine? What was she thinking when the angel Gabriel appeared to her out of nowhere with words that have shaped human history?

Greetings, O favored one, the Lord is with you! Do not be afraid, Mary, for you have found favor with God. And behold, you will conceive in your womb and bear a son, and you shall call his name Jesus. He will be great and will be called the Son of the Most High. And the Lord God will give to him the throne of his father David, and he will reign over the house of Jacob forever, and of his kingdom there will be no end. The Holy Spirit will come upon you, and the power of the Most High will overshadow you; therefore the child to be born will be called holy—the Son of God. (Luke 1.28–35)

Mothers have quite naturally wanted the best for their children for thousands of years. What mother holds a newborn baby in her arms and does not yearn for her son or daughter to enjoy success, fulfillment, and happiness? But this? What does one do with such promises of greatness? Mary's son, a king after the royal lineage of David? An unending reign? The Son of God? How? Why her?

What did she do for the rest of that fateful day? How did she even dream of telling Joseph? What went through her mind the first time she felt the promised child flutter in her womb?

And what was that glorious and frightening night like in Bethlehem when the time came for her to give birth? Again, what mother does not daydream for months about what that moment will be like? Where she will be. Who will be with her. Her first moments with her firstborn. And yet, if ever there was a setting that did not go according to a mother's plans this must have been it. Swaddling cloths for the Son of the Most High? A manger for David's heir? Had God forgotten His promises?

If Mary had any doubt, it must have been calmed by the arrival of marveling shepherds. They quickly recounted how an angel of the Lord had appeared to them while they were keeping watch over their flock, and the glory of the Lord had shone around them. The angel had said, "Fear not, for behold, I bring you good news of a great joy that will be for all the people. For unto you is born this day in the city of David a Savior, who is Christ the Lord. And this will be a sign for you: you will find a baby wrapped in swaddling cloths and lying in a manger" (Luke 2.10–12).

Suddenly a multitude of the heavenly host had appeared, praising God and saying, "Glory to God in the highest, and on earth peace among those with whom he is pleased!" (2.14).

As the shepherds breathlessly made known the saying that had been told them concerning this child, "all who heard it wondered at what the shepherds told them" (2.18)—and understandably so! "But Mary treasured up all these things, pondering them in her heart" (2.19). Even in the most unlikely of circumstances and trying of times, the Almighty had not forgotten Mary and her child. There may not have been room for them in the inn, but the promised Son had been born exactly where His heavenly Father intended.

Nearly six weeks later, "The time came for their purification according to the Law of Moses" (2.22). As had been done by new parents for hundreds of years, Joseph and Mary brought the infant Jesus up to Jerusalem to present Him to the Lord. They came to the beautiful Temple of Jehovah with two birds to sacrifice, being too poor to offer a lamb to the priest of God. But as they approached, an old man named Simeon who had been "waiting for the consolation of Israel" (2.25) took Jesus in his arms and blessed God, saying, "Lord, now you are letting your servant depart in peace, according to your word; for my eyes have seen your salvation that you have prepared in the presence of all peoples, a light for revelation to the Gentiles, and for glory to your people Israel" (2.29–32).

It had been revealed to Simeon that he would not see death before he had seen the Lord's Messiah. Finally, that time had come, and he was exuberant! He blessed Joseph and Mary, who must have continued to marvel at what had been and continued to be said about their newborn son. But for the first time, a blot of darkness stained the beautiful chronicle of their child as Simeon looked directly at Mary and said, "Behold, this child is appointed for the fall and rising of many in Israel, and for a sign that is opposed (and a sword will pierce through your own soul also), so that thoughts from many hearts may be revealed" (2.34–35).

Her child would be great, but His greatness would draw some and repel others. He would be called Son of the Most High, God's anointed to rule on the throne of David, but His claims would serve as a stumbling block to those who opposed His sovereignty. Of His kingdom there would be no end, but its coming would coincide with a sword to pierce His mother's own soul. And not just any sword. The word used by Simeon is *rhomphaia* in Greek, a long and broad blade more comparable to a javelin than a dagger. *Rhomphaia* is the word used in the Greek translation of the Old Testament to describe the sword of the mighty giant Goliath. One day, Simeon said, such a sword would pierce Mary's own soul.

She must have felt at least the sword's prick twelve years later following the annual Feast of the Passover (2.41ff). According to Jewish custom, Joseph, Mary and Jesus went up to Jerusalem. "And when the feast was ended, as they were returning, the boy Jesus stayed behind in Jerusalem" (v 43). The problem was that "his parents did not know it." When they discovered Jesus' absence, Joseph and Mary must have searched frantically. Not just for hours, but for *days* they looked in vain, with each lead turning up empty. The Son of the Most High had been given to them for safekeeping and He was nowhere to be found! What must have gone through Mary's mind? How could she possibly hope to sleep not knowing where her firstborn son had gone?

> After three days they found him in the temple, sitting among the teachers, listening to them and asking them questions. And all who heard him were amazed at his understanding and his answers. And when his parents saw him, they were astonished. And his mother said to him, "Son, why have you treated us so? Behold, your father and I have been searching for you in great distress." (vv 46–48)

If you are a parent, you can easily relate to the feelings behind Mary's statements. What a powerful wave of relief, exasperation, confusion and frustration must have rolled over her in a moment! A mother whose son has wandered away unnoticed knows first-hand the urge to squeeze in love and strangle in irritation at the same time. "Jesus, don't you know that your father and I have been looking for you for days? How could you put us through such an ordeal?" But what must Mary have felt as young Jesus looked her in the eye and said, "Why were you looking for me? Did you not know that I must be in my Father's house?" (v 49). Did Simeon's foreboding promise from twelve years before echo in her mind?

Mary must have felt the sword's sting as Jesus "came to Nazareth, where he had been brought up" (Luke 4.16). Even if she was not present at the time, surely word would have eventually gotten back to her. One ordinary day, Jesus went to His hometown synagogue and was provided the great honor of publicly reading from the scroll of Isaiah. The opportunity to address all those who had gathered was His. And after reading the prophet's prediction of jubilee, of liberty to the captives, of healing to the blind and freedom to those who were oppressed, Jesus unashamedly claimed, "Today this Scripture has been fulfilled in your hearing" (v 21). The audience marveled but was naturally moved to ask, "Is not this Joseph's son?" (v 22). Hadn't these words been recorded nearly 700 years ago? But Jesus continued His address, revealing Himself as a prophet and implicating this audience's hardness of heart. Their reaction? In wrath, "They rose up and drove him out of the town and brought him to the brow of the hill on which their town was built, so that they could throw him down the cliff" (vv 28–29). Jesus escaped unharmed, but what must Mary have felt when she heard the news? Did she think of Simeon's dark prediction?

How easy would it have been for Mary to hear Jesus' emphatic statement in Luke 8? Great multitudes had been following Jesus wherever He went for some time. His mother and His brothers had sought Him out in an effort to spend time with Him, "but they could not reach him because of the crowd" (v 19). The message slowly spread through the masses, "'Your mother and your brothers are standing outside, desiring to see you.' But he answered them, 'My mother and my brothers are those who hear the word of God and do it'" (8.20–21). What mother wouldn't have had a difficult time accepting such a response?

How must Mary have felt if word got back to her that some were spreading the rumor, "Jesus casts out demons by Beelzebul, the prince of demons" (Luke 11.15)? Was she in the crowd when a woman raised her voice and said to Jesus, "Blessed is the womb that bore you, and the breasts at which you nursed!"; was she listening as Jesus responded, "Blessed rather are those who hear the word of God and keep it" (11.27–28)? Was she a part of the multitude when Jesus turned and said, "If anyone comes to me and does not hate his own father and mother and wife and children and brothers and sisters, yes, and even his own life, he cannot be my disciple" (14.26)? Was she within earshot as Jesus made prediction after terrible prediction about what would soon happen to Him in Jerusalem (9.22, 44; 18.31–33)? Did she try to dissuade Him from making the journey? Was she present to watch as her son wept over the city of God (19.41–44)?

How long was it before she heard of Judas' betrayal? What must she have imagined as Jesus spent that darkest of nights as a common criminal? Was she in the crowd the next morning to watch as her firstborn son was mockingly presented as the "King of the Jews" with a crown of thorns pressed into His scalp and a purple robe sticking to His freshly scarred back? Could she hear the bloodthirsty cries of the multitude—the prevailing call for her son's hands and feet to be nailed to a cross—echoing off the stone walls?

There is so much that we do not know about Mary during Jesus' fleeting time on this earth: how she would have handled hearing the accusations that her son was a drunkard and a glutton; what she must have thought as the Pharisees' animosity toward Jesus became more and more evident; the confused feelings she must have had as Jesus consistently and publicly placed so much more emphasis on spiritual relationships than on those with His own family; how she handled her first face-to-face meeting with Peter after his bitter denials of her son. There is so much that we do not know.

But we *do* know this: Mary was at Golgotha. "Standing by the cross of Jesus were his mother and his mother's sister, Mary the wife of Clopas, and Mary Magdalene" (John 19.25).

Jesus' mother watched as the hands that had reached out for her comfort on a dark night in Bethlehem were pierced with nails on a dark day outside Jerusalem. She watched as the same feet that had kicked within her virgin womb were brutally fastened to a rugged wooden beam. She watched as the same body she had carefully wrapped in swaddling cloths and laid in a manger was raised toward the heavens on a cross.

Wherever she was during the intervening years, Mary was with Jesus as He took His first breaths and His last. Whatever she was doing as Jesus went from city to city fulfilling the will of His heavenly Father, she was there to hear Jesus' first cries and His last. Regardless of the ways she had dealt with some of Jesus' most difficult teachings, she stood at the foot of the cross and heard her oldest son make sure that His mother would be provided for after His death (John 19.26–27).

Mary's tear-filled eyes easily could have wandered from the Roman soldiers who were gambling for Jesus' tunic, to the Temple across the valley where she and Joseph had brought their infant son more than thirty years earlier, to the darkened heavens above. And she must have remembered:

"Behold, this child is appointed for the fall and rising of many in Israel, and for a sign that is opposed (and a sword will pierce through your own soul also), so that thoughts from many hearts may be revealed." (Luke 2.34–35)

The soldier's spear that pierced the side of Jesus is often mentioned as we reflect on His great sacrifice. Let us never forget, however, that a mother's own soul was pierced through with a javelin-like sword as well. "Blessed is she who believed that there would be a fulfillment of what was spoken to her from the Lord" (Luke 1.45).

John: The Disciple Whom the Crucified One Loved

"Behold!" The ways that simple word shaped the life of the apostle John could never be measured. He wrote an entire gospel in an effort to tell the story, but ended his testimony with this affirmation: "Now there are also many other things that Jesus did. Were every one of them to be written, I suppose that the world itself could not contain the books that would be written" (John 21.25).

"Behold, the Lamb of God who takes away the sin of the world!" (John 1.29). So the story begins. The idea of a lamb being sacrificed to atone for sins was by no means novel. For thousands of years, blood had been shed to reconcile wayward human beings with a holy God. But something was missing. Something better was required; more accurately, some*one*. At the appointed time, in accordance with an eternal plan, he who had come in the spirit and power of Elijah made the greatest announcement in human history. The Lamb provided by the Father Himself for the sins of humanity had finally arrived in the form of Jesus of Nazareth. The apostle John, among others, listened to the announcement. He responded to the call. He followed God's Lamb, and kept following for three years.

He heard Jesus boldly predict, "Destroy this temple, and in three days I will raise it up" (John 2.19). He documented that most famous of promises, "God so loved the world, that he gave his only Son, that whoever believes in him should not perish but have eternal life" (John 3.16). John was present to hear Jesus assure His disciples, "My food is to do the will of him who sent me and to accomplish his work" (John 4.34). He was a part of the crowd when Jesus asserted, "I am the living bread that came down from heaven. If anyone eats of this bread, he will live forever. And the bread that I will give for the life of the world is my flesh" (John 6.51).

John was witness to Jesus' comforting proclamation, "I am the Good Shepherd. The Good Shepherd lays down his life for the sheep" (John 10.11). He alone records Jesus' foreboding statement, "The hour has come for the Son of Man to be glorified. Truly, truly, I say to you, unless a grain of wheat falls into the earth and dies, it remains alone; but if it dies, it bears much fruit" (John 12.23–24). John's firsthand account provides precious insight into the mindset of Jesus as the end of His ministry drew near—"Now is my soul troubled. And what shall I say? 'Father, save me from this hour'? But for this purpose I have come to this hour" (John 12.27).

How rich the climactic promises of Jesus preserved by John for all time!

> Let not your hearts be troubled. Believe in God; believe also in me. ...I am the true vine; you are the branches. Whoever abides in me and I in him, he it is that bears much fruit, for apart from me you can do nothing. ...A little while, and you will see me no longer; and again a little while, and you will see me. ...I have said these things to you, that in me you may have peace. In the world you will have tribulation. But take heart; I have overcome the world. (John 14.1; 15.5; 16.16, 33)

"Behold, the Lamb of God who takes away the sin of the world!" That is how this story began, and in perfect harmony with the Creator's will, it culminated at the only point possible for mankind's redemption. God's Lamb had come to die.

> So they took Jesus, and he went out, bearing his own cross, to the place called The Place of a Skull, which in Aramaic is called Golgotha. There they crucified him, and with him two others, one on either side, and Jesus between them. ...So the soldiers did these things, but standing by the cross of Jesus were his mother and his mother's sister, Mary the wife of Clopas, and Mary Magdalene. When Jesus saw his mother and the disciple

whom he loved standing nearby, he said to his mother, "Woman, behold, your son!" Then he said to the disciple, "Behold, your mother!" And from that hour the disciple took her to his own home. (John 19.16–18, 24–27)

"Behold!" This simple word changed John's life forever. He had heard it countless times over the course of the last three years as Jesus encouraged His disciples to look, to listen, to ponder. What must have gone through his mind on this darkest of days as his Lord hung suspended between heaven and earth? Did he understand? Did he remember what that voice crying out in the wilderness had said three years before?

So much of the life of every disciple of Christ is based upon perspective. A healthy appreciation of the past can help to define the present. A grasp of the present can cultivate a constructive chart for the future. That being said, of all the writers of the New Testament, who could claim a better perspective on the fulfillment of God's amazing plan to redeem mankind than John? He heard the final cries of the Lamb with his own ears. He watched as the drops of blood with the divine power to atone fell to the dusty ground. John stood beneath the cross when all other men fled.

Mary, by this time, was very likely a widow. Nothing is said of Joseph after the narratives of Jesus' birth and childhood, though Jesus' brothers are mentioned throughout the gospels (Mark 3.31–35; Luke 8.19–21; John 2.12). Matthew even calls them by name—James and Joseph and Simon and Judas (Matt 13.55). Where were they as their mother stood at the foot of her first-born's cross? "Not even his brothers believed in him" (John 7.5).

Peter had left the Savior's side to weep in the gall of bitterness. Judas, immersed in the guilt of betrayal, had already hanged himself. Andrew? James? Philip? Bartholomew? Thomas? Matthew? James the son of Alphaeus? Thaddaeus? Simon? Jesus had told them the night before, "You will all fall away because of me this night. For it is written, 'I will strike the shepherd, and the sheep of the flock will be scattered'" (Matt 26.31). And just as Jesus had predicted, "all the disciples left him and fled" (Matt 26.56).

"Yet it was the will of the Lord to crush him" (Isa 53.10). The

Good Shepherd had always known that He would lay His life down for His sheep. For this purpose He had come to this hour. What must it have meant to the Good Shepherd, then, to look down from the cross with the weight of all the darkness in all the world on His shoulders, and to see John? "There is a friend who sticks closer than a brother" (Prov 18.24). As His time on earth drew painfully short, the Son was naturally concerned about the future of His mother. And as He looked down from the cross, seeking someone to watch over her in the difficult days ahead, there was John—a lamb who had stuck close by the shepherd to the bitter end. No wonder he is described on more than one occasion as the disciple whom Jesus loved!

At the close of God's book, it is John through whom Jesus speaks. For decades following the crucifixion, John used his firsthand perspective gained at the foot of the cross to inform, to encourage, to rebuke, to inspire—just as his Lord had done. It is John who finally reveals Jesus' last promise for all humanity of all time. The same word that so powerfully shaped John's life, here, at the end, beckons us also to look, to listen, and to respond to the assurance of God's Lamb. "Behold, I am coming soon" (Rev 22.7, 12, 20).

May our own confident assertion be, "The Lord is my shepherd; I shall not want. ...Even though I walk through the valley of the shadow of death, I will fear no evil, for you are with me" (Psa 23.1, 4). May we appreciate and continue to be inspired by John's precious perspective. May our prayer, though all others flee, be: *Jesus keep me near the cross....*

The Seven Sayings of Jesus

Brent Hunter

The seven sayings Jesus uttered on the cross speak volumes about the selfless nature, power, and kindness of our Savior. I believe they serve as some of the greatest testimonies to the divinity of Jesus. They caused a disbelieving Roman centurion, after witnessing these sayings and events, to proclaim, "Truly this man was the Son of God!" (Mark 15.39).

First, Jesus uttered a word of *forgiveness:* "Father, forgive them; for they know not what they do" (Luke 23.34). Most people being crucified would rail and curse at their tormentors, but Jesus showed selfless concern for them and thus fulfilled Isaiah 53.12: "[He] was numbered with the transgressors: yet he bore the sin of many, and made intercession for the transgressors."

Then Jesus spoke a word of *promise* to a nameless, condemned, guilty thief who had shown remorse and asked Him, "Jesus, remember me when thou comest in thy kingdom." Jesus responded, "Verily I say unto thee, Today shalt thou be with me in Paradise" (Luke 23.43). Perhaps the thief is nameless so that all of us guilty-but-penitent sinners can hang our names and hopes for Paradise at Calvary along with him; the promise is not just for this thief, but for all penitent believers throughout time. Consider 1 Peter 1.3, where we read that through the resurrection of Jesus, the Father "begat us again unto a living hope." It is this living hope that makes the memorial Supper so important to us. Its power stretches from Calvary over two millennia and touches each of us even today.

The last word Jesus spoke from the cross in the light of day is a word of *care* (John 19.26–27). When Jesus saw His mother and the disciple whom He loved standing by, He said to her, "Woman, behold, thy son!" Then to John, "'Behold, thy mother!' And from that hour that disciple took her unto his own home." Here is Jesus, a few hours before His death, showing concern not for Himself but for others. And this is not a word of care just for 2,000 years ago, but for today as well. In Matthew 12.49–50 we read that Jesus "stretched forth his hand towards his disciples, and said, 'Behold my mother and my brethren! For whosoever shall do the will of my Father who is in heaven, he is my brother, and sister, and mother.'" We are Jesus' mother and brethren if we do His will. He speaks words of care to all of us as a part of His spiritual family.

It is high noon—the sixth hour of the day. Jesus has been on the cross for three long, agonizing hours. The sun should be at its highest and brightest point in the sky, but darkness covers the land for three hours. At the ninth hour, Jesus pushes up on the nails in His feet to get a breath and utters one of the most perplexing statements ever spoken: "'Eli, Eli, lama sabachthani?' that is, My God, my God, why hast Thou forsaken me?'" (Matt 27.46). This is actually a quotation from Psalm 22.1. The idea of *forsake* is to abandon. 'My God, my God, why have you abandoned me?' is the question.

None of the sayings of Jesus on the cross are more controversial and thought-provoking than this fourth one. Theologians often refer to this statement as the cry of *dereliction*. Why did Jesus say this? What did it mean? Is it significant that He spoke these words in darkness?

Why did Jesus utter this cry? I believe it was so that we would never miss the real price that had to be paid for our redemption. Jesus' physical death was the penalty for sin (Rom 6.23); that was part of it, but not all of it—nor even the most important part.

Ezekiel 18.20 says, "The soul that sinneth, it shall die." Notice: the *soul* shall die, not just the body. Physical death was the result of sin and has been the consequence of sin since Adam and Eve, but the penalty for sin is separation from God—spiritual death.

This cry of anguish, spoken in the darkness of night, represented the zenith of all Jesus came to do. Isaiah 59.2 poignantly declares that "your iniquities have separated you and your God, and your sins have hid his face from you, so that he will not hear." Sin equals separation. Second Corinthians 5.21 says, "Him who knew no sin he made to be sin on our behalf."

At this moment Jesus bore the guilt of the world's sin. Picture all of the sins from the beginning of time to the cross and all of the sins from the cross until the end of time, and in one huge noxious mass—Jesus bore it all.

Scripture also says, "God is light, and in him is no darkness at all" (1 John 1.5). As Jesus became sin, God had to separate His presence from Jesus for the first time in eternity. As He did, darkness fell upon the earth, symbolizing the departure of God's presence. Jesus suffered spiritual death; His soul was snuffed out. And as He bore our guilt, He suffered alone without the presence of the Father. Hebrews 2.9 says that He tasted death for all men. He tasted and experienced spiritual death on our behalf so we would never have to.

The fifth saying was a word of *suffering* (John 19.28). As bodily functions begin to break down, one's mouth becomes dry as cotton. Jesus says, in what may have been nothing but a parched whisper, "I thirst." In response to His statement, they bring Him vinegar to drink and thus fulfill Psalm 69.21. Even in immense physical anguish, His concern was for fulfilling God's word.

One of the reasons He was so thirsty was because He had refused a drink offered earlier, a mixture of gall and vinegar (Matt 27.34). Gall is an opiate, offered to the condemned to dull the pain of the crucifixion. While it certainly would not have made the execution pleasant, it would have taken some of the edge off it. But Jesus would have none of it; His purpose was to suffer for our sins—to bear the full force of the punishment that we deserved. He came offering water of life to the lost, but such a gift could not be offered freely if He did not first fully drink the cup of suffering and fully pay the price Himself. And so He wanted to take the full force of the crucifixion. He was thirsty so that we need never thirst.

The sixth saying is my favorite. Jesus utters toward the very end a word of *triumph* (John 19.30). It is one Greek word, *tetelestai*, which translates into three English words, "It is finished." His mission of atonement was complete. Most men are born to live, but Jesus was born to die. He had completed His destiny. When the Roman centurion heard it, he cried out, "Truly this man was the Son of God" (Mark 15.39). What was there about this statement that so impressed this hardened soldier and skeptical Gentile?

The centurion knew that what Jesus said was more than just a statement of completion. *Tetelestai* was a Roman battle cry for victory. After defeating an enemy and securing new territory, soldiers would rush in and place the Roman banner in the ground and, usually at the top their voices, proclaim, *"Tetelestai!"* ('I've won! The battle is over! The victory is mine.')

Jesus found victory in death and proclaimed *"Tetelestai!"* ('Mission accomplished!') Jesus did not die in defeat, but in *victory*. This centurion had no doubt witnessed scores of men dying on crosses in disgrace and defeat, but never had he witnessed a man who hung there with such dignity and in the end claimed victory. And so, at that moment, this Gentile pagan (like the nameless thief who had expressed faith in Jesus earlier) became a believer.

One last push up on the nail and Jesus breathed His last, proclaiming, "Father, into thy hands I commend my spirit." This final statement, just moments before His death, is a word of *reconciliation* (Luke 23.46). Jesus was now ready to meet His Father once again, having borne our sins as the perfect sacrifice; He became the "firstfruits of them that sleep" (1 Cor 15.20). Jesus' word of reconciliation—His confident proclamation that His spirit would be one with God in Paradise—is what gives us confidence, assuring us that when we die, our spirits will also go to be with God.

Brothers and sisters, may it be so that when we die, we can

say with Jesus, *'Tetelestai!*—I have fought the good fight of faith, I have finished my course, the battle is over, and now I can join Jesus and secure the victory over sin and death which He obtained for me on the cross.' As we partake of the Lord's Supper, its emblems can remind us of Jesus' intercession for the forgiveness of sinners, of the promise He offers the guilty, of His unending care for His family, of the anguish of the separation He has borne for us, of the physical thirst suffered by the One who satisfies our spiritual longing, of His triumph which ensures our victory, and of the confidence with which we can commit our souls to Him. In his words from the cross our Lord reminds of of the hope with which we partake of His Supper.

The Stones Cried Out

Nathan Ward

As he was drawing near—already on the way down the Mount of Olives—the whole multitude of his disciples began to rejoice and praise God with a loud voice for all the mighty works that they had seen, saying, "Blessed is the King who comes in the name of the Lord! Peace in heaven and glory in the highest!" And some of the Pharisees in the crowd said to him, "Teacher, rebuke your disciples." He answered, "I tell you, if these were silent, the very stones would cry out." (Luke 19.37–40 ESV)

It wasn't long before the Pharisees' wish came to fruition. Those who were here shouting "Hosanna!" would soon be shouting "Crucify him!"

When Jesus stood on trial, no witnesses were called on His behalf. Plenty of false witnesses were called *against* Him, but no opportunity was given for a defense. And even if a witness had been called, no one would have answered. The crowd's opinion had changed in one short week. His disciples had fled. Peter stood nearby, but he wouldn't even admit his acquaintance with Jesus to a slave girl; surely, he wouldn't have testified in open court for him.

"I tell you, if these were silent, the very stones would cry out."

There's no doubt that Jesus' statement is something of a hyperbole. He certainly couldn't have meant that stones would *literally* speak on His behalf. At the same time, however, it mustn't be overlooked that what happens after everyone falls silent on

Jesus' behalf is that He receives testimony from some most un-likely sources.

Pilate was the first to testify on Jesus' behalf. He listened to the testimony of the high priests and the mob, he spoke privately with Jesus, and then he made his ruling: not guilty (John 18.38). Even though he is infamous for his spinelessness, he stood before all and said for the record—most likely the official Jewish and Roman records—that Jesus had no guilt and should not be executed.

The mob, of course, won the day and Jesus was led away to His crucifixion. On either side hung a thief being executed at the same time and at the same place. While we cannot know for certain, it is not a far stretch to suppose that these were career criminals, being executed not for a single lapse of judgment, but for a life of crime. One of these disreputable men turned to Him, confessed belief in Him, and received salvation (Luke 23.39–43).

And those who had Him put on the cross—those gloating over their supposed victory—testified for Him: "He saved others; let him save himself" (Luke 23.35). Did you catch that? *He saved others.* They admit it! They had never denied the miracles of Je-sus—only the source of His power. And now, even as they celebrate their victory, they can't help testifying for Him. Their words betray them and they speak the eternal truth: *He saved others.*

The centurion overseeing the crucifixion saw the manner in which Jesus died—and the events surrounding His death—and testified as well. As a Roman, he most likely shared in the polythe-istic views of his countrymen, so he may have been willing to accept another god without truly being converted. Even so, he became God's tool of testimony. Of Jesus, the centurion said that He was a righteous man (Luke 23.47) and the Son of God (Mark 15.39).

But not all of the testimony Jesus received was from unlike-ly sources. God Himself testified when everyone else fell silent (Matt 27.51–53): He tore the veil of the temple from top to bot-tom; He covered the land with darkness; He raised the dead, who came into the city after the resurrection; He caused the earth to quake—*and the stones to split.*

"I tell you, if these were silent, the very stones would cry out."

The world fell silent when Jesus needed testimony. There wasn't a believer to be found who would speak on His behalf. And so God raised up testimony from His enemies. And God reached down into the temple and testified Himself. And God raised up testimony from nature. Yes, when the world fell silent, even the stones cried out.

This Jesus, whom we memorialize when we commune with one another and Him, is God's Messiah. God has made this fact very clear. And in taking of the Supper *we* have become the stones: proclaiming His death—adding our own testimony to the chorus—until He comes.

The Blood of the New Covenant
Hebrews 12.18–24

Ben Greiving

When Jesus established the Lord's Supper, He said, "This cup that is poured out for you is the new covenant in my blood" (Luke 22.20, ESV). When He instituted the feast which would remind His followers of His sacrifice, Jesus did not say that the cup merely symbolized His blood in some mystic way, but that it should remind the partaker of the *new covenant* His blood established. That Jesus refers to this covenant as "new" should make us think about what makes this *new* covenant different from the *old* covenant.

In the first place, what is a covenant? Covenants are sometimes considered no more than a contract: an agreement between two parties that carries certain obligations, rewards, and punishments. *Covenant,* as the term is used in the Bible, however, is much more than a mere business agreement. For example, the friendship of David and Jonathan is said to be based on a covenant (1 Sam 18.3), and Malachi says that marriage is "by covenant" (Mal 2.14). Covenant, then, can describe not just a formal agreement between two parties, but a special degree of relationship—a relationship so serious its participants must make a solemn agreement about it.

God dealt with Israel, and deals with His people today, through special covenant relationships. In fact, the book of Hebrews is largely about the contrasts between the old covenant established by God with Israel at Mount Sinai and the new covenant established by Christ. In Hebrews 12.18–21, the writer recalls that, when the old covenant was established, the people were forbidden from even touching the mountain where God's presence rested:

> For you have not come to what may be touched, a blazing fire and darkness and gloom and a tempest and the sound of a trumpet and a voice whose words made the hearers beg that no further messages be spoken to them. For they could not endure the order that was given, "If even a beast touches the mountain, it shall be stoned." Indeed, so terrifying was the sight that Moses said, "I tremble with fear."

The Lord's Supper symbolizes in part the close fellowship we can have with God and with Christ under the new covenant. The closeness of relationship Jesus established, however, can be better appreciated in comparison with the relationship between God and His people under the old covenant.

The entire Mosaic covenant, which began at Sinai, emphasized the vast distance that existed between God and His people because of sin. For example, God's presence under the old covenant rested in the Most Holy Place in the Temple. As Hebrews 9.6–7 emphasizes, only one person out of the entire nation—the high priest—could enter the Most Holy Place, and even he could enter it on only one day out of the entire year. Even then, the high priest had to perform elaborate ceremonies before entering, under penalty of death. In Romans 7.7–24, the apostle Paul agonizingly describes how the old law functioned to make its adherents aware of their sin. Paul's description of this function of the law is summed up in verse 10: "The very commandment that promised life proved to be death to me."

Fortunately, God never intended for the old covenant to be the sum total of His relationship with humankind. After Paul expresses in Romans 7 his disgust with his own inability to keep the law perfectly, he rejoices throughout Romans 8 at the relationship with God he now experiences through Christ. As a result of the new covenant Christ establishes, Paul says in Romans 7.14–17, we are adopted children and heirs of God. It is no accident that Paul and the other New Testament writers use imagery like adoption and inheritance to describe the new covenant fellowship we share with God.

As the Hebrew writer tells us in Hebrews 10.1, the law was but "a shadow of the good things to come." In stark contrast to the arduous distance between God and man that the old covenant emphasized is the special relationship with God that Christ established through His blood. Hebrews 12.22–24 describes this new relationship:

> But you have come to Mount Zion and to the city of the living God, the heavenly Jerusalem, and to innumerable angels in festal gathering, and to the assembly of the firstborn who are enrolled in heaven, and to God, the judge of all, and to the spirits of the righteous made perfect, and to Jesus, the mediator of a new covenant, and to the sprinkled blood that speaks a better word than the blood of Abel.

God's people under the new covenant need not be afraid of approaching God. Under the new covenant, we have a mediator—Jesus—who brings us to the very city of God and directly into His presence.

In the Lord's Supper, we experience something of the majestic vision the writer of Hebrews describes. We come to the table in an "assembly of the firstborn"—the assembly of saints (the "righteous made perfect") that comes together to memorialize our Lord's sacrifice. We come to the table not only in fellowship with each other, but in real fellowship with Christ and with the Father Himself. In the Lord's Supper, we approach God in a way people under the old covenant never could.

The Lord's Supper symbolizes in part the new covenant that Christ established through His blood. When we eat the bread and drink the cup, we remember not only the physical sacrifice Jesus made, but also the special spiritual relationship we share with Him and with the Father—the relationship He died to make possible. We no longer approach God through an exclusive priesthood or through bloody sacrifices that must be offered several times a year. Rather, we have a direct relationship with our Heavenly Father—a relationship that is compared to that between an earthly father and son.

Rather than cowering in fear at the base of Mount Sinai, we come to the very presence of God at Mount Zion and share true spiritual fellowship with Him and with His saints. That fellowship can be seen when we eat the Lord's Supper, a "family meal" where the children gather at the table in the very presence of the Father and the Son, not in fear, but "with a true heart, in full assurance of faith, with our hearts sprinkled clean from an evil conscience, and our bodies washed with pure water" (Heb 10.22).

Outside the Gates
Proclaiming a Perfect Sacrifice

Robert A. Ogden

In an effort to strengthen the faith of wavering Jewish Christians, the writer of Hebrews sought to show that the new covenant of Jesus fulfills (and is therefore superior to) the Mosaic covenant. His argument for Christ's superiority includes a discussion of the sacrifice of Jesus as compared to the sacrifices of the Mosaic covenant (9.1–10.18). While Hebrews does not directly address the Lord's Supper, the indirect relationship between this memorial feast (which is designed to remind the participant of the significance of the sacrifice of Jesus) and the book of Hebrews (which argues for the superiority of that sacrifice) should be obvious.

Although the similarities between the death of Jesus and the Mosaic sacrifices are plentiful—especially the sin offering and the sacrifices made on the Day of Atonement—it is really in the differences that the superiority of the new covenant is revealed. Thus, the writer of Hebrews contrasts the ceremonial cleansing of the Mosaic law with the spiritual cleansing of the new law, the material nature of the Mosaic redemption with the heavenly nature of the redemption in the New Covenant (9.24), and the temporary nature of the Mosaic sacrifices with the permanent nature of Jesus' sacrifice (10.11–14).

Among the final exhortations of the book, the writer mentions one last contrast between the sacrifice of Jesus and the Mosaic system (13.10–16). Under the Mosaic covenant the body of the most important sacrifice was burned outside the camp as an unclean thing, but under the new covenant, the people are invited to join the sacrificial lamb outside the gate. A deeper look will show that this invitation represents a radical departure from the Mosaic limitations on true atonement and divine fellowship. A closer examination of this difference between the old and new covenants also brings to light additional significance in the Christian memorial feast. The Lord's Supper, we will see, is a symbolic reminder of the internal nature of the cleansing, the unprecedented degree of fellowship that is offered in Jesus, and the burdens that such cleansing and fellowship place on the believer.

Blood and Body

Many of the details of specific Old Testament sacrifices are uncertain because the text is often ambiguous or simply silent in answer to the modern student's inquiries. Presumably, this ambiguity or silence is due to the fact that the original readers and participants were well aware of the details that elude us. However, though there is much that we would like to know, the text does clearly answer two questions we might ask about the sacrifices in the Mosaic covenant: What was to be done with the blood? What was to be done with the flesh? The Old Testament gives symbolic significance to the answer of both of these questions, but the true significance of these details is fully revealed only when one discovers how these Mosaic regulations relate to the body and blood of Jesus the sacrifice of the new covenant.

The law gave specific instructions regarding the blood for each of the various sacrifices, except the grain offering (for obvious reasons). Though scholars debate the specific meanings of the emphasis on blood, there is little doubt that blood was significant, in part because no writings of other ancient Near Eastern religions include such an emphasis.[1]

From the beginning, God attributed a special significance to blood,[2] and it should come as no real surprise that such significance is later reflected in the Mosaic sacrificial code. In the burnt, guilt, and peace offerings, the blood was to be sprinkled on the sides of the altar itself (Lev 1.5; 3.13; 7.2). Presumably, this was intended to cleanse the vehicle of sacrifice ceremonially and thus to make the sacrifice acceptable. Similarly, the blood of the sin offering was applied throughout the temple, including on the veil and the altar of incense (4.17, 18). The consecration offerings, used in the appointment of new priests, included the application of blood to the priests' ears, hands, and toes (8.24). Concerning the most significant sacrifices, those made on the Day of Atonement, the law included instructions to sprinkle the blood in the Holy of Holies and on the Ark of the Covenant (16.15)—as if to say that the filth of the people's sins had polluted even the most strictly protected area of the Temple (16.16).

In all these instructions pertaining to the blood of the sacrifice, there is not a single instance in which anyone connected to the sacrifice is permitted to drink the blood. In fact, such would be a blatant violation of the general command not to eat the blood of animals (Lev 17.14). Herein lies a stunning contrast beween the old and new covenants: whereas under the Law of Moses, no one was allowed to drink the blood, under Christ the beneficiaries of the sacrifice are not only to apply the blood to themselves but to consume it in a perpetual symbolic feast (Matt 26.27–29). Jesus' words "Drink of it, all of you, for this is my blood of the covenant" (ESV) had a shocking significance to Jewish listeners that is mostly lost on modern Gentile readers.

Observe another contrast: in the Mosaic sacrifice, the blood was taken to the object in need of ritual purification and sprinkled on it for an external, ceremonial cleansing. In the new sacrifice, the blood is symbolically consumed by the individual who seeks the spiritual purification and cleansing which the blood makes available. Therefore, the blood of the memorial feast serves as a symbolic reminder of the internal, spiritual nature of the cleansing made possible by the sacrifice of Jesus, as opposed to a mere "purification of the flesh" (Heb 9.13). Jesus' blood is not superficially applied to the exterior but symbolically and perpetually applied to the soul.

There is also significant contrast between the use of the flesh from the Mosaic sacrifice and the use of the flesh from the sacrifice of Jesus. The Mosaic code is very specific in its instructions regarding the sacrificial flesh. With the exception of the daily burnt offerings, portions (usually the fatty portions) from the most common sacrifices were to be burned on the altar and the remaining portions eaten by the priests. For instance, the "flesh" of the grain offering was partially burnt on the altar but the rest served as the daily source of bread for the temple priests (Lev 2.3). The guilt offering, perhaps the second most common sacrifice, also included a portion to be burned and a portion given to the priests for eating—though in this case, there is a further stipulation that the meat must be eaten on the temple grounds (7.6). In both cases, the idea appears to be that though the sacrifice is wholly the Lord's, a portion of it is shared with the priests. With these two sacrifices, it is as though the priests are permitted to eat from the scraps of the Lord's table. Thus, the disposition of the sacrificial body under the Mosaic law carried with it a cold, limited sense of fellowship.

However, the most important sacrifices of the Mosaic code did not include even this limited, symbolic fellowship. For example, the instructions for burnt offerings called for the entire sacrifice to be burned on the altar, leaving none for the priests (Lev 1.9). If not for the sin and consecration offerings, this further limiting of fellowship would not seem so great. That is, if the priests are fed from the "scraps" of the Lord's table, surely it would be understandable that for some sacrifices there would be no "scraps." However, the instructions for sin and consecration offerings—as well as those for the sacrifices of the Day of Atonement—are even more exclusive in their insistence that the portion that would normally be for the priests be taken outside the camp and burned (4.11–12; 8.17). Ironically, it is in these sacrifices—the purpose of which was to purify, consecrate, and atone for the sins of the people—that there was so little fellowship, even symbolic fellowship, between man and the sacrifice.

Under the Mosaic law, the sacrifices intended to bring man close to God—most notably those made on the Day of Atonement—seem to have been designed to emphasize a lack of fellowship with God. These sacrifices were, by virtue of their very design, reminders of their own inefficacy.

It is important to note, then, that in Jesus, who was our sacrifice taken outside the camp, one finds not only true atonement and purification, but also, through that cleansing, the occasion for a divine fellowship unheard of since the days of Eden. Symbolically, this opportunity for communion with God is proclaimed in a memorial feast in which participants are permitted to eat the flesh of the sacrifice and are invited to dine in God's presence. Now we are at no altar; worshippers are here invited to His table where He breaks the bread, passes the cup, and reclines with His faithful ones (*cf.* Matt 26.26–29).

Outside the Gate – The Cost of Fellowship

There is another aspect of our memorial feast that significantly relates to the Mosaic sacrifices. Hebrews 13.10–16 says:

> We have an altar from which those who serve the tent have no right to eat. For the bodies of those animals whose blood is brought into the holy places by the high priest as a sacrifice for sin are burned outside the camp. So Jesus also suffered outside the gate in order to sanctify the people through his own blood. Therefore let us go to him outside the camp and bear the reproach he endured. For here we have no lasting city, but we seek the city that is to come. Through him then let us continually offer up a sacrifice of praise to God, that is, the fruit of lips that acknowledge his name. Do not neglect to do good and to share what you have, for such sacrifices are pleasing to God.

The writer points out one final contrast. The Mosaic law instructed that the atonement sacrifice be burned outside the city and that the one who carried out this duty was to be considered unclean (Lev 16.27–28). Jesus, who was the perfect atonement sacrifice and was Himself sacrificed outside the gate, invites His cleansed followers to join Him there. The implications of such an invitation are numerous. The disciple of Jesus is called upon to take up the stigma of one who has been taken outside the gate.[3] This means joining Him in humble acceptance of the scorn of the world and the rejection of "this city." Just as He suffered the scorn and rejection of His own people; so also must His disciples "bear the reproach he endured" (Heb 13.13). It also means joining Him in accepting the role of service and the burden of sacrifice. Just as He was willing to serve even to the point of sacrificing Himself for the good of others (Eph 5.2), so also must His disciples serve and offer themselves up as sacrifice (Heb 13.15–17). The writer specifically mentions the sacrificial praise of the lips and the self-sacrifice of good works, but joining the Lord outside the gate will at times call for even greater and perhaps more painful sacrifices.

The writer of Hebrews does not refer directly to the Christian memorial feast, but an indirect application is apparent. Because the feast proclaims true cleansing and divine fellowship, it also reminds the participant of the Lord's call to join Him outside the gate, and of the burdens this call places on him. Thus, the feast should be a solemn reminder of the implications of fellowship with the sacrificial lamb. Joining Jesus outside the gate means that the disciple must also join Him in the route He took to get there. To join the sacrificial lamb, one must himself become rejected and sacrificed—to take up his own cross.

The writer of Hebrews reminds his readers not only of the importance of the sacrifice of Jesus, but also of the symbolic significance of the feast intended to remind them of that sacrifice. Drinking the blood of the Lamb, disciples proclaim the true, spiritual nature of the cleansing it provides—not externally but internally, not temporally but eternally. Eating the sacrificial flesh, disciples proclaim a degree of fellowship with God unheard of under the old law. Implied in the proclamation of this fellowship is a challenge to those who desire it. Such fellowship with God demands great humility and service, a willingness on the part of participants to accept the role of a living sacrifice (Rom 12.1). However, this proclamation of fellowship also brings with it the hope of glory. The feast should remind disciples of the joy such fellowship with God offers, for if they suffer with Him, tey have the hope and promise that they "may also be glorified with Him" (Rom 8.17).

The Rainbow Covenant

Keith Ward

Wherein few, that is eight souls were saved through water. (1 Pet 3.20)

The NASB's translation of this verse—"eight persons were brought safely through the water"—makes it sound as if they were saved *from* the water rather than being saved *by* the water. Regardless of what some Greek scholars may suggest—although most agree the grammar indicates that the water is the agent of salvation—in the next verse, Peter makes it clear that the water saved them: "which after a true likeness doth now save you, baptism" (v 21 ASV).

So if Noah was saved *by* (not from) the same water that destroyed the world, what did God save him and his family *from*? The wicked world.

When God surveyed the world of Noah's day, He saw nothing but wickedness. Only Noah found favor in God's eyes. After Noah preached 120 years—with the ark a growing monument to the sincerity of his plea—only seven other people believed and entered the ark. Just over a year later, they entered a world that was clean and pure, all the wickedness having been washed away—exactly what baptism accomplishes for sinners.

After the flood, God made a promise that He would never again destroy the world by water, and He set a rainbow in the sky to be a sign of that unilateral covenant. We tend to think that the rainbow marks an ending of a specific method of God's judgment, but God intended it as a beginning: the hope for a world washed clean from sin. God would not deal with wickedness again by flooding the whole earth; He would resolve the issue of sin another way.

Thousands of years later, Jesus died on the cross as the fulfillment of the hope inherent in the rainbow: God solved the problem of sin by means other than universal destruction. Rather, one man bore the flood of God's wrath in our place. We deserved destruction; He underwent that baptism for us.

Just as the rainbow reminded the Jews that God would never again destroy the sinful world by water, each week we take the Lord's Supper to remind us that God fulfilled the rainbow covenant in Christ. The bread and the fruit of the vine shine with the color of the hope of forgiveness. God made a covenant in Christ. These emblems are the signs of that covenant to us.

War in Heaven

Gary Fisher

When we partake of the Lord's Supper we are not only remembering the Lord's suffering; we are also remembering the incredible blessings that His suffering has brought us. We are honoring Him for having accomplished such a spectacular redemption for us. But do we truly understand the results of what Jesus did?

The book of Revelation uses stunning pictures and drama to help us visualize the results of Christ's death:

> And there was war in heaven, Michael and his angels waging war with the dragon. The dragon and his angels waged war, and they were not strong enough, and there was no longer a place found for them in heaven. And the great dragon was thrown down, the serpent of old who is called the devil and Satan, who deceives the whole world; he was thrown down to the earth, and his angels were thrown down with him. (Rev 12.7–9 NASB)

War in heaven!? That's startling. Not just a minor skirmish either, but all-out conflict between the archangel with his troops and Satan with his angels. The result: the dragon is cast out of heaven and thrown down to the earth. Wow!

What's the time frame of this event? Some people imagine that this refers to some fall of Satan prior to the creation of the world. Others imagine this to be the ultimate defeat of Satan at the end of time. But the text identifies the timing in the next verse: "Now the salvation, and the power, and the kingdom of our God and the authority of His Christ have come" (v 10).

The salvation and kingdom of Christ come with Jesus' death and resurrection. This war in heaven does not occur before time nor at the end of time, but when Jesus died and rose again. The correspondence is no surprise. The Scriptures frequently present Jesus' death as the crisis point in the battle with the devil. As Jesus said just before His death, "Now the ruler of this world will be cast out"; this casting out He immediately connects with His being "lifted up" (John 12.31–32; see also John 14.30; 16.11). In His death Jesus disarmed Satan's troops and triumphed over them (Col 2.15) and rendered the devil powerless, delivering his prisoners (Heb 2.14–15). After all, He had come for this purpose (1 John 3.8). Thus the death and resurrection of Jesus is the time of Jesus' bruising His heel as He crushes the serpent's head—when the judgment that was pronounced against Satan is finally executed (Gen 3.15)—the time of the binding of the strong man (Matt 12.28–29), and the time of Satan's falling from heaven like lightning (Luke 10.18).

This fits the picture given in the Old Testament. Notice how in Job 1–2 and Zechariah 3 Satan is shown in heaven. Even the serpent's appearance in Eden may fit this picture: the enemy of God is in His paradise on earth (Gen 3). When Jesus comes to the earth to reclaim His own, Satan claims the world as his own (*e.g.*, Satan's uncontested offer of all the kingdoms to Jesus in Matthew 4) and tries to drive Jesus out by turning the world against Him. He accomplishes this quite well; indeed, he leads one of Jesus' twelve into betraying Him (John 13.27) and His own people to rejecting Him (John 1.11). It seems that Satan wins; Jesus is killed. But what Satan thinks is Christ's defeat is really His victory. Consider the following verses:

> Through death He might render powerless him who had the power of death, that is, the devil. (Heb 2.14)

> They overcame him because of the blood of the Lamb. (Rev 12.11)

Yes, Christ was *lifted up*. But this allowed Him to *draw all men* to Himself—and to *cast out* Satan (John 12.30–31).

But what does all this really mean for us? In what sense is the devil thrown down? Note Revelation 12.10 again: "For the accuser of our brethren has been thrown down, he who accuses them before our God day and night." We sometimes see Satan in that accuser role in the Bible—again consider Job or Zechariah 3. Think of Satan's whole mission. He hates everything good. He hates God. He hates people. He wants as many people in hell with him as possible. So he uses sin (1 Cor 15.55–56). If he can present himself before God and show that a certain person is a sinner, then he can essentially 'claim' him.

If Jesus had not come and died, Satan would have been 100 percent successful; all men have sinned. But with Jesus' death ("the blood of the Lamb," Rev 12.11) there is forgiveness, and through this forgiveness we overcome Satan's accusations. Now he cannot come before God and accuse a faithful Christian of sin. God can simply respond that there is not a single sin on the record (*cf.* Rom 8.33).

Perhaps it is easy for us to talk glibly about forgiveness of sins. Understanding that the accuser has been disarmed, however, gives us more appreciation of the great forgiveness Jesus' sacrifice provides.

Just imagine what it would be like if Jesus had not died. Since we have all sinned, Satan could—and would—use that sin to stake his claim to each of us. Our sin would cut us off from God without remedy. Thus, at the moment of death, we would be plunged into inevitable banishment from God's presence, into utter darkness.

Jesus' death completely absolves the faithful believer from all sin and guilt (1 John 1.7, 9). There is no sin whatsoever on the record of the Christian. Jesus' death turns out to be the crushing blow to Satan. Jesus came, bound the strong man, and plundered his property: the souls that had been in his domain. We are free, victorious, with a glorious hope of being with God forever—all by Jesus' sacrifice. Praise God!

While we rejoice in our salvation, Satan, on the other hand, is furious. When a tyrant is whipped he becomes enraged. So Satan furiously pursues the only remaining way he can reclaim Christians. He seeks to act on earth in such a way as to get them to turn away from God and back to him. To do that he employs the sea beast (persecution), earth beast (false religion) and Babylon (worldliness). But as long as we take advantage of the blood of the Lamb, hold fast to the word of our testimony, and sacrifice ourselves to the point of death, if necessary, we are absolutely protected from Satan's schemes (Rev 12.11). Paul makes this clear when he applies the language of the serpent's original judgment to the Christian: "The God of peace will soon crush Satan under your feet" (Rom 16.20).

What marvelous results of Jesus' death!

Part Three

Meditating on the Cross

What Does Christ's Suffering Lack?

Keith Ward

Now I rejoice in my sufferings for your sake, and fill up on my part that which is lacking of the afflictions of Christ in my flesh for his body's sake, which is the church. (Col 1.24 ASV)

Upon reading this verse, one is immediately struck with the thought: 'What could possibly be lacking in the afflictions and anguish that Christ bore on the cross?'

As a person, He was mocked and humiliated and held in contempt to a degree that in most people would destroy all self-esteem.

As a man, He was beaten nearly to death with vicious, cutting scourges that likely bared the bones of His back. Then He was nailed to the cross, where He had to scrape His lacerated back up the rough wood, pushing on the spike through His feet, in order to relieve the strain on His lungs and to gasp life-giving breaths. When the agony in His feet became too great, He would scrape painfully back down to hang on the spikes in His wrists—over and over and over....

As the Son of God—holy, blameless—He felt the crushing weight of all the horrifying filth of sin as He was "made to be sin on our behalf" (2 Cor 5.21). Having been in fellowship with the Father from eternity before time was, He was ripped from the presence of the Father by my sins, by your sins, and cried out, "My God! My God! Why have you forsaken me?" (Mark 15.34). The ravished concubine of Judges 19 was not as defiled as He was by our sins.

To what could Paul possibly be referring? What is lacking in such suffering? *We are.* We must continue to suffer for Christ because we are His body still on earth. Paul rejoiced in his sufferings for the Colossians' sake. Jesus was no longer in the world suffering that they might have the gospel; Paul was doing that in Christ's stead. This was as God intended, that we may have the privilege of sharing in Christ's sufferings.

So the Supper, the bread and juice, are not merely a memorial to His sufferings so long ago; they also are a commitment to fill up on our part that which is lacking in Jesus' sufferings.

It should be obvious that this suffering does not refer to cancers, blindness, disasters; these also happen to the wicked and are not "for his body's sake." What, then, are we committing to suffer when we take this bread and drink this cup? Paul was imprisoned for preaching the gospel, suffering much to carry the gospel to the lost and to see that churches grew from infancy to self-sufficiency (2 Cor 11.21–28). Our opportunities to suffer for the sake of the gospel in behalf of Christ are not likely to be so dramatic. It seems trivial to place giving up my favorite television show, my privacy, my precious routine, the big game, and other such things alongside Jesus' suffering or Paul's work to fill up the lack in it. At least, it seems trivial until we consider that we seldom manage to accomplish even these small sacrifices on behalf of the body. Just what, if anything, have we managed to give up for the sake of His body this past week?

Perhaps when we reach the next level—when giving up even these smallest things becomes second nature to us—God will grant us the privilege to join with Paul in filling up that which is lacking in the suffering of Christ.

The Word of the Cross

Mark L. Hatfield

For the word of the cross is foolishness to those who are perishing, but to us who are being saved it is the power of God. (1 Cor 1.18 NASB)

In recent times some have said not to focus so much on the cross, but to focus only on the Christ. But this is hardly possible! If Jesus hadn't died on the cross He couldn't be the Christ. The Scriptures tell us that the Christ would be pierced for our transgressions (see Psa 22); if Jesus had not died on the cross He could not bear our iniquities or take on the curse of sin. The Scriptures say, "Cursed is everyone who hangs on a tree" (Deut 21.23); if Jesus had avoided the cross there would be no gospel message. Paul said that we preach Christ *crucified*, not just that we preach Christ (1 Cor 1.23).

Most of us know that Jesus died on a cross. But how often do we take the time to consider the significance of what that means? From pieces of jewelry, to pictures in houses, to images on pulpits or other items in church buildings throughout the world, the cross is used to help people remember the death of Jesus.

But do we *really* remember it? Do we really understand and appreciate all that the cross represents? Why do we sing songs about clinging to the "old rugged cross"? Why do we pray and thank God for giving His Son on the cross?

Let us go back to the cross and the biblical record to understand more fully what the cross should mean to us—each day and as we partake of the Supper.

The Cross Means a Crucifixion

One way a criminal might be punished under the Roman government was to be nailed to and hung on a cross. This method of torture would subject the victim to a despicable and excruciating death. Since the body was hung in a position that prevented the free flow of air into the lungs, most who were crucified died slowly. By pushing up on the nails in his feet and pulling up on the nails through his wrists, the condemned could put himself in a position that allowed a breath—until the pain caused by the nails was unbearable and he had to slide back down the cross. This process would go on until the criminal was too fatigued to continue it any longer, or until the soldiers decided to end it and broke his legs. Either way, the final means of death was suffocation, unless the crucified survived long enough to die of exposure or dehydration. The Romans were specialists with this type of execution, and it was a death that would put the condemned to public shame.

The principal difference with Jesus' death by crucifixion is that He was *not* a criminal—yet He was numbered with the transgressors and died for every sinner in the world (Isa 53.12; 1 Pet 2.21–24). Although He was tried and found not guilty, the people still cried out, "Crucify, crucify Him!" (Luke 23.21). Jesus, knowing that it was the Father's will for His life (Luke 22.24), suffered that painful death. The cross should mean to us the innocent death of God's Son for all who are sinful.

The Cross Means a Willing Sacrifice

We often hear about criminals who run from the consequences of their lawlessness. Not only was Jesus innocent, but He *freely* gave His life for all sinners. He offered no resistance in the garden when the soldiers came to arrest Him. He uttered no threats of revenge as He was beaten, spat upon and mocked. Never do we see Jesus trying to avoid what was ultimately the will of the Father in heaven. Rather, Jesus said, "No one takes [my life] from Me, but I lay it down of Myself" (John 10.18). No one made Him pay the price for sin. As Paul said, "Christ has redeemed us from the curse of the law, having become a curse for us (for it is written, 'Cursed is everyone who hangs on a tree')" (Gal 3.13).

Jesus sacrificed Himself by going to the cross and dying. With this sacrifice He knew He was opening the door of peace and fellowship between God and man, even bringing glory to Himself again (Heb 12.2). The cross should mean to us the willingness of Jesus to do God's will.

The Cross Means a Message of Salvation

After Jesus' death, the crucifixion and the wonderful blessings that would come as a result became the central message proclaimed by His followers—and rightfully so. Paul said that the gospel is the power of God unto salvation (Rom 1.16). When people hear about what Jesus did for them—and what they have done against Him—it pierces their hearts and causes them to consider their stance before God.

The Corinthian brethren were told about the good news and their responsibility to accept and hold fast to these truths in order to be saved:

> Moreover, brethren, I declare to you the gospel which I preached to you, which also you received and in which you stand, by which also you are saved, if you hold fast that word which I preached to you—unless you believed in vain. For I delivered to you first of all that which I also received: that Christ died for our sins according to the Scriptures, and that He was buried, and that He rose again the third day according to the Scriptures. (1 Cor 15.1–4 NKJV)

This is why Paul said earlier that "to us who are being saved [the word of the cross] is the power of God" (1 Cor 1.18 NASB). The cross should mean to us the good news of salvation.

The Cross Means All of Our Glory

Paul helps us to recognize the basis for our glorying when he writes, "For I determined not to know anything among you except Jesus Christ and Him crucified" (1 Cor 2.2 NKJV), and, "But God forbid that I should boast except in the cross of our Lord Jesus Christ" (Gal 6.14).

Some people are concerned about "earning salvation" and being careful not to do any good works of obedience lest they try somehow to work their way to heaven. Although Jesus does want us to continue in His words as faithful disciples (John 8.31–32), it is clear that our glorying is not in what we do, but in what Jesus did on the cross. While we must obey the commands that Jesus has left for us, our only legitimate boast is not in our own work, but the cross of Christ and the works that God has done for those who desire to be His children through the shed blood of Jesus; the cross is all of our glory.

While it is true that the cross by itself could not save us without the Christ, it is also clear that the Christ without the cross is inadequate for salvation:

> Being found in appearance as a man, He humbled Himself by becoming obedient to the point of death, even death on a cross. For this reason also, God highly exalted Him, and bestowed on Him the name which is above every name, so that at the name of Jesus every knee will bow, of those who are in heaven and on earth and under the earth, and that every tongue will confess that Jesus Christ is Lord, to the glory of God the Father. (Phil 2.8–11 NASB)

Emptying Myself

C. Benjamin Hastings

We assemble every first day of the week to commemorate the death of our Savior, Jesus. There are many things that we consider as we remember Jesus—His life, His teaching, His suffering. Let's consider what Paul shared with the Philippian brethren regarding Jesus' sacrifice.

In the second chapter of Philippians, Paul begins by expressing his desire that the brethren be united. This is not only a goal that we feebly attempt to achieve or consider a good idea; it is something Jesus clearly desired, too (John 17.21). In order to achieve and maintain the unity that God requires, Paul tells us that we have to be willing to live with a humble attitude.

It is clearly important that we take care of the needs of both ourselves and our families, but our responsibility doesn't end there. To be unified, we must look out not only for ourselves, but for the needs of others as well. Ultimately, we must be willing to make sacrifices to achieve the unity God wants for us.

Christ clearly had the attitude of selfless sacrifice that we need to embody. Not only did Jesus live in what we would consider poverty (He had no fixed dwelling, no large wardrobe, and lacked almost everything we consider essential for life today); more importantly, Jesus left heaven, "emptied Himself" (or "made Himself nothing"), and came to live a life like ours (Phil 2.7 NASB).

His leaving heaven doesn't in any way mean that Jesus ceased to have the qualities of deity, but that He left the glory of heaven behind. Jesus had every reason to hold on to His position with our Father in heaven, but He left it to experience all that we experience—the pain, the difficulties, the humiliation that are part of our lives.

That Jesus emptied Himself could alone be considered the ultimate example of selfless humility, but Jesus didn't stop there. He submitted Himself to the lowliest punishment available. Capital punishment was frequent in Jesus' time, but one of the most humiliating of punishments was to be crucified—a death that was reserved for the worst criminals.

Jesus had absolutely no reason to submit Himself to this ridicule, torture, and suffering because of anything He had done. Instead, He counted our needs above His own desires. Because He did so, He stood in the place of one who is as far away from God as possible. Jesus took the place of the worst of sinners. Jesus took *my* place and *your* place.

As John the Baptist said of Jesus in John 3.30, "He must increase, and I must decrease." Because Jesus was willing to take my place and bear the punishment I deserved, I need to live as He wants me to. All of us must think of Jesus daily and empty ourselves, seeking to live like Him. Every day, we need to remember how He daily emptied Himself—and not only remember the sacrifice He made, but emulate it in our lives, sacrificing our own desires to meet the needs of others and to fulfill His desire for us.

Cleansing Our Sins

Gary Fisher

After David grievously sinned by committing adultery with Bathsheba and attempting to cover it up by arranging for Uriah to be killed, Nathan confronted him and brought him to conviction about what he had done. David was grieved over his sin. He asked God, "Wash me thoroughly from my iniquity and cleanse me from my sin" (Psa 51.2 NASB). He also requested, "Purify me with hyssop, and I shall be clean; wash me, and I shall be whiter than snow" (Psa 51.7). The fact that David insisted on being washed, cleansed and purified shows how dirty and defiled he felt.

Sin makes us filthy.

New Testament passages echo this idea. We look to the Lord to cleanse our conscience and heart (Heb 9.14; Acts 15.9) from all sin and unrighteousness (1 John 1.7, 9). As Saul was told to wash away his sins (Acts 22.16), every Christian is cleansed by the washing of water with the word (Eph 5.26), the washing of regeneration (Tit 3.5; see 1 Cor 6.11). Those Christians who die and go to heaven are those who "have washed their robes and made them white in the blood of the Lamb" (Rev 7.14).

I am not personally a fanatic about cleanliness, but even for me some filth is disgusting. When I was a teenager our family collected eggs from 5,000 caged laying hens. Every couple of months the pits had to be cleaned out by a front-end loader on a lawn tractor. This was a repulsive job made even worse by the fact that both the building and the watering system leaked quite a bit; the manure was the consistency of a hearty soup. After a day of 'fun' with scooping out the pits, I welcomed a shower with lots of soap.

Our sins smell worse than chicken manure. The picture in Zechariah 3 describes this: "Then he showed me Joshua the high priest standing before the angel of the LORD, and Satan standing at his right hand to accuse him. ...Now Joshua was clothed with filthy garments and standing before the angel" (Zech 3.1, 3). The sources I have consulted suggest that "filthy" here means excrement-soiled. Barker in the *Expositor's Bible Commentary* quotes Feinberg, who labels this term "the strongest expression in the Hebrew language for filth of the most vile and loathsome character." [1] That expresses the real nature of our sins: they stink and they make us vile, filthy and wretched.

The setting of Zechariah 3 is astonishing. Joshua was the high priest. As such he represents the people of Israel to God. Satan was standing before God to accuse Joshua and the people of sin and thereby lay claim to them. But God rebuked Satan and said that the Lord had chosen Jerusalem and rescued her from the fire. Therefore God was going to defend His people. Then—amazingly—God took away the filthy garments from Joshua and gave him festal robes and even a clean turban (Zech 3.4–5). God took away Satan's grounds for accusation and relieved Joshua of the smelly filth that he was wearing. The fact that He gave Joshua festal robes shows that God not only cleanses the saved but outfits them for celebration.

Perhaps we should also consider how Joshua is used in Zechariah as a symbol for God's Servant, the coming Branch (Zech 3.8). In this role, Joshua was crowned by God, prefiguring Jesus, who would unite the priesthood and kingship in one person (Zech 6.9–15). Such a union was prohibited by law, since kings were from Judah, priests from Levi, but as ancient Melchizedek had done, so Jesus would unite the two functions. It was appropriate that Joshua symbolize Jesus, since Jesus is the Greek form of the same name. Having considered these things, perhaps we can see that Joshua's wearing filthy clothes foreshadows the way that Jesus, as our sin offering, would take our filthy sins on Him.

The Lord's Supper should help us reflect on how dirty and soiled we are in our sins. As we feel extremely uncomfortable with and sickened by this, we come to appreciate even more the fact that God by His grace and by Jesus' sacrifice has cleansed and purged us. We are truly clean, with not a smudge, a stain or a hint of odor remaining. Thanks be to God!

He Died for Me
Passover and the Lord

Sewell Hall

It was a night long to be remembered when God passed through Egypt, taking the life of the firstborn of every family not eating the Passover meal and without blood on the doorpost. The Israelite families had been very careful to follow the instructions God had given (Exod 12). On the tenth of Abib, they had chosen an unblemished lamb in its first year and had killed it on the fourteenth. They had carefully placed the blood on the doorpost, roasted the lamb and gathered to eat it. Consequently, they were spared when God passed over. The Egyptians who had not prepared lost the firstborn of every family. As the wailing cry went up from the Egyptians, one can easily imagine every firstborn Israelite looking at the remaining carcass of the lamb on the table and saying, "He died for me."

As a result of the Passover, Israel was set free from Egyptian slavery. And God decreed that the feast that had preceded their deliverance should be repeated year after year as a memorial. Jewish historians record the annual observance of the feast. It was arranged so that children would ask its meaning. Then the father, or whoever presided, would explain each dish. "This is the lamb that was slain for deliverance of our forefathers. This unleavened bread is the haste with which they went out of Egypt. These bitter herbs are the bitterness of the slavery that they endured." Observed year after year, the ritual became increasingly familiar to each child.

Some fifteen hundred years later, Jesus presided at the Passover feast observed by His disciples on the night before His death. He likely followed the traditional explanation of each item, just as the disciples had heard it over and over all their lives. But Luke tells us that Jesus proceeded with something unfamiliar. "He took bread, gave thanks and broke it, and gave it to them, saying, 'This is My body which is given for you; do this in remembrance of Me.' Likewise He also took the cup after supper, saying, 'This cup is the new covenant in My blood, which is shed for you'" (Luke 22.19 NKJV). Jesus was instituting a new feast.

Just as the old Passover was first observed in expectation of deliverance from Egyptian slavery, this new feast was instituted in expectation of the deliverance from sin that would be accomplished the following day on the cross. And just as the Old Testament Passover was to be repeated annually as a memorial, so the Lord's Supper was to be repeated as a memorial. "This do," He said, "as often as you drink it, in remembrance of Me" (1 Cor 11.25).

If deliverance from Egyptian slavery justified an annual observance, surely deliverance from sin justifies a more frequent memorial. It is not surprising, then, that when we read of early Christians' observance of this memorial feast, it was not on a particular day of the year or of the month; rather, "On the first day of the week… the disciples came together to break bread" (Acts 20.7).

The church in Jerusalem "continued steadfastly… in the breaking of bread" (Acts 2.42). And it seems altogether likely that on the first day of every week since then, disciples have come together somewhere in the world to break bread in remembrance of their Savior. Let each one of us resolve to keep the memorial chain unbroken by continuing steadfastly in its observance.

The apostle Paul wrote, "For indeed Christ, our Passover, was sacrificed for us" (1 Cor 5.7). And as we look upon the bread and the fruit of the vine, we should say, as the firstborn of Israel said of the lamb, "He died for me."

Free for the Son's Sake
Ephesians 4.32

Kenneth L. Chumbley

Domrémy (dôm-rə-mē´), population 300, is situated on the Meuse River in northeastern France. Those who supposedly know such things say the village hasn't changed much since the time, nearly six hundred years ago, when it stepped onto the pages of history.

> We are told that in Paris they still show the old state books in which under every town and village there were entered the taxes due from each; and that on the page headed Domrémy . . . there were the usual official figures, but written across them in red ink, "Free for the Maid's sake."[1]

Domrémy, you see, was the home of Joan of Arc. In gratitude for her service to France, the newly crowned king Charles VII asked the Maid of Orleans to name her reward. In response, she asked that the people of her village be exempted from paying taxes. And this the king decreed. Indee, the paper in which he issued the order can still be seen; it is dated the last of July, 1429.[2]

As I read this story, another book comes to my mind—one as old as creation—in which is written my name, along with the names of all the small and great (Rev 20.12). Under my name (or so I envision it) is listed the debt I owe a King. But the debt I find written there is too great; like those mentioned in Luke 7.42, I owe what I am unable to pay.

But there is something else I find on my page. For written

across it—in blood, not ink—are the words *free for the Son's sake.* And when I see that, I remember what Paul wrote: "And be ye kind one to another, tenderhearted, forgiving one another, even as God *for Christ's sake* hath forgiven you" (Eph 4.32 KJV).

In the matter of forgiveness—of being free from a debt—there are two things from this verse that especially impress me.

First, the words *even as* tell me that **my forgiveness of another should be modeled after God's forgiveness of me.** When I read such texts as Psalm 103.8–12, I see the example I need to follow when there is another I need to forgive:

> The LORD is merciful and gracious, slow to anger, and
> plenteous in mercy.
> He will not always chide: neither will he keep his
> anger for ever.
> He hath not dealt with us after our sins; nor rewarded us
> according to our iniquities.
> For as the heaven is high above the earth, so great is his mercy
> toward them that fear him.
> As far as the east is from the west, so far hath he removed
> our transgressions from us.
> Like as a father pitieth his children, so the LORD pitieth them
> that fear him. (Psa 103.8–12; *cf.* Jer 31.34; Jer 50.20)

Second, the words *for Christ's sake* tell me that **forgiveness is not granted on behalf of the one who receives it.** Do not miss the connection between the *even as* part of this verse and the *for Christ's sake* part. We don't forgive others' debts because they deserve it any more than God forgave us because we deserve it (Rom 5.6). If our forgiveness is modeled after the One who forgave us for Christ's sake, then we, too, will forgive others for Christ's sake. We ought to treat others the way God, through Christ, has treated us (Matt 18.32–33; Rom 7.24–25).

Thanks be to God that there was One who, when asked to name His reward, asked that I be set free.

Scarlet though my sins may be,
God, for Christ's sake,
Has forgiven me.

Not As I Will, but As You Will
Matthew 26.39–56

T. Mark Lloyd, Sr.

The scene is the garden of Gethsemane. Jesus, with His three beloved disciples, Peter, James and John, is separated from the other apostles. The others are at a different location in the garden. Judas has already departed. Jesus is a stone's throw from the three, in deep, agonizing prayer. Drops of sweat like blood are coming from Him.

He is alone; the three are there to keep watch, but are sleeping. The single event that brought Him to earth is about to happen. As the horrible mental, moral, spiritual and physical suffering He is to endure is beginning, He says, 'Father, this may be too much for me to bear. Is there another way?'

"Let this cup pass from me!"

Let's think about this: was there possibly another way? Jesus knew what had been planned, but now, He was *experiencing* the agony. Was it more than He had anticipated? In the same breath, He says, "Not as I will, but as You will." Will is power of choice and deliberate action. Jesus' will may be wavering at the moment, ever so briefly, a strong reminder of His humanity. He is asking, 'Can I handle this?' Yet quickly His complete obedience comes forth when He says, 'I will do what You want me to do.' In other words, 'God, I know Your power and what Your choice is.'

Jesus Himself emphasized to Peter that He had options, when He said in verse 53, "Do you not think I could appeal to the Father and He would send twelve legions of angels?" He had an ultimate decision to make. Jesus would do what God wanted and needed from Him—a death and a sacrifice.

Can you imagine twelve legions of angels descending on this motley band of soldiers and Jews? Just think what one angel of God did to 185,000 Assyrians in the Old Testament (2 Kings 19.35). When I consider that episode, the thought crosses my mind of how awesome it would have been to witness such a divine intervention—yet, I quickly thank Jesus for not choosing that option.

What Jesus understood is that we—you and I—did *not* have options. A few hours later Jesus died on the cross. He lived and died experiencing the horror He had dreaded and about which He had prayed. If it was Jesus' will to do the will of His Father, what should our will be today? Should we not—in whatever circumstance we find ourselves—say, "Not my will, God, but Your will." May we always do what Jesus did and make our wills subservient.

As we partake of the memorial, we should remember Jesus' submission to the Father's will. Thank you, Jesus, for being the obedient Son that you are.

Remove This Cup

Mark Moseley

And He said to them, "My soul is deeply grieved to the point of death; remain here and keep watch." And He went a little beyond them, and fell to the ground and began to pray that if it were possible, the hour might pass Him by. And He was saying, "Abba! Father! All things are possible for You; remove this cup from Me; yet not what I will, but what You will." (Mark 14.34–36 NASB)

I'm convinced that most of us can identify, if not fully, at least closely with what Jesus was feeling. We have fallen to our knees in agony, crying to the Father, "Father God, You can do anything. Hear my prayer! Take away this pain! Lift this horrible burden! Remove this cup!"

Maybe we weren't even asking on our own behalf. Perhaps we were praying for a loved one, a beloved companion, a parent, a child, a dear friend.

The fact that we were praying for another person hardly made the anguish easier to bear. We may even have begged, "Father, if someone has to bear this burden, let it be me! Take it from him and let me bear it!"

Usually it is a comfort knowing that God is almighty. But there are moments when that knowledge only adds to the agony: "All things are possible for You."

The question isn't "If God?" but "Will God?" And the question "Will God?" naturally leads us to ask "Why, God?"

If God can, then why doesn't He?

This question has been a major stumbling block for countless unbelievers. "If God can end suffering, why doesn't He?" "If God is all powerful, then why does He allow catastrophic tragedy?" "Why doesn't God feed the starving children?" "Why does God allow the ruthless and cruel to have their way?" "Why doesn't God do something about cancer? AIDS? tsunamis?"

Why must men drink so deeply and so often from the cup of pain and suffering? I don't know.

But I do know that at one great moment in history the Son of God came to earth to take the world's burden upon Himself. I know that He fell to the ground beside us in Gethsemane, bearing the pangs of impending doom and death in His heart. I know this Lamb of God wrestled in agony, despising the shame that loomed ahead, crying, "Father! All things are possible for You; remove this cup from Me!"

Above all this, I know that Jesus uttered His prayer in unwavering trust in the Father's will: *"Yet not what I will, but what You will."* His faith could hear a promise of glory despite the awful silence of God that weighed so heavily in the garden. His faith enabled Jesus to see beyond the black pit of death to the joy set before Him.

And because of this, I know that when I fall to the ground in my Gethsemane, I am not alone.

Most True to Those
Who Are My Greatest Grief

Joseph Bingham

Is it nothing to you, all you who pass by? Look and see if there is any sorrow like my sorrow, which was brought upon me, which the LORD inflicted on the day of his fierce anger. (Lam 1.12 ESV)

Jeremiah's best-remembered lines may be the cry to passersby in his Lamentations: "Was ever grief like mine?" When he wrote them, his words may have been hyperbolic; Jesus, centuries later, made them ironic. Jeremiah's lament over the filthy, fallen state of Jerusalem and his misery as a part of that sinful people find their answer in Christ, who cleanses and heals. Jeremiah's implicit claim, that the suffering of the Jews of his day is history's greatest, also finds its answer in Christ, as the Savior is ruthlessly beaten, mocked and killed by the very people He has come to rescue. Jeremiah's grief was great, but the greater grief would be felt by the one sent by God in answer to His people's laments.

The story of the crucifixion is of course rich with such ironies. The history of God's dealings with His people is rather ludicrous; each generation is stunned by the folly of its fathers in their response to the mercy of the Almighty, and each generation continues to rush headlong to sinful pursuits and rebellion. It is only fitting that the climactic event of this history of man's unfit behavior should be the murder of God by His beneficiaries, and that God should still manage to work through this very murder a blessing—His greatest blessing—for His people.

But in the course of that murder, each recorded event seems to underscore the absurdity of Christ's suffering, and it seems likely that only Christ, and perhaps His mother, were conscious of this absurdity as the events unfolded. Jesus is captured so that He may set people free; had it not been for Him, those capturing Him would still be slaves in Egypt. He is accused of making Himself equal with God—Jesus, who, though He did not consider it robbery to be equal to God, gave it up. He is accused of saying He would destroy and rebuild the temple; He built the world.

Who has not almost laughed aloud at the Jews' words to Pilate: "His blood be on us and on our children!" (Matt 27.25)? Little do they know that their words will become the heartbroken, penitent plea of millions over millennia. As they say these words, Jesus, the Prince of Peace, stands next to the one they choose to free: Barabbas, a seditious man. In blind rage, they torture and spit on Him; a thoughtful reader remembers when Jesus spat, and why: to heal the blind. The crown of thorns placed on Jesus' head contrasts with His late appearance at the transfiguration; it also sets up for contrast Christ's role as the vine and the thorns which represent the consequences of sin in the world. Jesus takes those painful consequences to be His crown as He bears the ultimate consequence, death, without having sinned Himself.

Poet George Herbert explores all these ironies, and many more, in his almost encyclopedic poem "The Sacrifice." Written from the perspective of Christ, each stanza ends with the words of Jeremiah, "Was ever grief like mine?" It is a poem worth reading in full, and carefully. Each of its sixty-three stanzas brings out another heart-piercing aspect of Christ's grief, employing passages from across the Scriptures, from Genesis to the epistles, to underscore the infinite, and infinitely poetic, injustice of the crucifixion.

On the cross, Jesus cries out to God, "Why have you forsaken me?" He echoes the perennial cry of the sinful Israelites after judgment, the cry of Jeremiah in Lamentations, but this time the cry is from an innocent man. This is, among all the griefs in history, one perfectly unique. There was never a man like this; there was never grief like His.

Excerpts from "The Sacrifice"[1]

by George Herbert (1593–1633)

O all ye, who pass by, whose eyes and mind
To worldly things are sharp, but to me blind;
To me, who took eyes that I might you find:
   Was ever grief like mine?

The Princes of my people make a head
Against their Maker: they do wish me dead,
Who cannot wish, except I give them bread:
   Was ever grief like mine?

Without me each one, who doth now me brave,
Had to this day been an Egyptian slave.
They use that power against me, which I gave:
   Was ever grief like mine?

Arise, arise, they come! Look how they run!
Alas! what haste they make to be undone!
How with their lanterns do they seek the sun!
   Was ever grief like mine?

With clubs and staves they seek me, as a thief,
Who am the way of truth, the true relief,
Most true to those who are my greatest grief:
   Was ever grief like mine?

See, they lay hold on me, not with the hands
Of faith, but fury; yet at their commands
I suffer binding, who have loosed their bands:
   Was ever grief like mine?

All my Disciples fly; fear puts a bar
Betwixt my friends and me. They leave the star,
That brought the wise men of the East from far:
   Was ever grief like mine?

The Priests and Rulers all false witness seek
'Gainst him, who seeks not life, but is the meek
And ready Paschal Lamb of this great week:
   Was ever grief like mine?

Then they accuse me of great blasphemy,
That I did thrust into the Deity,
Who never thought that any robbery:
   Was ever grief like mine?

Some said, that I the Temple to the floor
In three days razed, and raiséd as before.
Why, he that built the world can do much more:
   Was ever grief like mine?

Then they condemn me all with that same breath,
Which I do give them daily, unto death.
Thus Adam my first breathing rendereth:
   Was ever grief like mine?

They bind, and lead me unto Herod: he
Sends me to Pilate. This makes them agree;
But yet their friendship is my enmity.
   Was ever grief like mine?

Herod in judgment sits, while I do stand;
Examines me with a censorious hand:
I him obey, who all things else command:
   Was ever grief like mine?

The Jews accuse me with despitefulness;
And vying malice with my gentleness,
Pick quarrels with their only happiness:
   Was ever grief like mine?

Hark how they cry aloud still, *Crucify:*
It is not fit He live a day, they cry,
Who cannot live less than eternally:
   Was ever grief like mine?

Yet still they shout, and cry, and stop their ears,
Putting my life among their sins and fears,
And therefore wish *my blood on them and theirs:*
   Was ever grief like mine?

They choose a murderer, and all agree
In him to do themselves a courtesy:
For it was their own cause who killéd me:
   Was ever grief like mine?

And a seditious murderer he was:
But I the Prince of Peace; peace that doth pass
All understanding, more than heaven doth glass:
   Was ever grief like mine?

Ah, how they scourge me! yet my tenderness
Doubles each lash: and yet their bitterness
Winds up my grief to a mysteriousness:
   Was ever grief like mine?

Behold, they spit on me in scornful wise;
Who with my spittle gave the blind man eyes,
Leaving his blindness to mine enemies:
        Was ever grief like mine?

Weep not, dear friends, since I for both have wept,
When all my tears were blood, the while you slept:
Your tears for your own fortunes should be kept:
        Was ever grief like mine?

The soldiers lead me to the common hall;
There they deride me, they abuse me all:
Yet for twelve heavenly legions I could call:
        Was ever grief like mine?

Then on my head a crown of thorns I wear;
For these are all the grapes Sion doth bear,
Though I my vine planted and watered there:
        Was ever grief like mine?

So sits the earth's great curse in Adam's fall
Upon my head; so I remove it all
From th' earth unto my brows, and bear the thrall:
        Was ever grief like mine?

Then with the reed they gave to me before,
They strike my head, the rock from whence all store
Of heavenly blessings issue evermore:
        Was ever grief like mine?

They bow their knees to me, and cry, Hail, King:
Whatever scoffs or scornfulness can bring,
I am the floor, the sink, where they it fling:
        Was ever grief like mine?

The soldiers also spit upon that face
Which Angels did desire to have the grace,
And Prophets once to see, but found no place:
        Was ever grief like mine?

Thus trimmed, forth they bring me to the rout,
Who *Crucify him,* cry with one strong shout.
God holds his peace at man, and man cries out:
        Was ever grief like mine?

My cross I bear myself, until I faint:
Then Simon bears it for me by constraint,
The decreed burden of each mortal Saint:
        Was ever grief like mine?

O all ye who pass by, behold and see:
Man stole the fruit, but I must climb the tree;
The tree of life to all, but only me:
    Was ever grief like mine?

Lo, here I hang, charged with a world of sin,
The greater world o' the two; for that came in
By words, but this by sorrow I must win:
    Was ever grief like mine?

But, *O my God, my God!* why leav'st thou me,
The Son, in whom thou dost delight to be?
My God, my God————
    Was ever grief like mine?

Now heal thyself, Physician; now come down.
Alas! I do so, when I left my crown
And Father's smile for you, to feel his frown:
    Was ever grief like mine?

In healing not myself, there doth consist
All that salvation, which ye now resist;
Your safety in my sickness doth subsist:
    Was ever grief like mine?

Betwixt two thieves I spend my utmost breath,
As he that for some robbery suffereth.
Alas! what have I stolen from you? death:
    Was ever grief like mine?

A king my title is, prefixed on high;
Yet by my subjects am condemned to die
A servile death in servile company:
    Was ever grief like mine?

But now I die; now all is finishéd.
My woe, man's weal: and now I bow my head:
    Only let others say, when I am dead,
    Never was grief like mine.

Until He Comes

C. Benjamin Hastings

Because of the frailty of the human mind, especially its tendency to forget, Jesus established the memorial feast we refer to as the Lord's Supper. Each week, we obey His command by eating and drinking the emblems—but is that all He asks? Does this weekly observance involve more than remembering?

The command is not just that we remember; it specifies remembering until He comes. We are to remember His death while longing for His return. Children might long for the return of their father from a business trip. They talk to him on the phone, read his postcards, then—when the time is right—they wake up early, get ready, and go to the airport to meet him at the gate. They are longing for his return. In the same way—and even more eagerly—we need to long for the return of esus and await His arrival. Think of what Paul tells Timothy: "Now there is in store for me the crown of righteousness, which the Lord, the righteous Judge, will award to me on that day—and not only to me, but also to all who have longed for his appearing" (2 Tim 4.8 NIV).

We can look to the Bible for examples of how to wait for Jesus. Even before His birth, people were waiting and looking for Him. Adam and Eve could look for Jesus as the prophesied seed of woman who would bruise the head of the tempter (Gen 3.15). Israel looked for the Messiah as the Deliverer foretold by may prophets throughout the Old Testament. For many generations, this promise remained unfulfilled.

Having to wait so long, the men and women of old could easily have given up and could simply have accepted that everything would continue as they had experienced it in the past. It must have been difficult not to dismiss the fulfillment of promises as something that wouldn't happen in their lifetime. However, when God's timetable had been met, Jesus did come, and all of those who were waiting could see the realization of their hopes.

Before Jesus was born into this world, His presence caused excitement. When Mary approached and Elizabeth heard her voice (Luke 1.39–45), the baby leaped in Elizabeth's womb. Elizabeth knew that Mary was carrying the Lord who was to come. She was overjoyed that her Lord was coming, that the time had come when God was fulfilling His ancient promise.

Simeon was a righteous man "waiting for the consolation of Israel" (Luke 2.25–32). He was blessed beyond others who were waiting for the Messiah: the Holy Spirit had told Simeon that he would not face death before seeing the Lord's Christ. When the child Jesus was brought to the temple to be redeemed as Mary's firstborn (see Exod 13.1–16), Simeon took Jesus in his arms and praised God that he could now depart in peace. He had eagerly awaited the coming of this Savior and now saw the salvation to be revealed before the entire world—Jew and Gentile alike.

The prophetess Anna (Luke 2.36–38) had devoted herself diligently to worshiping in the temple. The hour that Jesus was brought, "she began to give thanks to God" and to tell others the good news that Jesus had come.

These were the reactions of faithful servants of God. After longing for the fulfillment of promises made many hundreds of years before, they could easily have become discouraged; instead, they trusted that all would happen as prophesied and responded with joy to see the coming of the Promised One.

We who await Jesus' return could also become discouraged that He has yet to come. Or we can instead long for His appearance, trusting that God will continue to fulfill His promises.

Like these faithful witnesses of Jesus' entry into this world, we should continue to look for His coming. When we face life's difficult moments, we can seek and express the consolation of our confidence in His return. We can know that, in our relationship with Jesus, God will provide solace. Like Mary, we can know that Jesus has already come, and we can look forward to His return. And just as Anna shared the news of Jesus' arrival, we can spread the gospel message that jesus has come and will come again.

Jesus told us to remember His death. We are also to remember His life, His teaching, and His commandments. Just as children long for the return of the father when he is away, we should feel that craving and longing for Jesus to come back, for the time when we will be able to be with God. We should be motivated daily not only by remembering His way of life, His devotion to the Father, and His supreme sacrifice, but also by anticipating His return. To please the Lord, we must demonstrate in the way we live both that we remember His death and that we long for His return. Let us live faithful until He comes again!

He Did It for Others

Nathan Ward

There is something remarkable about Jesus' sacrifice for us. That, of course, goes without saying—after all, He gave Himself for us while we were enemies to God. But beyond that, there is something remarkable about *the way* in which He gave Himself.

Consider Jesus in the upper room. After celebrating the Passover, He kneels to wash the disciples' feet to teach them a lesson about being servants. He takes the time to warn Peter about his arrogance and caution him about the night's coming events. He spends a great deal of time comforting all of the disciples about His impending departure and instructing them about the coming Comforter.

Consider Jesus in the garden. Even in the midst of praying about His own fears, He knows that His desire is not of ultimate importance. Then He wakes the disciples and warns them to be watchful and to pray that they won't fall into temptation. When the soldiers come and arrest Him, He stops the entire process in order to reach down and heal an injured slave.

Consider Jesus at His trial. In this, the biggest sham of a trial that has ever been performed, Jesus had every right to be indignant about the violation of His rights and of every legal and ethical standard. Yet when He heard the rooster crow, He took the time to find Peter standing nearby and give him that look—the convicting, yet loving and reassuring look—that was needed to drive him to repentance.

Consider Jesus on the road to the cross. After He has been sentenced, we find Him carrying His cross to Golgotha while a group of women follow Him and weep over Him. And again, He stops everything so He can turn and warn them of the coming destruction over which they should be weeping.

Consider Jesus on the cross. When every breath was precious and every word agonizing, Jesus remained concerned with others. He looked out for the spiritual well-being of those crucifying Him ("Father forgive them"), the thief being crucified with Him ("You will be with me in paradise"), and all of mankind ("It [The plan to redeem man] is finished"). He looked out for the physical well-being of His mother ("Woman, behold your son"). And He concerned Himself with the fulfillment of prophecy ("My God, my God, why have you forsaken me" and "I thirst").

We can see something remarkable about how Jesus faced the last hours of His life—a life designed to bring Him to the cross. Certainly, He was fully aware of what faced Him. Surely He knew that He was about to undergo the most horrific method of execution man has ever devised. There is no doubt that Jesus had every right to be preoccupied with Himself and His immediate future— more right than we have ever had for our constant self-concern.

Yet everything that Jesus said and did as He approached the cross had someone else as its focus—just as He had lived His entire life. So, why is it that sometimes we have such a hard time focusing on Him? And focusing on Him isn't something that we are only to do when gathered around the Lord's Table. We can meditate about Jesus' sacrifice for 15 minutes while taking of the memorial feast on Sunday, but still do so in an unworthy manner, if we later go out and live a life contrary to that sacrifice.

That, really, is the crux of the matter: we are to live lives that are focused on Jesus' sacrifice. And that shouldn't be too much to ask, since He made His sacrifice focused on us.

A Judicial Death

Kenneth Craig

I had committed the crime and I stood before the judge as he pronounced the verdict.

Guilty!

Now I awaited the sentence. I so desired mercy. But I knew that I was indeed guilty and had no reason to expect anything except justice. Then the judge pronounced the sentence.

Death!

My death was the judicial price that had to be paid for my offense. I sank into the darkness of despair with no hope. I realized that I had received the sentence fairly and justly and that there was nothing further I could do. Only the taking of my life would pay the judicial price that had been pronounced for my offense. Justice would be served only with the payment of my death.

This is precisely the situation that all of us have encountered in the spiritual realm. Each of us at some point has broken a law (committed sin) of the God of the universe. "Guilty," He declares (Rom 3.23). Our breaking of God's law also carried a serious judicial price pronounced by the Lord of the universe. "Death" is the judicial price, for "without shedding of blood there is no forgiveness" (Heb 9.22 NASB; *cf.* Ezek 18.20). The penalty of death reflects the seriousness of the crime—no higher fine could be required than the death of the law-breaker. God's justice requires that this price *must* be paid. I am in a desperate situation. I have broken God's law, separating myself from Him spiritually (Isa 59.2); the price of death now hangs over my head; it is a price I cannot pay. Yet if I die separated from God, I will be separated from Him eternally.

It is the certainty of God's justice that makes His mercy so amazing. In His love for His creation, God provided a means for the judicial price of death to be paid by an innocent party. This representative death is first observed in the Old Testament as animals are sacrificed to pay the judicial price for sin throughout the Patriarchal and Mosaic eras. Animals were innocent and thus qualified to provide representative death, since they were amoral creatures and could not sin. When carried out by faith—on the basis of faith in God's promises and according to His instruction—the death of the sacrificial animal provided atonement, cleansing from sin (Lev 16.30), and represented the death of the sinner (Lev 17.11). The judicial price of death having been paid, sins were removed and the sinner was made holy. The sinner, having been made holy, was then reconciled to a holy God.

More than a thousand years went by under the system of animal sacrifices with millions of innocent animals being sacrificed. Then the moment arrived when God revealed the preparatory nature and purpose of animal sacrifice. God sent His one and only Son to earth to fulfill and replace the animal sacrificial system (Matt 5.17). Look at how Christ is announced publicly for the first time by John the Baptist: "Behold, the lamb of God, that takes away the sin of the world" (John 1.29). In seeing Jesus as "the lamb of God" we make two critical observations: First, Jesus' purpose in coming to earth was to die for sin. By calling Him "the lamb of God," John designated Him as God's sacrifice. The purpose of a sacrifice was to die, to pay the judicial price for sin. Jesus did not die an "accidental death," as some skeptics assert. Second, Jesus qualified Himself by remaining sinless (1 John 3.5). If Jesus had sinned—even one sin—He could not have been the representative sacrifice for us. He would have been guilty for His own sins.

Second Corinthians 5.14 says, "One died on behalf of all, therefore all died." L. A. Mott observed:

> When He died, we all died. This conclusion could only be valid
> if that death on behalf of all was a death in place of all, that is, as

a substitute for all. The death of the Christ was for all. His death was our death. It satisfied the demand of the law for the death of each and every sinner. [1]

When I survey the wondrous cross, I am reminded of the judicial price that Christ paid for my sins. Each of us was

> formerly alienated and hostile in mind, engaged in evil deeds, yet He has now reconciled you in His fleshly body through death, in order to present you before Him holy and blameless and beyond reproach—if indeed you continue in the faith firmly established and steadfast, and not moved away from the hope of the gospel that you have heard. (Col 1.21–23)

All of us who have died with Christ by faith in His work (Rom 6.1–23; Col 2.9–12) have been united with Him in His death and had our sins washed away. We were thus made holy (sanctified), and had the judicial price of sin removed (justified) (1 Cor 6.11). The judicial price that Christ paid by dying for our sins—along with our response of faith—have allowed our reconciliation with a holy God.

From the Bath to the Table

Hill Roberts

The boy standing in their foyer had been plucked off the street almost Oliver-style. He was completely disgusting. His stench was *terrible*. He had obviously never had a bath in all his ten years. The boy vaguely remembered that an old lady had once washed off his face; he hadn't much cared for it. Now the face under his ragged cap was streaked black and gray from the grease, soot and grime that covered him from head to toe. Only his two white eyes gave any relief to the filth on the child's face.

Did I mention how *bad* he smelled? A mixture of fire smoke, sweat, body odor, years of caked food grime that had been wiped off his hands and mouth all over his clothes, a bit of skunk and rat essence, the manure and urine on his feet and splattered up his legs—not all of it from animals. Many of the stains on his clothes were from his own vomit and bowels due to the almost constant stomach problems that came with scrounging garbage for his daily bread.

All in all, he was horrible. His behavior was not too nice either: foul-mouthed, rude, arrogant, precocious, lying. He was picking their pockets even as they looked him over now. He figured he might be able to get work here as a servant boy—maybe cleaning stables, or sweeping the chimney, or scrubbing floors. But it would be worth it if he could get just one decent meal out of them—*and maybe a piece of their silverware!* Anyway, that's why he'd got himself caught. On the street he'd heard some pretty unbelievable rumors about these folks. They just couldn't be true.

Clearly the first order of action was to clean him up before he could live in this fine house. The boy was taken upstairs to "the bath." He had never seen such a place: spotlessly clean tile floors, big soft stacks of towels, and a huge tub filled with hot steaming water and *piles* of soaps. Gracie the maid stripped him to the skin. His old clothes were taken out (hurriedly) and destroyed (with just as much haste). He had never been without those clothes, and now he was quickly becoming embarrassed. Fear of this whole thing almost made him bolt for the door. Baths were the stuff that made for ridicule where he came from.

But Gracie plucked him up and dumped him in the tub before he knew what had happened. He swallowed about half of the water before coming up for air. After his initial panic passed, he discovered a bath was pretty nice! The warm water caressed him, cleansed him, washed off years of filth. Gracie scrubbed him all over. She pushed him under to wash even his *hair*—imagine that! The soap felt delightful and smelled even better, like the flowers in the market stalls. The bugs that crawled over his body were washed off, the itch of filth was soothed by the washcloth, the scabs of the cuts and scrapes were softened and cleansed.

Then out of the now-stained bath water he was whisked, patted dry in those big soft towels, and his wounds were treated with ointments, which immediately brought a relief he had never known before. *He was clean!* He didn't even resemble the pile of dirt that had walked into the bath. He smelled like the bath, not himself. But it wasn't over yet.

They took him into the adjoining room—a bedroom he supposed, though he had never slept in a bed. To the side, two large doors were opened to reveal more clothes than he had ever seen—fine clothes, warm clothes, soft clothes, *beautiful* clothes. He realized he must be in the quarters of the first son of the house's master. And this huge room was just his closet! A servant boy would surely get in *so much trouble* if he even touched the cuff of the night shirt that hung on the door.

Just then the son entered the room, walked over to the clothes and in a flash picked out one of the most beautiful set of pants, shirt, waist coat, overcoat, undergarments, shoes and socks *(socks!)* the boy had ever seen. He'd never worn a pair of socks. The son dressed the boy in his own finest clothes. He led the boy over to the mirror. What he saw was astounding! No longer did he look like the street urchin he was. He had taken on the look of a master's son.

The boy had been transformed for a new life as a servant in this house. But he didn't have a clue what to do now. It appeared that dinner was to be next. This was just too good to mess up. So the only thing he could think to try was to follow the older son and do just as he did. The boy wondered what this "inheritance" was the son kept talking about as he followed him down the steps.

No matter, the food smells wafting up the steps were *out of this world!* Maybe the rumors were right. Maybe this really could be a new life for him. Gracie opened the door to the dining room. *What a feast!* He could eat well here just from the *crumbs* under the Master's table. And there was an empty place right beside the son's with his own name written right on it, just like the son's. "Yeah," he thought, "I could get used to this." The cups were a bit odd, though, all running over like that. Oh, well, welcome to the master's table.

> For all of you who were baptized into Christ have clothed your-selves with Christ. (Gal 3.27 NASB)

> Therefore we have been buried with Him through baptism into death, so that as Christ was raised from the dead through the glory of the Father, so we too might walk in newness of life. (Rom 6.4)

The Lord's Supper and Covenant

Doy Moyer

The Lord's Supper is rooted in the Passover event. Jesus gave instructions for the Lord's Supper specifically in conjunction with the Passover meal (Matt 26.17–29). This highlights the typological significance of the Passover and the subsequent events of the Exodus all the way to Sinai and the giving of the covenant. Christ our Passover, the perfect Lamb of God, took away the sins of the world as He initiated an even greater covenant of forgiveness (1 Cor 5.7; John 1.29). This new covenant is in His blood (Luke 22.19), and the shedding of His blood means forgiveness for us.

Thus the Lord's Supper is very much tied to a covenant way of life. To the Israelites, the Passover and Exodus events meant freedom from bondage and entrance into a new covenant way of life with Yahweh. The significance of the Lord's Supper is the same for a child of God today. Christians have been set free from bondage and brought into a new life with Christ. But for Christians, the meaning is even greater, for we are not brought out of physical slavery. We are set free from sin itself and are preparing to cross over into our heavenly inheritance. How much greater is the freedom we enjoy! How much greater is this inheritance of heaven! "How much more will the blood of Christ, who through the eternal Spirit offered Himself without blemish to God, cleanse your conscience from dead works to serve the living God?" (Heb 9.14 NASB).

Partaking of the Lord's Supper should bring to our minds

our covenant relationship with God. When Moses spoke all the words of the covenant to the people, the people answered, "All the words which the LORD has spoken we will do, and we will be obedient!" Moses then took the blood of the sacrifice and sprinkled it on the people (Exod 24.1–8). Now we have been sprinkled with the blood of the Son of God. Our reaction should be the same: we will be obedient! We have been cleansed to serve.

So while we reflect on what Christ did for us on the cross, let us also reflect on *our part* of the covenant. Does the cross motivate me to work harder for Him? How much will I serve in the coming week? How grateful will I be for the shedding of Jesus' blood? And will my actions reflect that gratefulness? In other words, will I keep my part of the covenant with God? If the cross means anything to us, we cannot take lightly our responsibility to serve God every day.

When the first covenant with Israel was established, the people had to stand at a distance from the mountain. We need not stand at a distance. Now, in Christ, we draw near through His blood. We must not draw back in terror, but rather "let us draw near with a sincere heart in full assurance of faith" (Heb 10.22).

The Greatest Devotional Aid

Gary Henry

A deeper devotion to God should be an obvious goal for every Christian. The devout life is not an option or a luxury, but a necessity. But a deeper devotion will not be ours if we don't avail ourselves of the means that God has designed to produce that result. It does not happen by accident, nor is there any shortcut to spiritual purity and strength; either we do the things that produce growth or we don't grow. It's just that simple.

But what are these means to spiritual growth? We could make a long list of activities, disciplines, helps, and aids that would be good for us. Most of these relate in one way or another to prayer or Bible study. But the most powerful aid to greater devotion is one that we often overlook: the Lord's Supper.

The Importance of the Lord's Supper

The cross is, to put it quite simply, the heart of the gospel. Many other truths shine out from the cross, but the story of Christ's atoning death is the heart of the matter. So Paul could say, "I determined not to know anything among you except Jesus Christ and Him crucified" (1 Cor 2.2 NKJV). And again, "God forbid that I should boast except in the cross of our Lord Jesus Christ, by whom the world has been crucified to me, and I to the world" (Gal 6.14).

It is no exaggeration to say that the story of the cross is the most powerful story ever told. When it is presented clearly, it moves the human heart in a way that nothing else can. When Paul, for example, heard that the Galatians were defecting from the gospel, he marveled that such could be the case: "O foolish Galatians! Who has bewitched you that you should not obey the truth, before whose eyes Jesus Christ was clearly portrayed among you as crucified?" How could anyone who has ever "seen" Christ crucified not obey the gospel, or having obeyed it, ever go backwards and become unfaithful?

If we are among those who have obeyed the gospel but are wavering in our faith, there can be only one reason for that: we have taken our eyes away from the cross and have quit contemplating it. The regular remembrance of what we saw when we saw the cross for the first time is so essential to our faithfulness that God requires us to think about it at least once a week. Many are the acts of God in history that it might be helpful for us to remember, but only one is of such importance that a ritual was commanded for its remembrance every seven days. The Lord's Supper is where we are reminded of the cross—lest we forget and become unfaithful.

Yet for all our talk, we often fail to observe the Lord's Supper as we should, and we don't receive the inward benefit that God intends. Yes, we pay lip service to its importance, but on many Sundays we partake of the Lord's Supper and go away unmoved and unimproved in our devotion to God. As far as our spiritual growth is concerned, the Lord's Supper is, for many of us, a vast, untapped resource.

Two Suggestions

First, it would help us to *prepare* for the Lord's Supper more than we do. If we stay up late Saturday night pursuing social and recreational activities, sleep in until the last minute Sunday morning, and then arrive at the assembly having given no thought to the Lord's death until that moment, the Lord's Supper is probably going to mean less to us than it should. Wouldn't it help to begin thinking and praying about the Lord's Supper on Saturday, arise early enough on Sunday morning to spend some time alone with the Lord, and then arrive at the assembly with hearts eagerly prepared to commune?

Second, we need to *participate* in the Lord's Supper more fully. For many of us, the Lord's Supper is a passive event, something that just "washes over us" as we sit in the pew. But if the power of the cross is going to help us grow in devotion, we must engage our minds in the Supper as active participants. Paul warns us to think consciously about the meaning of the Lord's death as we partake:

> Therefore whoever eats this bread or drinks this cup of the Lord in an unworthy manner will be guilty of the body and blood of the Lord. But let a man examine himself, and so let him eat of the bread and drink of the cup. For he who eats and drinks in an unworthy manner eats and drinks judgment to himself, not discerning the Lord's body. (1 Cor 11.27–29)

As we commune, we need to pray and to pay sober attention to the one of whom it is said, "Behold! The Lamb of God who takes away the sin of the world!" (John 1.29).

Paul was not wasting words when, after noting the Corinthians' neglect and abuse of the Lord's Supper, he said, "For this reason many are weak and sick among you, and many sleep" (1 Cor 11.30). There is more than a coincidental connection between the Lord's Supper and the hearts of the Lord's people. Let the cross be truly contemplated and spiritual growth will not be far behind—but let the cross not be contemplated and death will be lurking at the door.

Part Four

Singing with Understanding

Surveying the Cross

Mark E. Bingham

The biblical accounts of Jesus' physical suffering during the hours between His arrest and His death are remarkable in avoiding sensationalism. It is difficult to imagine the pain the Lord must have felt—scourged, slapped, crowned with thorns which were then beaten into His head; forced, though weak and exhausted, to carry His cross; pierced with nails through His hands and feet, lifted with the cross, and then suspended so that His full weight bore down on His wounds. All of that is difficult to imagine, and the biblical accounts offer little sensory detail to particularize our mental images—even less detail, perhaps, than is offered in the preceding sentence. Paintings, films, and sermons sometimes leave less to the imagination than the Holy Spirit has done. We may be wise, when we recount Christ's suffering, to imitate divine restraint.

As remarkably spare as the biblical accounts are, the story they tell is unrivaled in its impact, which depends less on searing details that recreate thrilling physical sensations for us, than on painful and disturbing ideas that combine extreme physical pain with excruciating injustice. "He was oppressed, and he was afflicted," Isaiah says, and "he was wounded for our transgressions" (53.5, 7 ESV). Addressing the council in Jerusalem, Peter reduces the account to this: "[Him] you killed by hanging him on a tree" (Acts 5.30). In Acts 2 he is hardly more graphic: "This Jesus, delivered up according to the definite plan and foreknowledge of

God, you crucified and killed by the hands of lawless men" (v 23). In Acts 13.28–29, addressing the synagogue in Antioch of Pisidia, the apostle Paul also declines to wax sensational, stating simply that those in Jerusalem who had not recognized Jesus as the promised Messiah, "though they found in him no guilt worthy of death… asked Pilate to have him executed. And when they had carried out all that was written of him, they took him down from the tree and laid him in a tomb."

It is Paul who gives us our most specific instructions, in 1 Corinthians 11.23–29, for commemorating Jesus' death. One can easily imagine memorial rituals calculated to make the participants reflect more feelingly—or perhaps feel less reflectively. "This is my body," the Lord said, as Paul recounts it. "Do this in remembrance of me." The apostle's instruction that follows enjoins self-examination and warns against eating of the memorial bread and drinking of the cup "without discerning the body. To proclaim the Lord's death," it seems, does not mean probing His wounds, but rather reflecting on sin, sacrifice, and salvation.

One hymn that encourages such reflection both feelingly and fittingly is "When I Survey" by Isaac Watts. Its power, in my opinion, results in part from its restraint. The hymn directs our gaze to the cross and its burden, to the crucified body and the spreading blood of the Prince of glory. The focus, however, is on the meaning, not on the horror, of the cross; because that meaning involves the sinners for whom Christ suffered, the gaze aimed at the cross becomes a probing look at oneself. The hymn asks us to remember, to reflect, and to react. Indeed, the hymn devotes more words to expressing a response than to painting the picture of suffering that prompts the response.

Scripture offers us guidance in our reactions to the cross. The centurion and guards who witnessed Jesus' death—and the earthquake and other wonders that accompanied it—"were filled with awe and said, 'Truly this was the Son of God!'" (Matt 27.54). Mark's account (15.39) ties the centurion's reaction to his observing Jesus as He "breathed His last." Wonder is an appropriate response for anyone astounded at the innocence and convinced of the divinity of the one who allowed Himself (as Isaiah expresses it) to be "wounded for our transgressions." Humility is another: "Far be it from me to boast," the apostle Paul writes in Galatians 6.14, "except in the cross of our Lord Jesus Christ, by which the world has been crucified to me, and I to the world." One can hardly hold on to pride while confronting the humility and humiliation of the Son, who,

> though he was in the form of God, did not count equality with God a thing to be grasped, but made himself nothing, taking on the form of a servant, being born in the likeness of men. And being found in human form, he humbled himself by becoming obedient to the point of death, even death on a cross. (Phil 2.6–8)

Wonder and humility are fitting responses to the cross; another is gratitude, expressed as self-denial:

> But whatever gain I had, I counted as loss for the sake of Christ. Indeed, I count everything as loss because of the surpassing worth of knowing Christ Jesus my Lord. For his sake I have suffered the loss of all things and count them as rubbish, in order that I may gain Christ and be found in him… that I may know him and the power of his resurrection, and may share his sufferings, becoming like him in his death, that by any means possible I may attain the resurrection from the dead. (Phil 3.7–11)

Wonder, humility, and gratitude—these are responses the hymn "When I Survey" helps us experience and express. The cross becomes "wondrous" because of the glory of the one whose body it bears; the crown of thorns becomes incomparably rich as the source of blood, blood that signifies not just the sorrow of suffering, but a love transcendent and incomprehensible—love both amazing and divine. Echoing Philippians 3 and Galatians 6, the hymn expresses the humility of one who recognizes that the death of Christ exposes the emptiness of any human pride: "My richest gain I count but loss, / And pour contempt on all my pride," we sing in the first stanza; in the second, "Forbid it, Lord, that I should boast, / Save in the death of Christ my God!" And acknowledging a debt that cannot be repaid ("the whole realm of nature… were a present far too small"), the hymn expresses overwhelming and insatiable gratitude, shown in a determination to sacrifice not only all of life's enticing vanities, but even more—"my soul, my life, my all." In response to His sacrifice on the cross, though I have nothing more than myself to offer, how could I offer less?

May all of us, when we survey the cross, respond with wonder at the love of Christ—love that we can never deserve and that we cannot fully comprehend. May we respond with humility to the Prince of Glory's willingness to suffer humiliation. May we respond with endless gratitude for His sacrifice, by giving Him our souls, our lives, our all. And may we keep our eyes fixed, always, on His wondrous cross.

When I Survey the Wondrous Cross
Isaac Watts

When I survey the wondrous cross
On which the Prince of glory died,
My richest gain I count but loss,
And pour contempt on all my pride.

Forbid it, Lord, that I should boast,
Save in the death of Christ my God!
All the vain things that charm me most,
I sacrifice them to His blood.

See from His head, His hands, His feet,
Sorrow and love flow mingled down!
Did e'er such love and sorrow meet,
Or thorns compose so rich a crown?

His dying crimson, like a robe,
Spreads o'er His body on the tree;
Then I am dead to all the globe,
And all the globe is dead to me.

Were the whole realm of nature mine,
That were a present far too small;
Love so amazing, so divine,
Demands my soul, my life, my all.

Beneath the Cross of Jesus

Joseph Bingham

At Christ's arrest in the garden, His disciples fled in disarray. At His first trial, some apostles stood nearby—one only to betray Him. Their presence may have signified more morbid curiosity than readiness to aid Him, and it certainly did not signal readiness to be identified with Him by others. No disciple was available to help carry the cross. As the Lord hung dying on that Friday afternoon, John was the only apostle whose presence has been recorded. A few devout women stood by; even many of His enemies seem not to have thought His death worthy of much more than passing notice once it was secured—they mocked Him as they were passing by.

Beneath the cross was not a pleasant place to be, whatever one's position on whether Jesus merited this death. His loved ones not too cowardly to remain watched in agony as their Lord suffered. The soldiers whose duty it was to guard criminals were working; a piece of His tattered clothes could hardly be worth, to their minds, getting grimy with His blood, working up a sweat as they raised His cross, and being forced to stand around and wait hours for Him to die. His enemies perhaps experienced a malevolent satisfaction in seeing Him crucified; one would be hard-pressed, though, to call this experience enviable. Golgotha is a place for criminals, those who have rejected the order of the civilized world, and for soldiers, representatives of those who have judged and condemned these criminals.

It is here, though—beneath a cross at Golgotha—that Christians take their place when they accept Christ, not reluctantly, but gladly, embracing that from which the apostles fled. They find shelter beneath the wood intended to expose Christ to the elements. They find relief in the shape of that which formed His burden. They find security in God's mercy at the site of the ultimate expression of His severe justice. They find a ladder to heaven in the piece of timber from which Christ's lifeless corpse was torn. They come not with the trepidation of people approaching a scene no one should be forced to endure, but with the trepidation of lost souls who wonder that they are even allowed to approach such an awesome site, "for the message of the cross is foolishness to those who are perishing, but to us who are being saved it is the power of God" (1 Cor 1.18 NIV). The cross indeed represents the ultimate divide between those who place their faith in Christ and those who place their faith in the things and thoughts of the world. For to the people of the world, it is senseless to take one's place at the side of a criminal condemned to die—senseless, and dangerous. But to the Christian, this is the only place where sense and safety may be found.

In another sense, Christians take their place on a cross of their own. Jesus says, "If anyone would come after me, let him deny himself and take up his cross and follow me" (Matt 16.24 ESV). This does not mean simply that the Christian bears a number of burdens as he goes through life ('Oh, that's just another cross he has to bear'), but that he is willing to trace the steps of Jesus to His death, to crucify the old man—die to himself—that he may gain life. Denying oneself, of course, is the precise opposite of what Peter did: he denied Christ. According to tradition, his repentant life led him to a literal crucifixion.

The cross also symbolizes freedom from the old law and its exclusion of Gentiles. In his epistle to the Galatians, Paul repeatedly casts the issue of circumcision in terms of the cross. People offended by Gentile Christians' lack of circumcision, he says, are offended by the cross: "But if I, brothers, still preach circumcision, why am I still being persecuted? In that case the offense of the cross has been removed" (Gal 5.11). Those who press circumcision on others, he says, do so "only in order that they might not be persecuted for the cross of Christ" (Gal 6.12). When Christ canceled "the record of debt that stood against us with its legal demands... nailing it to the cross," (Col 1.20) He also brought about the end of the system which by itself could never free men from that debt of sin. In dying, thereby saving us from the old law—which brings death—Jesus became "a watchman set to guard the way from that eternal grave," standing "with two arms outstretched to save."

Elizabeth Clephane's hymn "Beneath the Cross of Jesus" is the meditation of a Christian approaching the cross, forsaking the world and its standards to take refuge at the foot of the Son of God, who was brought up in the world, lifted up on the cross, raised up from the dead, and taken up into heaven. The hymn expresses the joy of a redeemed soul, the relief of one saved from the pit, the sorrow of witnessing the Savior's death, and the grateful wonder of knowing what it means to stand here—beneath the cross in unworthiness—finding cause for exultation. For as the apostle Paul wrote, so say all true Christians: "God forbid that I should boast... except in the cross of our lord Jesus Christ, by whom the world has been crucified to me, and I to the world" (Gal 6.14 NKJV).

Beneath the Cross of Jesus
Elizabeth Clephane

Beneath the cross of Jesus I fain would take my stand,
The shadow of a mighty rock within a weary land;
A home within the wilderness, a rest upon the way,
From the burning of the noontide heat, and the burden of the day.

O safe and happy shelter, O refuge tried and sweet,
O trysting place where Heaven's love and Heaven's justice meet!
As to the holy patriarch that wondrous dream was given,
So seems my Savior's cross to me, a ladder up to heaven.

There lies beneath its shadow but on the further side
The darkness of an awful grave that gapes both deep and wide,
And there between us stands the cross, two arms outstretched to save,
A watchman set to guard the way from that eternal grave.

Upon that cross of Jesus mine eye at times can see
The very dying form of One Who suffered there for me;
And from my stricken heart with tears two wonders I confess:
The wonders of redeeming love and my unworthiness.

I take, O cross, thy shadow for my abiding place;
I ask no other sunshine than the sunshine of His face;
Content to let the world go by, to know no gain or loss,
My sinful self my only shame, my glory all the cross.

'Tis Midnight, and on Olive's Brow
Reflections on Jesus' Prayer in Gethsemane

Matt Harber

When my love to Christ grows weak,
When for deeper faith I seek,
Then in thought I go to thee,
Garden of Gethsemane.[1]

Among the body of hymns traditionally associated with the Lord's Supper, a relatively large percentage choose to focus on Jesus' ordeal in the garden of Gethsemane the evening before His crucifixion. While this percentage might seem disproportionate to the Passion narratives' brief treatment of the episode, the phenomenon is hardly surprising. The synoptic accounts of the garden episode—especially Luke 22—candidly portray Jesus' sorrow, mental anguish and fear, in sharp contrast to His calm, almost passive demeanor during His trial and execution. Naturally, then, authors and hymnists seeking to explore the emotional dimensions of the relatively terse Passion narratives have often "gone in thought" to Gethsemane for inspiration.

A particularly successful example of this effort in hymnody, I believe, is William Tappan's "'Tis Midnight, and on Olive's Brow," written in 1822. This beautifully crafted hymn, which draws heavily upon Luke's gospel,[2] concentrates on a single, powerful image: Jesus' prostrate figure, bowed in agonized prayer, forsaken by His companions. Tappan begins by highlighting the irony and injustice of this forlorn picture of Jesus, but slowly turns the somber tone of the hymn into a comforting message of hope as Jesus finds strength and determination as a result of His prayer.

Purpose of the Hymn

Before we attempt to explicate this hymn, it may be helpful to consider some of its key ideas. At least three themes became apparent to me as I read it:

1. **The value and necessity of prayer.** I believe that this hymn is, first and foremost, a lesson about prayer. Perhaps the most astounding fact about Jesus' anguished prayer in the garden is the very fact that Jesus *prays* in this circumstance. Alone and anxious on the eve of His death, knowing that hostile forces are quickly approaching, Jesus unhesitatingly devotes His final hours of freedom to prayer. The final verses of "'Tis Midnight" suggest that Jesus' decision to pray at this critical juncture is instrumental in His triumph over temptation. If He does not choose solitude in order to align His will with His Father's, He truly will be alone at the end.

Even Luke's account of the Gethsemane scene (22.39–46) stresses the prayer motif by bracketing the episode with Jesus' exhortation to "pray [so] that you will not fall into temptation" (40, 46, NIV). Because the disciples fail to engage in prayer, they leave themselves vulnerable to doubt and fear when opposition comes. In the words of the hymn, the divine comfort that Jesus enjoys is "unheard by mortals" who choose to sleep rather than pray. As a result, prayer enables Jesus to succeed where His disciples fail. Just as the disciples required admonishment in this regard, we too must recognize that our most difficult moments of sorrow and trouble will only be compounded if we do not take advantage of the salvific power of prayer.

2. **Man's abandonment vs. God's presence.** This theme provides some of the most striking and ironic imagery in the hymn. Whereas Emmanuel ("God-with-us") is abandoned by those whom He loves, God does not abandon Him. As the final verse indicates, Jesus' comfort ultimately comes from heaven rather than from His friends. Even though the disciples have not physically deserted

Jesus yet, both the gospel accounts and Tappan's hymn suggest that their abandonment has already begun during Jesus' prayer as they fail to maintain their vigil. This point is emphasized more strongly in Matthew 26 and Mark 14, both of which place Peter's rash vow of loyalty to Jesus immediately before the Gethsemane episode. It is also these two gospels which specifically state that the disciples disappear once the arresting officers arrive (Mark 14.50; Matt 26.56). In contrast, a God-sent angel appears suddenly to aid Jesus during His distress. This divine encounter becomes the climactic image of the hymn.

3. Perseverance and strength in suffering. What are the results of Jesus' prayer? It might seem as though the prayer is unanswered, in spite of the angelic intervention, simply because Jesus is still arrested, tortured and killed in the following hours. Did His Father not listen to His request? The final verse of the hymn, I believe, demonstrates that God answered the prayer by granting Jesus the necessary resolve to fulfill His purpose. In the end, Tappan says, the joy Jesus found in submitting His will to His Father was far greater than the relief of being spared the trial of obedience. Understanding the value of suffering will encourage us not to evade pain unnecessarily, but rather to persevere through it—especially as we consider the disparity between our affliction and the burden carried by our Lord.

Explanation of the Hymn

"'Tis Midnight, and on Olive's Brow" compactly expresses many intriguing ideas about Jesus' prayer in Gethsemane, some of which we will attempt to clarify here by referencing pertinent biblical passages and other relevant commentary. It is my hope that the following explanation will neither insult the reader's intelligence by overstating what is obvious about the hymn, nor try the reader's patience by exploring ideas that may not be directly present in the hymn. Since a well-crafted hymn is both art and admonition, I will try to emphasize both the poetic and practical value of "'Tis Midnight," keeping in mind that any beauty or power found in this hymn serves only to glorify God, not the author.

Stanza One

'Tis midnight. This short declaration introduces each stanza and is repeated in the second couplet of stanza 1. Since none of the gospel accounts mention the specific time of night at which Jesus prayed, the author is probably using the phrase for dramatic purposes. Its repeated usage certainly provides an ominous tone for the hymn. *Midnight* suggests total darkness (note the parallel idea, "the star is dimmed," in the next line), a darkness that in this context is spiritual as well as physical. In this period of testing, Jesus is battling "against the powers of this dark world and against the spiritual forces of evil in the heavenly realms" (Eph 6.12). However, it may be that the use of this phrase in stanza 4 is less ominous than before, and that *midnight* there represents a turning point: a transition from night to morning, from suffering to joy.

And on Olive's brow / The star is dimmed that lately shone. The geographical reference here is to the Mount of Olives, the ridge east of Jerusalem upon which the garden of Gethsemane was located. Jesus often visited this hill with His disciples (*cf.* Luke 19.29; 21.37) and began His triumphal entry into Jerusalem from this area (19.37). The main point of these lines is striking: the same Jesus who enjoyed such an enthusiastic, kingly reception from the crowds on this mountain only a few days before is now sitting on the mountain alone, awaiting the abuse that those same crowds will inflict. The royal imagery is subtly emphasized by a play on the word *brow:* just as the brow (peak) of a mountain is darkened at night by the dimming of the stars, so a king's brow (forehead) is dishonored by the tarnishing of his star-studded crown. Interestingly, the Messianic oracle in Numbers 24.17 creates royal overtones for the word *star* by using it in parallelism with *scepter.*[3]

Lately, I think, has the double sense of "until recently" and "late at night." Jesus' royal star has shone *lately* in the triumphal entry, but His imminent trial and conviction by the Jewish leaders will cause His popularity to decrease rapidly. This first couplet as a whole is an elegant summary of the quick reversal of Jesus' fortunes in Jerusalem the week before His crucifixion.

In the garden now / The suffering Savior prays alone. With the word *garden*, the author focuses specifically on Jesus' solitary prayer in Gethsemane. This particular garden was probably an olive tree grove near the foot of the Mount of Olives.[4] We may question whether the mention of a garden/grove within this section of the Passion narrative is theologically significant. Obviously, the best-known reference to a garden/grove in the Old Testament is the garden of Eden in Genesis 2–3, a place of fellowship with God but also a place of temptation. By showing Jesus' combat with temptation in a garden, the gospels essentially portray Him as a second Adam who will succeed where His predecessor failed (*cf.* Rom 5.12–21). Although this allusion to Adam's fall may not have been specifically in the mind of the hymnist, it is most likely present in the synoptic accounts of Gethsemane.

The first of three titles for Jesus in this hymn appears here: *the suffering Savior.* As we discuss the hymn, it should become apparent that none of these titles is used thoughtlessly. The author has carefully chosen appellations from the book of Isaiah to show the ironic and unexpected ways in which Jesus fulfills Messianic expectations. As this first title indicates, Jesus displays all of the characteristics of the "suffering servant" of Isaiah 52–53, who saves the people even as He is rejected and killed by them.

Keep in mind the three key themes mentioned above, which are all represented here in the last line: *suffering, prays,* and *alone.* These ideas will be fleshed out in the following stanzas.

Stanza Two

And from all removed / Emmanuel wrestles lone with fears. As Jesus prays, He is alone. Although Luke specifies that Jesus intentionally *withdrew Himself* a little way from the disciples (22.41), this hymn stanza is talking about more than physical presence. Jesus' solitude is mental and spiritual in nature: none of His followers understands or appreciates what is about to take place, meaning that none of them is able to sympathize with Him in His time of distress. As a result, Jesus must struggle alone with complex emotions and temptations. *With fears* is simply an alternate translation of the Greek phrase *en agōnia* in Luke 22.44, commonly rendered *in agony*. The irony of the title *Emmanuel* (Isa 7.14; Matt 1.23) is clear: "God-with-us" has no one with Him, no one to share His affliction and sorrow. Man has deserted God.

There may be a (somewhat less obvious) echo of hope in these lines, however. The wording of the couplet is strikingly similar to that of Jacob's lone encounter with God:

> Then Jacob was left alone,
> and a man wrestled with him until daybreak. (Gen 32.24 NASB)

> And from all removed
> Emmanuel wrestles lone with fears. (Tappan)

If this verbal correlation is intentional, it may be that the author also intends for us to correlate the outcomes of these two stories. Since Jacob's struggle evidently had a positive effect on his life (*i.e.*, teaching him to depend more fully on God), we can become encouraged as we read this hymn that Jesus' strife will also result in victory for Him, even though all seems bleak at the moment.

E'en the disciple whom He loved / Heeds not his Master's grief and tears. This second couplet drives home the point of the first: namely, the injustice and irony of Jesus' virtual abandonment by His companions, especially those closest to Him. *The disciple whom He loved* is of course John (John 13.23), although Peter and James are clearly targeted in this indictment as well. Both Matthew and Mark mention that only these three men—Jesus' "inner circle"—accompany Him to the place of prayer. Yet even they, who had enjoyed particularly close fellowship with Jesus and witnessed His transfiguration, are poor friends in a crisis. The use of this title for John creates a sharp contrast: while Jesus had always dutifully loved and served the disciples, they respond by falling asleep in His hour of need, despite His repeated pleas for attentiveness.

Perhaps Paul's rebuke in 1 Corinthians 11.30 is not entirely out of place here: "For this reason many among you are weak and sick, and a number sleep." Although Paul is particularly reprimanding those with poor attitudes toward fellow Christians during the Lord's Supper, there is likely an implicit command in that passage to develop proper attitudes toward Him for whom the Supper is observed. Anyone who *heeds not his Master's grief and tears* during this memorial is spiritually asleep, as it were. If we fail to appreciate Jesus' agony, we fail to appreciate that we are the ones for whom He agonized—that we are the ones whom He loved enough to go to the cross.

Stanza Three

And for others' guilt / The Man of Sorrows weeps in blood. These lines refer specifically to Isaiah 52.13–53.12, in which the Servant of the Lord is humiliated and struck down for the sins of the people. The hymn's third title for Jesus, *Man of Sorrows,* is taken from 53.3, which describes the rejection and loneliness that the Servant experiences. The people's hostile reception of the Servant becomes even more astonishing as we learn that He willingly accepts the punishment they deserve: "He was pierced through for our transgressions, He was crushed for our iniquities" (53.5). The injustice of Jesus' situation again manifests itself, although this time it is not only the disciples who are at fault, but all of mankind! Why should one who is blameless be made to suffer for the immorality of the world? How could one man even bear such a burden? The rest of the hymn can help us answer some of these questions.

None of the gospel accounts mentions that Jesus *weeps,* although this is stated in Hebrews 5.7. This verb is chosen primarily to complement the *Man of Sorrows* terminology of Isaiah 53. *In blood* is a reference to Jesus' profuse sweating during His prayer: "And His sweat became like drops of blood, falling down upon the ground" (Luke 22.44).

Yet He Who hath in anguish knelt / Is not forsaken by His God. The word *yet* signals the turning point in this hymn. Whereas the previous lines have been essentially negative, stressing the fickleness of man, this couplet highlights Jesus' most valuable resource: the faithfulness of God. God is palpably present in the garden, strengthening His Son to accomplish the purpose for which He was sent.

What enables Jesus to enjoy the divine presence here in the garden? The answer is simple: in His extreme need, He *knelt* in prayer, thereby surrendering Himself to His Father's will. "He was heard because of His piety," as the writer of Hebrews says (5.7, NIV). As was mentioned above, this hymn showcases the efficacy of prayer through the example of Jesus. The connection between prayer and deliverance from trouble is well established in the Old Testament (2 Chron 7.13–14; Psa 34.15–18) but was rarely appreciated by God's people, despite the instruction and admonition of the prophets. Stories in which great suffering does in fact lead people to prayer (*e.g.*, Hannah's barrenness in 1 Sam 1–2) inevitably result in increased faith for the supplicants and praise for the One who listens to those prayers.

I have heard this couplet criticized as a contradiction of Mark 15.34, in which Jesus cries on the cross, "My God, My God, why have You forsaken Me?" We must remember that in His final moments Jesus is intentionally echoing Psalm 22, a psalm that relates not only the distress but also the eventual salvation of its author! As Rikk Watts notes, "It is hard to understand why Mark would work so hard at evoking Psalm 22 if he did not also expect his informed readers to know exactly what was coming next: a startling reversal and deliverance."[5] Even at the cross, seemingly abandoned by God, Jesus demonstrates His confidence in His Father's faithful presence—a confidence that is powerfully vindicated by His resurrection.

Stanza Four

And from ether plains / Is borne the song that angels know. The final stanza focuses on the visitation described in Luke 22.43: "Now an angel from heaven appeared to Him, strengthening Him." Commentators disagree about the function of the angel in this episode, but possibly the most natural interpretation is that "the presence of the angel empowers Jesus to engage in even more ardent prayer."[6] Angels are primarily messengers of comfort in the book of Luke (1.13–14; 2.10); in this case, too, the angel is an encouraging sign of the Father's continued presence with the Son.

From ether plains is a poetic way of saying "from heaven," ether being "the element believed in ancient and medieval civilizations to fill all space above the sphere of the moon and to compose the stars and planets."[7] The comfort that this angel brings from heaven is described here as a *song*. This term may allude to the "song in the night" that God gives to those who cry out to Him in despair (Job 35.10; Psa 42.8; 77.6), or it may refer more generally to the soothing qualities of music.

Unheard by mortals are the strains / That sweetly soothe the Savior's woe. The hymnist sees in this angelic visit a fitting picture of the benefit Jesus received from His time in prayer—a benefit unknown to His sleeping disciples. The angel's message is not *unheard by mortals* because Jesus has an unfair advantage over His disciples as a result of His status as Son of God, but because He is more vigilant in prayer than they. In other words, Jesus receives divine help because of His piety, not His deity.

The key word in this final couplet is *strains,* which carries the double meaning of (1) musical sounds and (2) severe tests. The former meaning is more obvious because of its connection to the word *song,* but the latter meaning is the more potent one. By including this definition of *strains,* we might now paraphrase the couplet as follows:

Jesus is soothed by the fact that His suffering will be for His own benefit, although His disciples do not understand this.

As Joel Green observes, "God's response to Jesus' prayer is to provide strength for the ordeal, not to remove the cup."[8] Jesus' acceptance of this answer is the ultimate act of willing submission (*cf.* Heb 5.8). Although His fate is not changed as a result of His prayer for deliverance, Jesus finds reassurance and joy in the fact that His suffering accomplishes the will of His Father. In this sense, His *strains* enable Him to overcome His *woe.*[9]

Jesus' prayer in Gethsemane bears a striking resemblance to Paul's prayer, recorded in 2 Corinthians 12.7–10, in which Paul begs God three times (as Jesus does) for relief from his physical affliction. His request is refused by God, who reminds him that "My grace is sufficient for you, for My power is made perfect in weakness" (12.9 NIV). Paul's reaction is stunning: "That is why, for Christ's sake, I delight in weaknesses… for when I am weak, then I am strong" (12.10). Through Paul's Christ-like example, we should learn to be prudent in our prayers, realizing that God may have uses for our suffering and pain that we might never consider.

Application of the Hymn

"'Tis Midnight, And On Olive's Brow" ought to be just as useful in developing our attitude toward prayer as in developing our attitude toward the Lord's Supper. In truth, our approach to prayer can only improve as we learn to appreciate and emulate the humble, sacrificial spirit of our Lord. This hymn should inspire us to revisit the garden of Gethsemane again and again "when our love to Christ grows weak."

Tappan's hymn contains a wealth of biblical allusions that were certainly not covered exhaustively here. A hymn that makes us think more deeply about the complexities of God and His word is, I believe, a good hymn. Recent (and not-so-recent) hymn-writing trends that focus only superficially on the love of Jesus tend to overlook the weighty truths of His submission and piety, as well as the moral imperatives for us that result from these truths. If it is true that a primary purpose of our hymn-singing is for us to teach one another about Scripture, as Colossians 3.16 implies, then it is also true that hymn-writers are primarily teachers. By continuing to welcome hymns such as this in our assemblies, we will continue to grow in our desire for helpful instruction and insight into the word of God.

'Tis Midnight, and on Olive's Brow
William B. Tappan

'Tis midnight, and on Olive's brow
The star is dimmed that lately shone;
'Tis midnight, in the garden now
The suffering Savior prays alone.

'Tis midnight, and from all removed
Emmanuel wrestles lone with fears;
E'en the disciple whom He loved
Heeds not his Master's grief and tears.

'Tis midnight, and for others' guilt
The Man of Sorrows weeps in blood;
Yet He Who hath in anguish knelt
Is not forsaken by His God.

'Tis midnight, and from ether plains
Is borne the song that angels know;
Unheard by mortals are the strains
That sweetly soothe the Savior's woe.

Night, with Ebon Pinion

Matt DeVore

"Night, with Ebon Pinion" is a classic hymn rich in meaning. The lyrics recount Jesus' time in the garden of Gethsemane immediately before He was betrayed by the kiss of Judas, arrested, tried, and crucified. It covers His mental anguish, His loneliness, and His prayer to the Father.

The following are excerpts from Isaiah 53, Mark 14 and Luke 22, the foundational texts for this hymn.

> He was despised and rejected by men;
>   a man of sorrows, and acquainted with grief;
> and as one from whom men hide their faces
>   he was despised, and we esteemed him not.
> Surely he has borne our griefs
>   and carried our sorrows;
> yet we esteemed him stricken,
>   smitten by God, and afflicted.
> But he was wounded for our transgressions;
>   he was crushed for our iniquities;
> upon him was the chastisement that brought us peace,
>   and with his stripes we are healed. (Isa 53.3–5 ESV)

And they went to a place called Gethsemane. And he said to his disciples, "Sit here while I pray." And he took with him Peter and James and John, and began to be greatly distressed and troubled. And he said to them, "My soul is very sorrowful, even to death. Remain here and watch." And going a little farther, he fell on the ground and prayed that, if it were possible, the hour might pass from him. And he said, "Abba, Father, all things are possible for you. Remove this cup from me. Yet not what I will, but what you will."

And there appeared to him an angel from heaven, strengthening him. And being in an agony he prayed more earnestly; and his sweat became like great drops of blood falling down to the ground.

And he came and found them sleeping, and he said to Peter, "Simon, are you asleep? Could you not watch one hour? Watch and pray that you may not enter into temptation. The spirit indeed is willing, but the flesh is weak." And again he went away and prayed, saying the same words. And again he came and found them sleeping, for their eyes were very heavy, and they did not know what to answer him. And he came the third time and said to them, "Are you still sleeping and taking your rest? It is enough; the hour has come. The Son of Man is betrayed into the hands of sinners. Rise, let us be going; see, my betrayer is at hand." (Mark 14.32–36; Luke 22.43–44; Mark 14.37–42)

"Night, with Ebon Pinion" draws from these texts in a beautiful way that can aid us in meditating upon the suffering of our Savior. But the hymn suffers from difficult, archaic language—even in the title—which can serve as a barrier to the modern English-speaking Christian's understanding of the message and thus hinder the hymn's usefulness. Since we are instructed to sing with the spirit and with understanding (1 Cor 14.15), we need to overcome this difficulty in order for the hymn to have its intended effect.

What follows are the original words of "Night, with Ebon Pinion" on one line followed by a paraphrase using words that are more easily understood by the modern worshiper. The paraphrase is intended as a sort of commentary—not as a replacement for the excellent poetry of the original hymn.

Night, with ebon pinion, brooded o'er the vale;
Night that was as dark as the wing of a black bird covered the Kidron Valley;
All around was silent, save the night wind's wail,
It was quiet except for the howling of the wind,

When Christ, the Man of Sorrows,/In tears, and sweat, and blood,
Christ, shedding tears and sweating so profusely that the drops of
sweat were like drops of blood,
Prostrate in the garden, raised His voice to God.
Lay face down in Gethsemane and cried out to God in prayer.

Smitten for offenses which were not His own,
Punished for crimes that He did not commit,
He, for our transgressions, had to weep alone;
He had to weep alone because of **our** sins.
No friend with words to comfort,/Nor hand to help was there,
Since the disciples were sleeping, He had no friends there to say
comforting words to Him nor to help Him,
When the Meek and Lowly humbly bowed in prayer.
When Jesus, submitting to the Father in humility, prayed to Him.[1]

"Abba, Father, Father, if indeed it may,
Dear and respected Father, if it is possible,
Let this cup of anguish pass from Me, I pray;
Allow Me to avoid the terrible suffering I am about to go through.
Yet, if it must be suffered, by Me, Thine only Son,
But if it is necessary that I go through this suffering, even though
I am Your only Son,
Abba, Father, Father, let Thy will be done."
My dear respected Father, let **Your** will be done.

As we consider the meaningful content of this hymn, we should
be able to identify more fully with the sickening grief that Jesus
endured in the time before His arrest. We should feel the darkness of the night and the chill of the wind as He was fervently
praying without any earthly friend. We should be able to hear
His sorrowful praying and feel the warm sweat-drops falling from
His face. We should feel shameful as we consider that He was receiving the wages of our sins, having no guilt of His own. And as
we see His ultimate example of submissive obedience, we should
be both awestruck and zealous to emulate His great example.

Night, with Ebon Pinion
Love H. Jameson

Night, with ebon pinion, brooded o'er the vale;
All around was silent, save the night wind's wail,
When Christ, the Man of Sorrows,
In tears, and sweat, and blood,
Prostrate in the garden, raised His voice to God.

Smitten for offenses which were not His own,
He, for our transgressions, had to weep alone;
No friend with words to comfort,
Nor hand to help was there,
When the Meek and Lowly humbly bowed in prayer.

"Abba, Father, Father, if indeed it may,
Let this cup of anguish pass from Me, I pray;
Yet, if it must be suffered, by Me, Thine only Son,
Abba, Father, Father, let Thy will be done."

Alas! and Did My Savior Bleed?

John D. Trimble

Alas! and did my Savior bleed
And did my Sovereign die?
Would He devote that sacred head
For such a worm as I?

Can any hymn begin with such a cry and leave the reader untouched? From the beginning, we are verbally and emotionally wrenched from any form of self-contentment and brought low. It is the cry of humanity over something irretrievably and irrevocably lost. It is the same cry as the one uttered in despair by a son of the prophets as he felled a tree and watched the axe head fly off into the Jordan River, never to return under ordinary means: "Alas, my master! It was borrowed" (2 Kings 6.5 ESV). Indeed, it is the realization that God sent His own Son to earth "and we have seen his glory, glory as of the only Son from the Father…and we esteemed him not" (John 1.14; Isa 53.3).

First, it is the loss of a Savior and Sovereign. Who can fully express the shock America felt when Abraham Lincoln, who led the nation through its greatest period of strife and anguish, was suddenly taken away by a bullet? In a time when news had only just begun to spread quickly through the lines of the telegraph, the nation was suddenly assaulted with the news that, just as the Civil War had passed, so had their leader.

Jesus had been offered the kingdoms of the earth by Satan, He had nearly been crowned by force, and His disciples followed

Him to Jerusalem still expecting that He would take His rightful place as heir of the kings and save their people. He was welcomed into the city of His father David with palm branches and shouts of praise and hope—and within the week scourged, beaten, struck, crucified and sent out of the world which He came to save. Who would treat their Savior and Sovereign so?

Not only does the hymn's initial statement express the loss felt over a Savior and Sovereign, it makes that loss personal. Rather than saying "the Savior," "the Sovereign," we sing "*my* Savior," "*my* Sovereign." Each of us is the Israelite who sinned unintentionally, who has to bring his offering before the Lord and lay his hand upon the animal, hearing its breath, seeing its eyes, feeling the warmth and movement of life, and then end that life, watching the blood gush from the wound. Just as we ache to see a child who has been injured, seeing blood pour from a cut or wound and knowing that the blood is not supposed to be there—that the child should be clean and smiling and laughing—the writer Isaac Watts forces us to look at the Christ, the Savior, to see the blood where blood ought not to be seen, running down His skin and falling to the earth—and all because we have sinned. Not only is the loss personal; we caused the loss.

Who are we to have caused such a loss? Watts' original words were "for such a *worm* as I," echoing the sentiment of David: "But I am a worm and not a man,/Scorned by mankind and despised by the people" (Psa 22.6).

While we recognize this as a Messianic psalm, it is still from the mouth of David, expressing his feelings and his struggles. If such a man as David can describe himself as a worm—David, who was described as a man after God's own heart, raised up by God to be king of Jerusalem and of God's covenant people—surely we have no room ourselves to rise above that description. In some hymnals, however, the line "for such a worm as I" has been changed to such offerings as "for such a one as I," or "for sinners such as I"—a change to our loss. In comparison with our Savior and Sovereign, we *are* worms. This contrast makes it all the more glorious that He would descend to live among us—and all the more wondrous and horrifying that He offered up His blood and body to the cross because of us.

Thy body slain, sweet Jesus, Thine,
And bathed in its own blood,
While all exposed to wrath divine
The glorious Sufferer stood.

This stanza is not usually included in modern hymnals, but it was originally published in Watts' *Hymns and Spiritual Songs*.[1] It seems almost out of place, since the following stanza continues in the form of a question as in the first stanza, but this stanza adds important aspects of the sufferings of Christ. It gives the picture of the body, bathed in blood—Christ's physical sufferings—and then blends the physical with the spiritual. His body is nearly completely exposed on the cross, as His clothing has been removed by the Roman soldiers, yet He is exposed in another way:

> Surely he has borne our griefs
>   and carried our sorrows;
> yet we esteemed him stricken,
>   smitten by God, and afflicted.
> But he was wounded for our transgressions;
>   he was crushed for our iniquities;
> upon him was the chastisement that brought us peace,
>   and with his stripes we are healed.
> All we like sheep have gone astray;
>   we have turned—every one—to his own way;
> *and the* Lord *has laid on him*
>   *the iniquity of us all.* (Isa 53.4–6)

For our sake *he made him to be sin* who knew no sin, so that in him we might become the righteousness of God. (2 Cor 5.21)

We know that Christ, being raised from the dead, will never die again; death no longer has dominion over him. *For the death he died he died to sin,* once for all, but the life he lives he lives to God. (Rom 6.10)

He himself bore our sins in his body on the tree, that we might die to sin and live to righteousness. By his wounds you have been healed. (1 Pet 2.24)

For Christ also suffered once *for sins*, the righteous for the unrighteous, that he might bring us to God, being put to death in the flesh but made alive in the spirit. (1 Pet 3.18)

Having had the sins of unrighteous man placed upon Him on the cross, the suffering Savior stood naked before the wrath of God—"it was the will of the LORD to crush him" (Isa 53.10). Everything that would provoke the divine wrath of God was laid on Him, and He died for it. As another hymn writer put it, it was the "trysting place where heaven's love and heaven's justice meet."[2] It was justice that there be a death for sin, but Christ loved the ungodly enough to take that punishment upon Himself, even though He Himself "knew no sin." It is this thought that leads Watts to exclaim:

Was it for crimes that I had done
He groaned upon the tree?
Amazing pity! grace unknown!
And love beyond degree!

As the first three stanzas link together to present the thought of the sufferings of Christ—and the expressions of amazement—the last three stanzas link together to make application and to formulate the response of the writer and his readers. All the stanzas are dependent upon one another, and the absence of one diminishes the effect of the others.

The fourth stanza begins a new thought by referring to the darkness that came "over the whole land until the ninth hour, while the sun's light failed"—while Jesus was on the cross (Luke 23.44–45).

Well might the sun in darkness hide
And shut his glories in,
When Christ, the mighty Maker died,
For man the creature's sin.

The first act of God in creation was to divide the light from darkness (Gen 1.3–5). By making this reference to creation, Watts ties together the crucifixion with this statement of John:

> In the beginning was the Word, and the Word was with God, and the Word was God. He was in the beginning with God. All things were made through him, and without him was not any thing made that was made. In him was life, and the life was the light of men. The light shines in the darkness, and the darkness has not overcome it. …And the Word became flesh and dwelt among us, and we have seen his glory, glory as of the only Son from the Father, full of grace and truth. (John 1.1–5, 14)

The sun shut his glories in because the glory of his Creator, his Maker, was put to the ultimate humiliation and shame: that Christ died for the sins of beings He had created.

Not only does the sun represent all of creation in distress, it represents the covenant of God with His people:

> Thus says the Lord: If you can break my covenant with the day and my covenant with the night, so that day and night will not come at their appointed time, then also my covenant with David my servant may be broken, so that he shall not have a son to reign on his throne, and my covenant with the Levitical priests my ministers. (Jer 33.20–21)

The Jews' action in putting Christ to death signified their rejection of the Messiah, the son of David and the one who would stand as high priest before God and make intercession for their people and for all the peoples of the world. They had rejected the mediator of the new covenant promised by God through Jeremiah and the prophets, and inaugurated with the blood of His son, and God allowed the light of the sun to fail in answer. Well might the sun hide as God's chosen one was rejected by beings He had created.

Thus might I hide my blushing face
While His dear cross appears,
Dissolve my heart in thankfulness,
And melt my eyes to tears.

Although the Jews had rejected the Messiah, we have done no better: "there is no distinction, for all have sinned and fall short of the glory of God" (Rom 3.22–23). We have all rejected God and His covenant. None of us stands innocent. In the weekly observance of His death, we are brought up far short of the measure of the stature of the fullness of Christ. The dissolving of the heart brings to remembrance the writings of Ezekiel:

> Therefore I will judge you, O house of Israel, every one according to his ways, declares the Lord God. Repent and turn from all your transgressions, lest iniquity be your ruin. Cast away from you all the transgressions that you have committed, and make yourselves a new heart and a new spirit! Why will you die, O house of Israel? For I have no pleasure in the death of anyone, declares the Lord God; so turn, and live. (Ezek 18.30–32)

> Therefore say, "Thus says the Lord God: 'I will gather you from the peoples and assemble you out of the countries where you have been scattered, and I will give you the land of Israel.'" And when they come there, they will remove from it all its detestable things and all its abominations. And I will give them one heart, and a new spirit I will put within them. I will remove the heart of stone from their flesh and give them a heart of flesh, that they may walk in my statutes and keep my rules and obey them. And they shall be my people, and I will be their God.
> (Ezek 11.17–20; *cf.* 36.24–28)

When we consider the death of the Lord, our heart of stone is melted, dissolved, and we are moved emotionally. It is the consideration that He died for our sins that convicts us, shakes us and forces us to consider our failings with such a cry as "Alas!"; yet Watts will not allow simply for an emotional outburst, but forces us to take action:

But drops of grief can ne'er repay
The debt of love I owe:
Here, Lord, I give myself away—
'Tis all that I can do.

The inclusion of the fifth stanza brings clarity to the expression of the last stanza. Though we may be moved—even moved to tears—by the death of Christ, our response makes no difference if it does not prove a change in us. In the above passages from Ezekiel, God's promise to give the people a new heart is not independent of action, but requires repentance, the turning and casting away of sinful practices, the removal of "detestable things," of idols and their abominations. An idol does not only mean an object of wood or stone that represents a pagan deity; it can mean anything that we put before our service to God. Ultimately, it is the putting away, the crucifying of ourselves—just as the mighty Maker Himself was made in the form of men—that makes us like our Lord. Even that offering, however, is meager when compared with what He gave, yet "tis all that I can do."

The power of this hymn cannot be mistaken. Indeed, the refrain that would later be added by Ralph E. Hudson in 1885 ("At the Cross")—long after Watts' death—seems superfluous, especially if it causes hymnals to exclude some of the stanzas to make room for it. It was this hymn in its original form (minus the second stanza) that dissolved the heart of Fanny J. Crosby:

> [In] the autumn of 1850...revival meetings were being held in the Thirtieth Street Methodist Church [New York City]. Some of us went down every evening; and, on two occasions, I sought peace at the atlar *[sic]*, but did not find the joy I craved, until one evening, November 20, 1850, it seemed to me that the light must indeed come then or never; and so I arose and went to the altar alone. After a prayer was offered, they began to sing the grand old consecration hymn, "Alas, and did my Saviour bleed, And did my Sovereign die?" And when they reached the third line of the fourth *[sic]* stanza, "Here Lord, I give myself away," my very soul was flooded with a celestial light. I sprang to my feet, shouting "hallelujah," and then for the first time I realized that I had been trying to hold the world in one hand and the Lord in the other.[3]

Let us all examine ourselves in the light of the sacrifice of Christ, and determine that we, too, will put away all other desires, all other signs of self, and give ourselves away in the service of the Lord who died for us.

Alas! and Did My Savior Bleed?
Isaac Watts

Alas! and did my Savior bleed
And did my Sovereign die?
Would He devote that sacred head
For such a worm as I?

Thy body slain, sweet Jesus, Thine,
And bathed in its own blood,
While all exposed to wrath divine,
The glorious Sufferer stood.

Was it for crimes that I had done
He groaned upon the tree?
Amazing pity! grace unknown!
And love beyond degree!

Well might the sun in darkness hide
And shut his glories in,
When Christ, the mighty Maker died,
For man the creature's sin.

Thus might I hide my blushing face
While His dear cross appears,
Dissolve my heart in thankfulness,
And melt my eyes to tears.

But drops of grief can ne'er repay
The debt of love I owe:
Here, Lord, I give myself away—
'Tis all that I can do.

Our God Reigns

Steve Wallace

There are beloved figures in both history and fiction who bravely put themselves in mortal peril for the sake of their friends or family. Sometimes it is even an adversary who does this and in some way redeems himself for his past actions by being the savior of others. This type of selfless behavior is atypical of man: "For one will scarcely die for a righteous person—though perhaps for a good person one would dare even to die" (Rom 5.7 ESV).

Although self-sacrifice is atypical of man in general, it is not unusual to see characters in the Bible put themselves in danger and zealously forfeit their lives for the sake of the people they loved and the God whom they served, under both the Old and New Covenants:

> He said, "I have been very jealous for the LORD, the God of hosts. For the people of Israel have forsaken your covenant, thrown down your altars, and killed your prophets with the sword, and I, even I only, am left, and they seek my life, to take it away." (1 Kings 19.10)

> Woe to you! For you build the tombs of the prophets whom your fathers killed. So you are witnesses and you consent to the deeds of your fathers, for they killed them, and you build their tombs. Therefore also the Wisdom of God said, "I will send them prophets and apostles, some of whom they will kill and persecute." (Luke 11.47–49)

Similarly, on a day before Passover Sabbath began, another religious zealot was added to the list of those martyrs who had been put to death.

Yet this man was unlike those prophets who had died doing Jehovah's work before. The difference is that this martyr didn't merely die. And this difference is summed up in three brief words which are the title of a hymn by Leonard E. Smith, "Our God Reigns."

This hymn echoes superbly the imagery of the slain Messiah from Scripture, borrowing heavily from Isaiah 53; however, it is the simple repetition of the title phrase in the chorus that brings such power and emotion: *Our God Reigns!*

Our God Reigns. *Our* relates to some group of which we are a part, and denotes relationship and often possession. This adjective appears with descriptions of deity many times in the New Testament: *Our Lord* (75 times), *Our God* (25 times), *Our Father* (12 times) and *Our Savior* (9 times). Of course, He is not someone we possess; rather it is He who possesses us (1 Pet 2.9).

Our has great significance based on the fact that we have a covenant relationship with God. He chose to offer a relationship with us, and we chose to accept that offer. He is ours as we are His (*cf.* Exod 6.7).

Our **God** Reigns. *God* has special meaning in this title, because the deity under consideration is not the One whom we usually refer to by this term, but God the Son. Usually when God is mentioned, it is God the Father who is under discussion. Yet the Son and the Holy Spirit are just as much the all-powerful deity of God that the Father is. Christ is creator, sustainer, savior, redeemer—He certainly is God.

God is of critical significance in this song, as it was not just another man who died that day, but divinity. He is the kind of God who would leave His home in Heaven to give His creation a perfect example of how the Law of Moses could be kept and what it actually meant. This God intended to fulfill all prophecy concerning the Messiah and establish a new kingdom.

Then God died. What an unfathomable end to the story!

Our God **Reigns.** But the unfathomable *isn't* the end. Here we find the triumph. The curtain which separated the mercy seat of

God from the rest of the holy place was torn in two, probably striking fear into the hearts of anyone who entered the sanctuary, because there was no longer a barrier between God and man. And the crucified Son appeared alive again, "the firstfruits of those who have fallen asleep" (1 Cor 15.20).

The fact that the Father raised the Son gives us assurance for God's promises: victory over death through our resurrection when Christ comes to gather up His own, *and* an eternal dwelling in heaven with Christ our brother.

"Our God reigns" over creation, over demons, over the elements, over principalities, over death, over His church, and over our lives. Praise the Lord!

Our God Reigns
Leonard E. Smith

How lovely on the mountains are the feet of Him
Who brings good news, good news;
Announcing peace, proclaiming news of happiness:
Our God reigns, our God reigns!

He had no stately form, He had no majesty
That we should be drawn to Him.
He was despised and we took no account of Him.
Our God reigns, our God reigns!

It was our sin and guilt that bruised and wounded Him.
It was our sin that brought Him down.
When we like sheep had gone astray our Shepherd came
And on His shoulders bore our shame.

Meek as a lamb that's led out to the slaughterhouse,
Dumb as a sheep before its shearer,
His life ran down upon the ground like pouring rain
That we might be born again.

Out from the tomb He came with grace and majesty;
He is alive, He is alive.
God loves us so, see here His hands, His feet, His side
Yes we know, He is alive.

Our God reigns! Our God reigns! Our God reigns! Our God reigns!

O Sacred Head

Joseph Bingham

In the truncated account of the Passion presented in the gospels, inclusion constitutes emphasis. The crown of thorns, mentioned in three of the gospels, with the implied accompanying image of blood running down Christ's face, is one of the most compelling snapshots selected by the authors for their accounts. The thousand-year-old hymn "O Sacred Head," generally attributed to Bernard of Clairvaux,[1] is a meditation on the tragedy of the abuse inflicted on Jesus' head, and the believing observer's inevitable response of penance and anguish.

One of the more familiar versions of "O Sacred Head" prints two hybrid stanzas of the hymn.[2] The full hymn, which comprises eleven stanzas, explores the face of the crucifixion in considerably more depth. Christ might not have possessed "form or majesty that we should look at him, / And no beauty that we should desire him" (Isa 53.2b ESV), but His was a face which had inspired followers. His was a head held high, if not with regal pride, with the integrity of a sinless man—and now the writer sees it weighed down with sorrow, grief and shame. It is now truer than ever that the king does not look kingly. "O sacred Head, what glory, what bliss till now was Thine! / Yet though despised and gory, I joy to call Thee mine." Christ at His most revolting draws the penitent the most powerfully, because the believer cannot see the wounds of Christ without his own responsibility for them, as Clairvaux goes on to express in the second stanza.

The third stanza addresses another irony, as Christ's "noble countenance" is mocked and jeered by mere men, "Though mighty worlds shall fear Thee and flee before thy glance." The next two lines and the fourth stanza contrast Christ's face in heaven and at the transfiguration, where His face "shone like the sun" (Matt 17.2), with His face now, "pale with anguish" and ultimately lifeless.

The rest of the song expresses the sinner's grieved and almost frenzied pleas for mercy from the One who suffered such evils for him. He grasps in desperation for words to express his gratitude, and can find only another plea, voiced in stanza six as he begs the Lord to make him His. Invoking the penitent thief on the cross, who expressed his faith in Jesus as both of them were dying, the author writes, "O Lord of Life, desiring Thy glory now to see, / Beside thy cross expiring, I'd breathe my soul to thee." At the same time, the hymnist is aware that it will be difficult for a flawed servant to maintain—beyond this brief reflection—the burning devotion inspired by concentrating intensely on the Savior's wounded face; the worshipper's awareness of his own weakness is a central focus of the hymn, as again and again it repeats its vows of constancy and its entreaties for help in maintaining that constancy until the time of his death.

Christ's head, crowned with thorns, covered in blood, pale, bruised, beaten, spurned and scorned, represents His weakest, lowest hour. The singer of this hymn, following the author's thoughts as he gazes at this vision of pitiful weakness, disgusting gore, and shameful humiliation, experiences the power of this weakest hour of Christ to work the Lord's ultimate goal and greatest achievement: the penitence and transformation effected in the heart of the believer at the sight of his Head's suffering. The face of a man willing to endure such torture on my behalf is a face worth dying to see.

O Sacred Head (selected stanzas)
Bernard of Clairvaux (James W. Alexander, translator)

O sacred Head, now wounded, with grief and shame weighed down,
Now scornfully surrounded with thorns, Thine only crown;
O sacred Head, what glory, what bliss till now was Thine!
Yet, though despised and gory, I joy to call Thee mine.

What Thou, my Lord, hast suffered, was all for sinners' gain;
Mine, mine was the transgression, but Thine the deadly pain.
Lo, here I fall, my Savior! 'Tis I deserve Thy place;
Look on me with Thy favor, vouchsafe to me Thy grace.

Men mock and taunt and jeer Thee, Thou noble countenance,
Though mighty worlds shall fear Thee and flee before Thy glance.
How art Thou pale with anguish, with sore abuse and scorn!
How doth Thy visage languish that once was bright as morn!

Now from Thy cheeks has vanished their color once so fair;
From Thy red lips is banished the splendor that was there.
Grim death, with cruel rigor, hath robbed Thee of Thy life;
Thus Thou has lost Thy vigor, Thy strength in this sad strife.

My burden in Thy Passion, Lord, Thou hast borne for me,
For it was my transgression which brought this woe on Thee.
I cast me down before Thee, wrath were my rightful lot;
Have mercy, I implore Thee; Redeemer, spurn me not!

What language shall I borrow to thank Thee, dearest friend,
For this Thy dying sorrow, Thy pity without end?
O make me Thine forever, and should I fainting be,
Lord, let me never, never outlive my love to Thee.

The joy can never be spoken, above all joys beside,
When in Thy body broken I thus with safety hide.
O Lord of Life, desiring Thy glory now to see,
Beside Thy cross expiring, I'd breathe my soul to Thee.

Be Thou my consolation, my shield when I must die;
Remind me of Thy Passion when my last hour draws nigh.
Mine eyes shall then behold Thee, upon Thy cross shall dwell,
My heart by faith enfolds Thee. Who dieth thus dies well.

Christ Arose
It's Why We Take This Supper

Coulter A. Wickerham

Often, our talks at the Lord's table focus only on the death and crucifixion of Jesus. Perhaps there is another important aspect of what we should focus on at the Lord's table. When Paul writes to the Corinthian Christians about their observance of the Lord's Supper, he tells them that when they partake, they are proclaiming something: "For as often as you eat this bread and drink the cup, you proclaim the Lord's death until He comes" (1 Cor 11.26 NASB). Obviously, the Corinthians were proclaiming that their Lord had died. However, they were also proclaiming that He was risen and alive—and coming back.

This proclamation of Jesus' resurrection is crucial to the believer. Paul goes on to argue near the end of the same letter that "if Christ has not been raised, then our preaching is in vain, your faith also is vain" (1 Cor 15.14). Disciples of Jesus of Nazareth need to realize why we are able to call *Him* the Christ: it is because of His predicted and accomplished death *and* resurrection. Much could be said about the power of this argument—that Jesus, in dying and being raised, proved that He was who He said He was. This proof should influence believers and unbelievers alike; it certainly had a prominent place in the apostles' doctrine. However, instead of focusing on the resurrection as powerful apologetic evidence, let us highlight the relationship of the Lord's resurrection to the Lord's Supper.

One of the songs we often sing during our reflection at the Lord's table is "Christ Arose," by Robert Lowry. Lowry based his hymn on the proclamation of the angel at the empty tomb: "He is not here, but He has risen" (Matt 28.6). The testimony of the angel here is a dramatic turning point in the story. Reading the previous verses in Matthew's account, we find that trained guards shook with fear in the presence of the angel of the Lord. Luke says that the women who had come to the tomb were themselves terrified (Luke 24.5). The whole passage dealing with the aftermath of the crucifixion, beginning with Matthew 27.57, has a very somber, serious, almost sad tone. But the words of the angel, "He is not here, but He has risen," change everything. The picture becomes very bright, as bright as a flash of lightning in the night sky.

The lyrics of "Christ Arose" need little commentary; they are simple and straightforward. Yet perhaps we need to meditate on their profound simplicity. In the first stanza, we are reminded just how "low" a state our Savior accepted when He humbled Himself on our behalf. If "taking the form of a bondservant" wasn't bad enough, now we see Him humbled to "the point of death" (Phil 2.7–8). Not only is the image of a Jesus laid low in the grave a way to show how far He really descended from the Father; it is also, it seems, a picture of the seeming permanence of His death. Jesus, we must remember, was a dead man; His corpse was actually wrapped in burial garments; He was really placed in a tomb, a tomb His disciples surely thought was to be His final resting place. The grave lay still and "waiting" for the grand miracle. Outside were soldiers, and weeping, and a world of chaos. But Christ's body was at rest and waiting. As the world saw it, He was as far from being alive as could be.

The second stanza discusses the vanity of attempting to keep Jesus from coming back to life—how foolish it was to "watch His bed" or to "seal the dead." This vanity was on the part of both the guardsmen who watched the tomb and the Jewish leaders who sent them there. If "seal the dead" is a reference in the hymn not to the sealing of the stone in front of the tomb, but to the attempts of the women disciples to embalm the body of Jesus, "sealing" him with burial clothes and spices, Lowry here is lumping together the efforts of the unbelieving disciples with the efforts of the unbelieving Jews. Either way, the point is clear: no one, nothing, not any action of man could keep the Father from raising Christ from the dead.

The third stanza reveals the climax of the great story of Jesus of Nazareth. He defeated even Death, here personified as a predator or the keeper of a prisoner. As the second stanza describes the futility of men trying to keep Jesus from life, the third shows the Lord and His Christ as victors over the great and final foe, Death (1 Cor 15.26), the curse that had stung man since his sin in the garden. In the resurrection of Jesus, the bars of death are torn away and Jesus lives again, just as He said He would.

The third stanza, a grand transition from the somber first two verses, leads us into the grand chorus, a confession of our faith: Yes, "God raised Him from the dead" (Rom 10.9). In His resurrection, Christ triumphed over all those who rebelled against Him, who killed Him, who wanted Him gone. He triumphed over sin and the grave, both dominions of darkness. And what does the Lord do in His triumph? This One whom "God has made both Lord and Christ" (Acts 2.36) makes us to reign with Him in His victory. He will not live forever alone; He will live and reign forever with His saints. What a mighty thought! God will raise us up as He raised Jesus, and we will then reign with His Son in Heaven. Though it is difficult to imagine what reigning in Heaven will be, the idea is found throughout the New Testament (*cf.* 2 Tim 2.11–13; Rev 2.26; 3.21; 22.5). What a glorious victory we share with Christ Jesus! He is the Conqueror, the great King of kings, and He makes us to share in His victory.

I am afraid I have been guilty of coming to the table out of routine rather than with great reverence. I have 'observed' like the guards of the tomb who were merely doing their job. However routine those guards must have felt that day was, we know they were participating in something much more than another day of work: they were among the first eyewitnesses of the event that changed the world! So we too, when we observe the feast, are doing more than a routine. We are testifying to His resurrection. We are proclaiming His life after death!

I am afraid I have come to the table with great sorrow and fear rather than with great rejoicing. I have 'observed' like the women who were uncomfortably paying their last respects. However awkward the women might have felt as they mourned over their separation from Jesus, their mourning was overcome with great rejoicing. Jesus' resurrection meant to them—as it means to us—that Jesus lives, and that He is the Christ, and that all the promises of the Christ are now true.

We need to realize that the Lord's table is not just about His death. The table exists because this man Jesus was raised from that death, and His being raised is a part of what we proclaim. The resurrection is indeed why we observe the Supper on the first day of the week and not the second-to-last. We are gathered to worship not on the day that He died but on the day when He came back to life. We should offer grand hallelujahs to the Lord both for offering His Son and for raising Him from death into victory.

Hallelujah! Christ arose!

Low in the Grave He Lay
Robert Lowry

Low in the grave He lay,
  Jesus my Savior,
Waiting the coming day,
  Jesus my Lord!

Vainly they watch His bed,
  Jesus my Savior;
Vainly they seal the dead,
  Jesus my Lord!

Death cannot keep its Prey,
  Jesus my Savior;
He tore the bars away,
  Jesus my Lord!

Up from the grave He arose,
With a mighty triumph
  o'er His foes,
He arose a Victor from the
  dark domain,
And He lives forever, with His
  saints to reign.

He arose! He arose!
Hallelujah! Christ arose!

I Come to the Garden Alone

Ralph Walker

C. Austin Miles was born in 1868 in Lakehurst, New Jersey. He was a pharmacist when he wrote his first published religious song, which prompted him to quit his job and devote himself to that career.

Miles' most popular gospel song was one which gave me concern as a young Christian, partly because of its location in the *Sacred Selections* songbook. Song #25 was "The Beautiful Garden of Prayer," a symbolic description of the blessings of meeting Jesus in prayer: "There My Savior awaits, and He opens the gates to the beautiful garden of prayer."

On the facing page was #26: "In the Garden." At first it appeared to be a similar song, both in title and concept: someone comes and meets Jesus in a garden, and the chorus declares, "And He walks with me, and He talks with me, / And He tells me I am His own, / And the joy we share as we tarry there, / None other has ever known."

Yet the stanzas were troubling. This person hears the literal voice of Jesus in stanzas 1 and 2, and then stanza 3 states the most puzzling thought of all: "I'd stay in the garden with Him / Though the night around me be falling, / But He bids me go; through the voice of woe / His voice to me is calling."

Why would Jesus ever want us to quit praying and leave Him? My best efforts to symbolize and generalize this song left me unsatisfied. For a few years I refused to lead it, and I sat in quiet protest while others sang it.

Then I read a short blurb about the intent of Mr. Miles. Here is what he said about this song:

> I read… the story of the greatest morn in history: "The first day of the week cometh Mary Magdalene early, while it was yet very dark, unto the sepulcher." Instantly, completely, there unfolded in my mind the scenes of the garden of Joseph. …Out of the mists of the garden comes a form, halting, hesitating, tearful, seeking, turning from side to side in bewildering amazement. Falteringly, bearing grief in every accent, with tear-dimmed eyes, she whispers, "If thou hast borne him hence"… "He speaks, and the sound of His voice is so sweet the birds hush their singing." Jesus said to her, *"Mary!"* Just one word from his lips, and forgotten are the heartaches, the long dreary hours… all the past blotted out in the presence of the Living Present and the Eternal Future.[1]

Suddenly it all made sense. This song is the perspective of Mary Magdalene, and is the story of her personal encounter with the risen Lord Jesus.

John says that she came to the garden early on the first day of the week (20.1), evidently apart from the other women who were also making their way through the pre-dawn to the tomb. She observes the opened tomb and runs to Peter and John to report the obvious: Jesus' body has been removed by His enemies.

Peter and John outrun her back to the tomb, observe that it is, in fact, now empty, and return to ponder the significance. Mary makes the arduous journey a second time that morning, but doesn't return with the two men. Instead she is overcome with grief (and probably exhaustion) and weeps outside the tomb. At that moment she becomes the most favored human in history—the first person to encounter the risen Lord.

So many questions arise from this encounter. Where were the angels when Peter and John entered the tomb, and why didn't they appear to them? Why would they ask Mary why she was weeping, when the answer seems obvious? But most disconcerting of all—why didn't she recognize Jesus when she saw Him? It had been only a few days since she saw Him alive. Surely He would be identifiable here!

I offer some possibilities, all of which have provided me comfort at times in my life.

1. She didn't recognize Him because she wasn't focused on Him. The construction of John's narrative in chapter 20 indicates that she glanced at Him when He addressed her, but then evidently turned her eyes to the garden, searching for the place where they had laid His body, and then turned back toward Him at His use of her name. The text says twice she turned toward Jesus (vv 14,16). She simply wasn't focused on Him long enough to realize His presence.

How like us. We know who Jesus is. We know what He means in our lives, if only we would take enough time to focus our spiritual eyes on Him. Cares of this world draw us. The "flicker" of the fleshly existence pulls our eyes from the spiritual center. We go for hours, days, weeks sometimes with only a glance at Him. And unless His 'voice' drags our eyes back to Him, we continue in that shadowy state of weakened faith.

2. She couldn't see through her tears. Tears blur the sight. Four times in verses 11–15, the text speaks of her weeping. She is a woman overcome with sorrow; she is wracked with grief. And eyes occupied in grief simply don't see clearly. Jesus is a fuzzy, obscured vision to her.

In a well-known parable, Jesus compared some disciples to rocky soil which rejects the seed when affliction or persecution arises (Matt 13.20–21). In the pain of those conditions, Jesus may not be very clear or dear to us. Our hopes—and our Lord—may be washed away in our tears.

3. She wasn't expecting Jesus to be outside the tomb, alive. The angels who addressed Mary also spoke to the group of women who came independent of her. The question they asked those women is deeply poignant: "Why do you seek the living One among the dead?" Why would one expect to see Jesus outside the tomb when that is not where He *should* be?

I've missed seeing some celebrities because I didn't expect them to be where I was. And sometimes I've even doubted my eyes when I saw someone who was famous but not in a familiar setting.

The word warns us that truth and the word will be found in unfamiliar settings. Babes will spout truths which remain hidden from the mature and wise (Luke 10.21). We may not see those truths because of where they are found. Some of us don't see Jesus in difficulties, afflictions, failures, error-ridden people, 'inadequate' or 'unsatisfying' worship, amateurs or the ignorant. But so often that is exactly where He chooses to be.

Mary's story turns out well. She adjusts her thinking and recognizes her Lord. She returns to the disciples and declares, "I have seen the Lord!"

"In the Garden" is a treasure because it brings us into the heart of one of Jesus' precious disciples. One who doubts as we do. Who miscalculates as we do. Who weeps when she should rejoice, because she misunderstands as we do.

What does this story, this song about Mary, mean to disciples breaking bread today?

She became the first evangelist of the resurrection. While we may not have the same impact on others, each week we proclaim the risen Lord. We declare that the tomb was empty and the Lord is reigning from heaven. Every week we celebrate the event she first testified of—He is risen from the dead.

Mary came away from that encounter more convinced than ever of her Lord's love for her and His power in her life. The Supper should serve that purpose for us. How can we believe anything less about our Lord and His feelings for us when we touch that broken body and lift up the cup of His blood? Doubt it all week if you can, but come Sunday, you have to believe He loves you. Everything on that table declares that He does.

Finally, Mary was ordered to leave Jesus and return to duties He gave her. Each week we leave that memorial table and return to the world and the tasks of the Lord. We have our work to bear, our message to declare, our faith to share. We cannot serve Him well by "clinging" to Him, but we can by spreading His message to others. We rise from the table of the Lord, as Mary rose from the feet of the Lord, renewed in faith, fervent in spirit and filled with love to do His will.

May your times with the Lord during the memorial be such that the joy you share as you tarry there none other has ever known. May we, like Mary, ultimately declare, *"I have seen the Lord!"*

In the Garden
C. Austin Miles

I come to the garden alone
While the dew is still on the roses
And the voice I hear falling on my ear
The Son of God discloses.

He speaks, and the sound of His voice,
Is so sweet the birds hush their singing,
And the melody that He gave to me
Within my heart is ringing.

I'd stay in the garden with Him
Though the night around me be falling,
But He bids me go; through the voice of woe
His voice to me is calling.

And He walks with me, and He talks with me,
And He tells me I am His own;
And the joy we share as we tarry there,
None other has ever known.

One Blest Chain of Loving Rite

Mark E. Bingham

For as often as you eat this bread and drink the cup,
you proclaim the Lord's death until he comes. (1 Cor 11.26 ESV)

As he prepared the children of Israel for their release from Egyptian bondage, Moses gave them the Lord's instructions for the Passover. Each household was to select and kill a Passover lamb, then use its blood to mark the doorposts and lintels, in faith that the Lord would pass over the marked houses when He killed the firstborn of the Egyptians. At the same time Moses gave the instructions the Israelites were to follow that evening, He was introducing the memorial observance with which they and their descendants would be reminded of their having escaped death and bondage:

> You shall observe this rite as a statute for you and for your sons forever. And when you come to the land that the LORD will give you, as he has promised, you shall keep this service. And when your children say to you, "What do you mean by this service?" you shall say, "It is the sacrifice of the LORD's Passover, for he passed over the houses of the people of Israel in Egypt, when he struck the Egyptians but spared our houses." (Exod 12.24–27a)

This "rite"—the killing of a Passover lamb, and the Feast of Unleavened Bread that accompanied it—is the observance that Jesus told Peter and John to prepare on the day of His betrayal and that He then kept with His disciples that evening. Their observance of the Passover thus became the occasion for a new memorial meal, the bread and cup Jesus served His disciples and instructed them to observe in His memory.

Moses' instructions to the Israelites in Egypt linked the death of the lamb with the death that was to be visited on the Egyptians; more precisely, the instructions linked the lamb's blood with the Israelites' imminent deliverance, from both death and bondage. Even as Moses connected the preparations they were to make that day with events they were about to witness, he described those preparations as a timeless "memorial," a "rite," and a "service." He said, in effect, 'You must do these things now; you will see their results before tomorrow,' and also, 'You and your descendants must observe these rites throughout future generations; you will recognize their significance forever.' From a twenty-first century perspective (or for that matter, a first-century Pentecost perspective) the real significance of the Passover lamb seems to lie in its anticipation of Jesus Christ, whom 1 Corinthians 5.7 calls "our Passover lamb"; curiously, however, God did not have Moses relate this rite to a promise for the future. For the Israelites it was to serve as a remembrance of things past—that "By a strong hand the LORD brought us out of Egypt, from the house of slavery" (Exod 13.14). For them it was not prospective, but retrospective.

Jesus' instructions to the twelve, on a Passover evening nearly 1,500 years later, also connect the simple meal He shares with them to events already unfolding, and also establish it as a ritual commemoration. "I have earnestly desired to eat this Passover with you *before I suffer,*" Jesus tells them (Luke 22.15). Soon afterward He breaks the bread, identifying it as "my body, which is given for you" (Luke 22.19). As Moses' words linked the lamb's blood with events the Israelites were to witness during the next few hours, Jesus' words link the bread and cup He offers His followers with His own imminent suffering and death. "Do this in remembrance of me," He adds, suggesting that He Himself will soon be a memory. At the same time, however, Jesus' words convert the eating of bread into a memorial, a rite—again, as Moses' instructions had done. He says, in effect, 'Eat this bread now; it indicates something that is about to happen,' and also, 'Observe this continually; it carries lasting significance.'

In significant ways, however, Jesus' language calls attention to contrasts between His memorial meal and the Passover. For one thing, Jesus mentions that the Passover's fulfillment is coming: "I have earnestly desired to eat this Passover with you," He says, explaining, "I will not eat it *until it is fulfilled* in the kingdom of God" (Luke 22.15–16). By suggesting that the Passover feast looked forward to a fulfillment, Jesus suggests that the Passover's end is approaching—that its observance will cease and that it will have achieved its true purpose. Moreover, by hinting at a connection between His own imminent suffering and the fulfillment of the Passover, Jesus also suggests that the new memorial He now offers His disciples will replace the Passover observance, that henceforth their memorial rite will recall not deliverance in Egypt, but rather "my body, which is given for you," and "the new covenant in my blood" (Luke 22.19–20).

A further contrast surfaces after the meal itself. When the apostles renew their dispute about rank in the kingdom, Jesus rebukes them by reminding them that He has made Himself their servant, even on this occasion and at this table. He then adds, "You are those who have stayed with me in my trials, and I assign to you, as my Father assigned to me, a kingdom, *that you may eat and drink at my table in my kingdom* and sit on thrones judging the twelve tribes of Israel" (Luke 22.28–30). The words of this promise suggest that the memorial meal He has just served, to be eaten *in remembrance,* contains also a flavor of expectation, that it will connect past with future events. In contrast to the Passover, which Moses introduced without revealing its relationship to future events, this supper is introduced as both backward- and forward-looking.

When the apostle Paul, writing to Christians in Corinth, rehearses for them what he has "received from the Lord" about this rite, he concludes thus: "For as often as you eat this bread and drink the cup, you proclaim the Lord's death until he comes" (1 Cor 11.26). This special meal, Paul reminds them, unites past

294 | *Beneath the Cross*

and future, recalling the Lord's death and anticipating His return. The apostle's words are the basis of George Rawson's 1857 hymn "By Christ Redeemed, in Christ Restored."[1] Among hymns focusing on the Lord's Supper, this one is unusual in the degree to which it emphasizes the aspect of anticipation. Each of its six stanzas concludes with a reminder of the Lord's return.

The first three stanzas explore the memorial aspect of this "rite." As we partake, according to the first stanza, we recall the Lord's death, recognizing in it our redemption and restoration; that remembrance moves us to adoration, or worship. The hymn (in this, its original version) devotes an entire verse to the bread's symbolism and another to that of the cup, emphasizing in one the love and in the other the agony shown in the Lord's death and remembered in the memorial supper. The refrain—"Until He come"—links each somber reflection on the past with the promise of the future. (That refrain would also have served well in a hymn for Passover, had God chosen to reveal to the Israelites that their Passover observance anticipated the sacrificial role of the coming Christ.)

The promise of the future becomes the hymn's focus, rather than just its refrain, in stanza five. "Until" expands to fill the stanza, which anticipates the sounding of the trumpet and the raising of the dead when (as the stanza's final line asserts emphatically) "The Lord shall come."

The link between this stanza of anticipation and the earlier stanzas of remembrance is stanza four, which describes the supper as a link between past and future. Since this crucial stanza is the hymn's most challenging, both in its syntax and in its imagery, a paraphrase may help us better understand (and perhaps better appreciate) the poetic language: With this memorial meal, this "rite," the stanza says, we bind together, as with a chain, the dark night on which the Lord was betrayed and the glorious day on which He will return; each time we observe the memorial, we extend the chain that links His dying, of which we are reminded by the bread and the cup, and His coming again in triumph, to which we look forward because of His death. By the end of stanza four, the hymn has imitated that chain by involving our hope for the future in our awareness of the past.

With stanza five, as we have already observed, the note of anticipation begins to dominate; the tone is triumphant, and the stanza builds to its confident affirmation: "The Lord shall come." After such a rousing climax (we may ask, along with the editors of hymnals), why add another stanza? Why risk anticlimax? The answer, I believe, lies in the hymn's purpose, to focus on the present and the impact in the present of the rite itself. Stanza six reminds us, as we observe the Lord's Supper in His memory and as we reflect on a prospect made bright by the body and blood we remember, that we inhabit a present of faith, with a hope that sustains us to wait, patiently and expectantly, until He comes.[2]

By Christ Redeemed, in Christ Restored
George Rawson

By Christ redeemed, in Christ restored,
We keep the memory adored,
And show the death of our dear Lord
  Until He come.

His body broken in our stead
Is here, in this memorial bread,
And so our feeble love is fed
  Until He come.

The streams of His dread agony,
His life-blood shed for us, we see;
The wine shall tell the mystery
  Until He come.

And thus that dark betrayal night,
With the last advent we unite,
By one blest chain of loving rite,
  Until He come.

Until the trump of God be heard,
Until the ancient graves be stirred,
And with the great commanding word
  The Lord shall come.

O blesséd hope! with this elate
Let not our hearts be desolate,
But strong in faith, in patience wait
    Until He come.

The Old Rugged Cross

John D. Trimble

Of all of the hymns focusing on the death of Christ, perhaps none is so loved—and yet so criticized—as "The Old Rugged Cross," by George Bennard. It is loved for its simple words and for the way that they cause the reader to step into the same mindset as the author; it is criticized for placing too much emphasis on the physical cross involved in the death of Christ. Often, however, the criticism fails to take into account both the intent of the author and the emphasis placed on the cross by New Testament writers.

From the beginning, Bennard makes it clear that the cross, while being the object of the hymn, is meant to focus the mind of the singer on much more:

On a hill far away stood an old, rugged cross,
The emblem of suff'ring and shame.

Bennard calls the cross an "emblem." *The American Heritage Dictionary* defines an emblem as "an object or a representation that functions as a symbol."[1] In modern times, many Christians use the same term to describe the bread and the fruit of the vine: they are "emblems" of the Lord's body and blood. Some hymns, instead of mentioning the body and blood of Christ, mention the bread and the fruit of the vine only,[2] yet have not drawn the criticism that "The Old Rugged Cross" has. To Bennard, the cross is not only a representation of the suffering and shame that Jesus endured on it; it represents the reason Christ died: to save a world of lost sinners. Bennard is not expressing his admiration for a physical piece of wood; he is expressing his admiration for everything that the cross represents.

And I love that old cross where the dearest and best
For a world of lost sinners was slain.

In his article on this hymn in *101 Hymn Stories*, Kenneth W. Osbeck recognizes that Bennard's focus was the meaning behind the cross:

> One time, after returning to Michigan, [Bennard] passed through a trying experience which caused him to reflect seriously about the significance of the cross and what the Apostle Paul meant when he spoke of entering into the fellowship of Christ's suffering. As Bennard contemplated these truths, he became convinced that the cross was more than just a religious symbol but rather the very heart of the gospel.[3]

In *Then Sings My Soul*, Robert J. Morgan offers the following:

> On one occasion, after a difficult season of ministry, [Bennard] realized he needed to better understand the power of the Cross of Christ. He later said, "I was praying for a full understanding of the Cross... I read and studied and prayed... the Christ of the Cross became more than a symbol... It was like seeing John 3.16 leave the printed page, take form, and act out the meaning of redemption. While watching this scene with my mind's eye, the theme of the song came to me."[4]

Osbeck and Morgan argue that Bennard's intent is not to worship the physical cross, but to admire the meaning the cross conveys.

Jesus used this same idea of the cross as an emblem in His teaching. The Jews, having been under the rule of the Roman Empire, would have been unhappily familiar with the picture of crucifixion, and such phrases as Jesus used would have called these things to mind: "Whoever does not take his cross and follow me is not worthy of me," and "if anyone would come after me, let him deny himself and take up his cross and follow me" (Matt 10.38; 16.24 ESV). Jesus was not commanding all of His disciples to be crucified, as He Himself would later be; He was using the cross as a symbol, an emblem of the ultimate loss of self, the giving over of one's life to Him.

Further evidence that Bennard's intent is to focus on the symbolic aspect of the cross can be seen as the hymn continues. In every stanza (except the last), Bennard uses the first two lines to describe the quality for which he admires the cross and the last two lines to explain the reason why. Stanza two describes the cross as being "despised by the world," yet to Bennard it "has a wondrous attraction." Why?

For the dear Lamb of God left His glory above
To bear it to dark Calvary.

If Bennard was focusing solely on the physical cross, the last two lines do not offer a satisfactory explanation of the wondrous attraction, for they merely describe a change in location; instead, it is the action of the Lamb that gives the cross its meaning. The cross may be despised by the world, yet Christ "despised" His "glory above" to come down to the world. When He came, He was ridiculed, beaten, scourged, and forced to exert His remaining physical strength to pick up the cross and carry it to the place where His body would be nailed to it, where the Son of Man would be lifted up for all the world to look to.

In that old rugged cross, stained with blood so divine,
A wondrous beauty I see,
For 'twas on that old cross Jesus suffered and died,
To pardon and sanctify me.

The author looks at the cross and experiences an emotional response; he sees beauty in an object that would be horrifying if just seen as an instrument of execution spattered with blood—because of the beautiful actions behind it. Similar thoughts are expressed by Issac Watts:

When I survey the wondrous cross
On which the Prince of glory died,
My richest gain I count but loss,
And pour contempt on all my pride.[5]

Viewing the cross, realizing that it was the means by which the Lord was offered up as a sacrifice, the onlooker cannot help having his heart stirred. Whether or not Bennard expresses his emotion as ably as Watts is not the question; the question is the motivation behind the expression. Both are motivated by the actions of the Christ, and both are motivated to action:

To the old rugged cross I will ever be true;
Its shame and reproach gladly bear....

The hymn comes full circle, beginning and ending with shame, first as an emblem seen from afar, now as an object adopted, held close and cherished. Based on his observations, Bennard will take up the same cross as his Master, denying himself, crucifying "the flesh with its passions and desires" (Gal 5.24), preparing to be "despised by the world," to "suffer dishonor for the name" (Acts 5.41), because he wishes to be like his Lord:

> For to this you have been called, because Christ also suffered for you, leaving you an example, so that you might follow in his steps. He committed no sin, neither was deceit found in his mouth. When he was reviled, he did not revile in return; when he suffered, he did not threaten, but continued entrusting himself to him who judges justly. He himself bore our sins in his body on the tree, that we might die to sin and live to righteousness. By his wounds you have been healed. (1 Pet 2.21–24)

As seen above, New Testament writers often made it a point to remind their readers of the method of the Lord's death as well as the event itself. Peter could simply have said, "He himself bore our sins in his body," yet he specifies and perhaps emphasizes that it was "on the tree." The same can be seen in several other passages:

> For Christ did not send me to baptize but to preach the gospel, and not with words of eloquent wisdom, lest the *cross* of Christ be emptied of its power. For the word of the *cross* is folly to those who are perishing, but to us who are being saved it is the power of God. ...We preach Christ *crucified*, a stumbling block to Jews and folly to Gentiles. (1 Cor 1.17, 18, 23)

For even those who are circumcised do not themselves keep the law, but they desire to have you circumcised that they may boast in your flesh. But far be it from me to boast except in the *cross* of our Lord Jesus Christ, by which the world has been *crucified* to me, and I to the world. (Gal 6.13–14)

But now in Christ Jesus you who once were far off have been brought near by the blood of Christ. For he himself is our peace, who has made us both one and has broken down in his flesh the dividing wall of hostility by abolishing the law of commandments expressed in ordinances, that he might create in himself one new man in place of the two, so making peace, and might reconcile us both to God in one body through the *cross*, thereby killing the hostility. (Eph 2.13–16)

And being found in human form, he humbled himself by becoming obedient to the point of death, even death on a *cross*. (Phil 2.8)

For many, of whom I have often told you and now tell you even with tears, walk as enemies of the *cross* of Christ. (Phil 3.18)

And through him to reconcile to himself all things, whether on earth or in heaven, making peace by the blood of his *cross*. (Col 1.20)

By canceling the record of debt that stood against us with its legal demands. This he set aside, nailing it to the *cross*. (Col 2.14)

Looking to Jesus, the founder and perfecter of our faith, who for the joy that was set before him endured the *cross*, despising the shame, and is seated at the right hand of the throne of God. (Heb 12.2)

In most of the above verses, the writers could simply have said "death" instead of "cross," yet, inspired by the Holy Spirit, they deliberately chose to bring to mind the full vision of the cross itself with full force. Can these men, and the Spirit that inspired them, be accused of focusing too much on the physical cross of Christ? Certainly not! Indeed, the reason that the cross is mentioned so often is that it is the absolute symbol of our faith. There is no more room for worshipping the physical cross than there would have been for the Israelites to worship the ark of the covenant as if it were an idol, yet they were to regard it as holy because it represented the most important concept to God's covenant people: the presence of God among them.

Paul and Peter did not worship the physical cross; they revered what had been done on it, the atonement for sins, the reconciliation of Jew and Gentile, the removal of the old law unable to make men perfect and the inauguration of a new covenant in His blood, the example given for His disciples to follow, all meanings that could be wrapped up and delivered to the reader with one word: *cross*. Paul did not simply preach Christ; he preached Christ crucified. Although he expresses so well the thoughts of Scripture, Watts made one error when quoting Paul:

> Forbid it, Lord, that I should boast,
> Save in the *death* of Christ my Lord![6]

> Far be it from me to boast except in the *cross* of our Lord Jesus Christ. (Gal 6.14)

May it never be said that Christians, determined to escape the foolishness of cross-worship and crucifixes, go so far as to distance themselves from the cross that their forerunners in the faith embraced. To them, bearing the cross was an honor, the symbol of the triumphant suffering and shame of the Lord that resulted in the ultimate victory, even though preaching the cross brought shame, reproach, and even death. Truly they would consider these things trophies, their endurance of these sufferings yet one more manifestation that they were becoming like their Master. With eyes of faith they looked upon their Lord, knowing that He saw their sufferings just as He had seen Stephen's, rising from His seat at God's right hand and standing, ready to welcome His servant who had shared with Him in death. They poured their lives out before Him, offering Him everything, laying it all down at His feet that they might be welcomed into His kingdom, leaving the suffering and shame of the world for the eternal glory of heaven. May all Christians take up their cross and endure it, despising the shame, and waiting for the day when all their sufferings will be rewarded.

I have fought the good fight, I have finished the race, I have kept the faith. Henceforth there is laid up for me the crown of righteousness, which the Lord, the righteous judge, will award to me on that Day, and not only to me but also to all who have loved his appearing. (2 Tim 4.7–8)

Then He'll call me some day to my home far away,
Where His glory forever I'll share.

So I'll cherish the old rugged cross,
Till my trophies at last I lay down;
I will cling to the old rugged cross,
And exchange it some day for a crown.

The Old Rugged Cross
George Bennard

On a hill far away stood an old rugged cross,
The emblem of suffering and shame;
And I love that old cross where the dearest and best
For a world of lost sinners was slain.

O that old rugged cross, so despised by the world,
Has a wondrous attraction for me;
For the dear Lamb of God left His glory above
To bear it to dark Calvary.

In that old rugged cross, stained with blood so divine,
A wondrous beauty I see,
For 'twas on that old cross Jesus suffered and died,
To pardon and sanctify me.

To the old rugged cross I will ever be true;
Its shame and reproach gladly bear;
Then He'll call me some day to my home far away,
Where His glory forever I'll share.

So I'll cherish the old rugged cross,
Till my trophies at last I lay down;
I will cling to the old rugged cross,
And exchange it some day for a crown.

Come Share the Lord

Daniel DeGarmo

"Come Share the Lord" has become a favorite among many congregations of Christians who assemble each Sunday to remember Jesus' sacrifice. The words, when united with its stirring melody, give worshippers both a practical perspective and a deeply emotional connection to the Supper for which they have gathered. In an effort to draw from this hymn all that we can, I invite you to "Come, Share the Lord."

Come. Invitations today are not unique in their quantity or quality. Whether from a local car dealership, a national credit card merchant or the community market downtown, I receive invitations by the hundreds in my mailbox every year. In their futile attempt to honor or reward me, these businesses will invite me to join them for their special extravaganza or "one-day-only" sale that I have been honorably selected to attend. Somehow, I'm certain my mailbox is not the only one to receive such noble requests.

Personal invitations, on the other hand, are unique—in both their quantity and quality. Nearly all personal invitations that I receive are addressed to me personally and are signed—not stamped—by the one extending the invitation. And I receive only a few of these each year. There is one invitation, however, that is far greater than anything I could receive in my mailbox: a personal invitation from the Lord of hosts to sit and eat with Him in His kingdom. "Behold, I stand at the door and knock. If anyone hears my voice and opens the door, I will come in to him and eat with him, and he with me" (Rev 3.20 ESV).

The disciple of Jesus Christ should take this invitation personally and seriously. The Lord will never dishonor His disciples by failing to attend the very Supper that commemorates His redeeming death. Every first day of the week the King of kings will arrive, on time, to dine with those who have confessed their faith in Him. And unlike the many invitations I receive each week, this is one that I cannot ignore. There is no need to RSVP. The Prince of Peace and Wonderful Counselor is hosting His Supper. He has personally invited me to "Come!" and join Him. He will be there waiting to serve me (Luke 12.37). I wouldn't miss it for the world.

Share. The Lord's Supper is a most refreshing time of sharing. When believers assemble together and eat the Supper of the Lord, they have fellowship, communion and participation with the Lord and with Christians all over the very earth that He created. As the lyrics to this hymn say, "Through the loving Son the Father makes us one. ...No one is a stranger here, everyone belongs."

I can think of no greater moment of equality and unity. No one sits higher than another, and all are served by the same Master. There is but one who sits at the head because He is *the* Head (Eph 4.15). The rest of His family gather around the same table and eat from the same body and drink from the same blood. "The cup of blessing that we bless, is it not a participation in the blood of Christ? The bread that we break, is it not a participation in the body of Christ? Because there is one bread. We who are many are one body, for we all partake of the one bread" (1 Cor 10.16–17). So the next time you pull your chair up to the table of the Lord, examine yourself (1 Cor 11.28) and not your brother, for the wine you are drinking represents shared blood that flowed from the shared body of a shared sinless Savior.

The Lord. Volumes upon volumes of books have been written about the One called the Christ. Neither time nor space would allow me to exhaust the magnitude of the boy who silenced the scribes or the man who walked on water. Simply said, "He was called Jesus" (Luke 2.21). Indeed, Jesus was His name, but those who truly believed in Him called Him "Lord" (*e.g.*, John 20.28).

The Bible recognizes the Lord of lords by many names and descriptions. He is the Alpha and Omega, Savior, Redeemer, Light of the World, Lamb of God, Bread of Life and more. He is our mediator, our judge and our friend. In light of our thoughts concerning His supper, He is the main course of which we all partake.

What an amazing thought: not only is our Lord present with us while we feast, He is present with us because He *is* the feast! The supper is all about Him, *every time* we partake. It's not about you or me. It's not about a placement within a scheduled order of worship. It's not about a preacher. It's not about a song. It is all about Jesus Christ. Don't ever let it be about anything else.

There is no greater reason to come. There is no greater gift to share. There is no greater meal than the Lord.

> I am the living bread that came down from heaven. If anyone eats of this bread, he will live forever. And the bread that I will give for the life of the world is my flesh. (John 6.51)

Come Share the Lord
Bryan Leech

We gather here in Jesus' name,
His love is burning in our hearts like living flame.
For through the loving Son the Father makes us one.
Come take the bread, come drink the wine, come share the Lord.

No one is a stranger here, everyone belongs.
Finding our forgiveness here, we in turn forgive all wrongs.

He joins us here, He breaks the bread.
The Lord who pours the cup is risen from the dead.
The One we love the most is now our gracious host.
Come take the bread, come drink the wine, come share the Lord.

We are now a family of which the Lord is head.
Though unseen He meets us here in the breaking of the bread.

We'll gather soon where angels sing.
We'll see the glory of our Lord and coming King.
Now we anticipate the feast for which we wait.
Come take the bread, come drink the wine, come share the Lord.
Come take the bread, come drink the wine, come share the Lord.

My Jesus, I Love Thee

Nathan Quinn

We love because He first loved us. (1 John 4.19 ESV)

"My Jesus, I Love Thee," written by William R. Featherstone, is a beautiful expression of these words from the beloved apostle. The song focuses on our ability to love God, which comes not from a superior skill possessed within our hearts, but as a response to the tremendous love God has shown us (1 John 4.10). The more we understand and know the love of Christ, which surpasses knowledge (Eph 3.19), the more we are enflamed to a complete dedication to our Father in heaven. This song testifies to how reciprocal the love of Jesus can be to those who respond to it.

The first stanza of "My Jesus, I Love Thee" introduces the two main themes of the hymn: the love of Christ and how we should respond to that love. The hymn begins: "My Jesus I love thee, I know Thou art mine." This is not an arrogant thought; it is a statement of sincere gratitude. Knowing Jesus and appreciating Him as our Savior provokes thankfulness in us. Jesus is our Lord and our Shepherd, and He cares for *us.*

This connects to the following line: "For Thee all the follies of sin I resign." As we grow in our understanding of Christ's love, we are armed and motivated to put off sin in our life. Growing in Christ means growing in our understanding of what He did for us, understanding that, despite our sinfulness, our Lord reached out and drew us near with the cords of love (Jer 31.3). This love releases us from the holds of sin and empowers us to resign all the vanity and emptiness of sin.

The love of our Master should be the most motivating influence in our lives. This is what Paul means when he says that "the love of Christ controls us because... he died for all, that those who live might no longer live for themselves but for him who for their sake died and was raised" (2 Cor 5.14–15). The love of Christ can thoroughly change lifelong habits, effectively creating (really *re-creating)* the worst among us into a new person. When we focus on the love of our Lord, we are daily being transformed into the very image of Christ (2 Cor 3.18). What power! What love our God shows, teaching us not only to resign sin, but to lay it down gladly! The first stanza of this hymn is a declaration that we will love our gracious Redeemer and Savior more than anything that would keep us from Him. Putting away sin, then, becomes the first way we proclaim our love to Christ: "If ever I loved Thee, my Jesus, 'tis now."

The second stanza begins with a paraphrase of 1 John 4.19: "I love Thee because Thou hast first loved me." Because 1 John 4.19 provides the foundation of the hymn, it is important to understand what this stanza is really saying. Christ's love is significant not because it came first chronologically, but because it teaches us what love is. It's not as simple as 'Christ loved us, so we should love Him back.' Instead, John teaches us that we don't even know *how* to love without Christ and, specifically, His death on the cross. As this hymn brings out, the pinnacle moment of Jesus' love was demonstrated on the day He willingly allowed a crown of thorns to be forced onto His head.

The cross is the undeniable evidence of God's love. Not only evidence, it is the sublime presentation of what love really is. In the cross, God called out to a sinful world and showed us that He would offer the ultimate sacrifice to redeem us and make us holy, despite our self-centeredness. In the cross, we see the purest distillation of love the world has ever known. When we understand the Lord's sacrifice, how can we respond with anything but the grateful declaration, "If ever I loved Thee, my Jesus, 'tis now"?

The third stanza is a promise to our gracious Redeemer: we will love Jesus regardless of what this life brings us. Though it might seem that this stanza is trying to draw attention to the greatness of our own love, in reality the words continue to demonstrate just how powerful God's love is. His divine and sacrificial love generates a deep response in His people, from those in severe persecution or in blissful peace, from those in want or in wealth—in other words, those in "life" or in "death." When we are in the love of Christ, even if everything we possess is destroyed or we lose everything of importance, we will still look to God as the only thing we really need. His love sustains us.

Christ's love not only provides us with breath each moment of life, but it began a relationship that will carry us even through our death. For the rest of our lives, nothing can rob us of the joy of serving our King. God provides a life—and death!—of love and abundance, even in the midst of sorrow and poverty. If we hold on to our Lord, even when the hours are cold with the dew of death, we will proudly proclaim, "If ever I loved Thee, my Jesus, 'tis now."

The fourth stanza takes us beyond death and into our blessed reward, heaven. Even in the hymn's reference to John 14 there is a reminder that these provisions come from Christ's love: we will dwell in "mansions of glory" after this life only because Jesus prepared them for us after His death. The Lord's love will bring every disciple to that wondrous dwelling place where we shall be together and fall in His blessed presence. In that "endless delight" we will experience an eternal opportunity to glorify Christ, since our temporal, often sick body will be transformed into a glorious, everlasting body (Phil 3.21). Surrounding the heavenly throne, we will sing with angels and spend an eternity enjoying blissful rest. Our deepest hope and desire will be met as we are restored to the presence of God. Surely, in those ages, as we realize God's love more and more completely, we will sing of the wonderful love of God with the throng: "If ever I loved Thee, my Jesus, 'tis now."

"My Jesus, I Love Thee" is a wonderful statement of what the love of God produces in His children. By highlighting both the love of Christ and what His love is able to perform in us, the song attests to the wonderful glory of the suffering and sacrifice of Jesus.

The hymn's most striking image is also its most helpful: Jesus, who willingly donned a thorny crown as a part of His great suffering, gives to us a glittering crown of life. We will receive a crown only because He willingly received His. Our endless delight is only a possibility because of His torturous cross. We shall live forever because He died. We can love because He first loved us.

This hymn challenges us to pray its refrain with boldness and honesty. Do we really love the Lord more now than we ever have before? Even if we realize as we sing those words that our love is not what it should be, they express an ideal worth striving for. When we break the bread, we see the event when God removed any doubt about His love. When we reflect on the love of Christ, the Lord's Supper should move us to say, with all doubt removed, "If ever I loved Thee, my Jesus, 'tis now."

My Jesus, I Love Thee
William R. Featherstone

My Jesus, I love Thee, I know Thou art mine;
For Thee all the follies of sin I resign.
My gracious Redeemer, my Savior art Thou;
If ever I loved Thee, my Jesus, 'tis now.

I love Thee because Thou hast first loved me,
And purchased my pardon on Calvary's tree.
I love Thee for wearing the thorns on Thy brow;
If ever I loved Thee, my Jesus, 'tis now.

I'll love Thee in life, I will love Thee in death,
And praise Thee as long as Thou lendest me breath;
And say when the death dew lies cold on my brow,
If ever I loved Thee, my Jesus, 'tis now.

In mansions of glory and endless delight,
I'll ever adore Thee in heaven so bright;
I'll sing with the glittering crown on my brow;
If ever I loved Thee, my Jesus, 'tis now.

Learning All the Worth of Pain
The Great Commands and the Lord's Supper

Nathan Ward

When asked about the greatest command, Jesus responded that it is to love God wholly (Mark 12.28–30). His response shouldn't be a surprise to the thoughtful Bible student, as this command is the root of all others. Why should I be pure? Why should I be humble? Why should I sacrifice myself? Why should I worship God and Him only? If one does not wholly love God, the answers to questions like these can be difficult to find; making practical application of the principles behind these questions will be next to impossible.

You have no doubt weighed Jesus' response and understand how foundational our love for God is. For you, then, the question is not what command underlies all others, but What do I do when my faith isn't as strong as it should be? What do I do when I don't love God as I should?'

The answer to this question is not as complicated as we often make it. Entire books—series of books—have been written to answer the lagging faith question. Advice has been given—good advice, for the most part—to study more, gather more, pray more. Yet in all of this, we sometimes miss the simplest answer: look to Jesus. More specifically, look to Jesus on the cross.

Do you want to see the fullness of what it means to love God wholly? Look to Jesus on the cross. Do you want to see what it really means to have faith in God? Look to Jesus on the cross. Do you want to understand better the practical application of your feelings about God? Look to Jesus on the cross. Study Jesus in Gethsemane and at Calvary. Come to know Him at the climax of His earthly life. Meditate on how He reacted to this ultimate trial.

Understand Jesus on the cross and you will understand what it means to love God. Fully grasp this and your valleys of faith will be short. And when those valleys come, turn your attention back to the cross.

When my love to Christ grows weak, when for deeper faith I seek,
Then in thought I go to thee—Garden of Gethsemane.
There I walk amid the shades while the lingering twilight fades,
See that suffering, friendless one—weeping, praying there alone.

A second command, Jesus said, was like the first: Love your neighbor as yourself (Mark 12.31). And again, this should not be surprising. God has created man for two relationships: with Him and with one another. The greatest command covers the first of these; the second covers the other. And just as the greatest command underlies all of the laws and principles about our relationship with God, the second provides the foundation for all the laws and principles about our relationship with one another (*cf.* Rom 13.9–10). In fact, this command is a natural outgrowth of the first—a connection confirmed by Jesus' volunteering the 'second greatest command' without prompt and by John's declaration that one cannot love his brother without loving God (1 John 4.20–21).

There may be no single command more disregarded by modern man than this one. Modern life is all about *my* rights; the thought of putting someone else above oneself is shocking—to be a servant to another is nearly horrifying. One must wonder if this emphasis is, in some part, due to the softening of Jesus in modern teaching. It is far too easy to replace the 'folly' of the cross with the more appealing aspects of the Lord—to our own loss:

One of the greatest mistakes that we have made in the preaching of the gospel to our neighbors and our children is to emphasize that service is an important part of Christianity, even the most important part of Christianity. The life of following Christ is *nothing but service*—selfless, sacrificial, suffering service that imitates the crucified Christ. We preach a sympathetic Christ who will fix people's problems, a helpful Christ who will meet people's needs, an encouraging Christ who will lift people's spirits, and an exciting Christ who will stir people's emotions. However, while Jesus is all of these things and can do all of these things, it is all a lie unless He is proclaimed first, foremost, and solely as a *crucified* Christ.[1]

And again, the cross provides the answer for our difficulty in loving others as we ought. When *my rights* well up inside, I should consider the only human who has ever lived who actually had fair claim to His rights—and how He gave them up. When pride rears its ugly head, I should look at Deity allowing Himself to be brutalized and murdered. When service sounds unappealing, I should meditate on the fullness of Christ's sacrifice.

When my love for man grows weak, when for stronger faith I seek,
Hill of Calvary, I go to thy scenes of fear and woe.
There behold his agony, suffered on the bitter tree.
See His anguish, see His faith—love triumphant still in death.

Do you want to understand fully the greatest commands that God has ever given? Do you want to grasp what it means—not just in theory, but in practice—to love God and your fellow man? The answer is simple: look at the crucified Christ.

And this may be the most overlooked aspect of our weekly memorial feast. Not only is it a memorial of His death. Not only is it a celebration of His resurrection. Not only is it a proclamation of His coming. Not only is it a occasion to examine ourselves. It is, of course, all of these things. But it is also another opportunity for us to see our crucified Christ—and in meditating on His Passion, to be taught how to follow God as we ought.

The Supper should go beyond the table, beyond the assembly, and into our lives. It should daily shape us, teaching us both how to love God and how to love our fellow man.

Then to life I turn again, learning all the worth of pain,
Learning all the might that lies in a full self sacrifice.

When My Love to Christ Grows Weak
John R. Wreford

When my love to Christ grows weak
When for deeper faith I seek,
Then in thought I go to thee,
Garden of Gethsemane.

There I walk amid the shades
While the lingering twilight fades,
See that suffering, friendless One,
Weeping, praying there alone.

When my love for man grows weak,
When for stronger faith I seek,
Hill of Calvary, I go
To thy scenes of fear and woe.

There behold His agony,
Suffered on the bitter tree;
See His anguish, see His faith,
Love triumphant still in death.

Then to life I turn again,
Learning all the worth of pain,
Learning all the might that lies
In a full self sacrifice.

Notes

Part One: Approaching the Lord's Table

Communion
1. Timothy Friberg, Barbara Friberg, and Neva F. Miller, *Analytical Lexicon of the Greek New Testament* (Grand Rapids, MI: Baker, 2000.

The Meal Format of the Communion
1. Pliny (the Younger), Epistle 0.96, *Epistulae,* trans. Betty Radice, Loeb Classical Library 59 (Cambridge: Harvard University Press, 1969), 284-91; Athenagoras, Leg. 3.1, available as "A Plea for the Christians," trans. B. P. Pratten, *Fathers of the Second Century,* The Anti-Nicene Fathers, eds. Alexander Roberts and James Donaldson, vol. 2 (Grand Rapids, MI: Eerdmans, 1962), 129-48.

The Lord's Supper: Four Meals in One
1. *International Standard Bible Encyclopedia,* (Grand Rapids: Eerdmans, 1956) s.v. "Covenant."

Communing in Memory of Him
1. C. R. Nichol and R. L. Whiteside, "The Lord's Supper," *Sound Doctrine,* vol. 1 (Clifton, TX: Nichol Publishing, 1920), 159-60.

2. James McClenny, "Taking It Seriously," *Plain Talk,* December 1983, 6.

In Anticipation of the Final Victory
1. Florentino García Martínez and Eibert J. C. Tigchelaar, *The Dead Sea Scrolls Study Edition* (New York: Brill, 1999), 1Q S 6.3-5 (page 83) and 1Q 28a.17-22 (page 103).

2. 1 Enoch 10.17-22; 60.7-10; 2 Baruch 29-30; b. Pesahim 119b; b. Berackhot 34b.

3. Martínez and Tigchelaar, 1Q28a.17-22 (page 103); 1 Enoch 62.12-14.

Part Two: Seeing Jesus Through the Bible

The Lord Will Provide

1. Bruce K. Waltke and Cathi J. Fredricks. *Genesis: A Commentary* (Grand Rapids: Zondervan, 2001), 302.

2. On the "absurdity" of God's command to Abraham, see Kierkegaard's well-known treatise, *Fear and Trembling*.

3. Gordon J. Wenham. *Genesis 16-50*. Word Biblical Commentary, Vol. 2 (Dallas: Word, 1994), 108.

4. *Ibid.,* 104–105.

Psalm 113

1. Franz Delitzsch. *Biblical Commentary on the Psalms*, trans. Francis Bolton (Grand Rapids: Eerdmans, 1970), 202–203.

The Suffering Savior in Zechariah

1. C. E. Couchman, "Immanuel, God with Us," *The Sumphonia Hymn Supplement* (Bowling Green, KY: Guardian of Truth, 2007).

If I am Lifted Up From the Earth

1. All Scripture quotations are the author's own translation.

The Departure of Judas

1. The order of events followed in this essay is based on a harmonization of Matthew, Mark and John. Matthew, Mark record the institution of the Lord's Supper immediately following the identification of Judas as the betrayer. John, who does not include the institution of the Lord's Supper, indicates that Judas left the group immediately following his identification.

The Triumph of the Cross

1. I wish to acknowledge, as a catalyst for the following ideas, Thomas E. Schmidt's *A Scandalous Beauty: The Artistry of God and the Way of the Cross* (Grand Rapids, MI: Brazos, 2002).

2. Dionysius of Halicarnassus, *Roman Antiquities* 4.59–61.

3. Schmidt muses that John Mark likely witnessed Nero's triumph in Rome.

Outside the Gates

1. E. E. Carpenter, *International Standard Bible Encyclopedia*, rev. ed (Grand Rapids: Eerdmans, 1988), s.v. "Sacrifices and Offerings in the OT."

2. It is interesting that, throughout Scripture, the ability to communicate truth to God seems to be attributed to blood. The blood of Abel called out to the Lord the truth of injustice (Gen 4.10), for example, and the blood of the first Passover lambs on doorposts and lintel communicated the true identity of God's people. In the Mosaic sacrifices, the blood appears to communicate ritual cleanliness.

3. F. F. Bruce, *The Epistle to the Hebrews,* The New International Commentary on the New Testament (Grand Rapids: Eerdmans, 1990), 381.

Part Three: Meditating on the Cross

Cleansing our Sins

1. Kenneth Barker, "Zechariah," *The Expositor's Bible Commentary: Daniel–Minor Prophets* (Grand Rapids, MI: Zondervan, 1985), 7:624.

Free for the Son's Sake

1. E. Stanley Jones, *How to Be a Transformed Person* (Nashville: Abingdon, 1981), 223.

2. Some translations of this document read: "Nothing. For the sake of the Maid." For the next three hundred years Domrémy paid no taxes; after the French Revolution, however, taxes were reinstituted.

Most True to Those Who are My Greatest Grief

1. The text here is based on that of George Gilfillan, ed., *The Poetical Works of George Herbert* (Edinburgh: James Nichol, 1853), available online at *http://books.google.com* (search term: Gilgillan). The full text is available there (on pages 20–29) and in many other editions of Herbert's *The Temple.*

A Judicial Death

1. L. A. Mott, *The Ministry of Reconciliation* no. 15 (Sunset Publishing).

Part Four: Singing with Understanding

Tis Midnight, And on Olive's Brow

1. John Wreford, "When My Love to Christ Grows Weak."

2. Since the imagery of "'Tis Midnight" is particularly indebted to Luke's account (22.39–46), I think it is appropriate to mention here a textual issue involving verses 43–44. Apart from these verses, Luke's account of Jesus' trial in the garden provides little information not included in the parallel accounts of Matthew 26 and Mark 14. Verses 43–44, however, provide these additional details not found elsewhere: "An angel from heaven appeared to Him and strengthened Him. And being in anguish, He prayed more earnestly, and His sweat was like drops of blood falling to the ground" (NIV).

Several early manuscripts of Luke do not include this paragraph, leading many commentators to believe that verses 43–44 were not original to Luke's gospel. These writers regard the sudden appearance of the angel and the vivid description of Jesus' stress symptoms as uncharacteristic of Luke's style. On the other hand, many authors argue that the verses fit the context very well and were excluded from certain manuscripts only because of doctrinal concerns. See I. Howard Marshall, *The Gospel of Luke* (Grand Rapids, MI: Eerdmans, 1978), 831-31.

The reasons for mentioning this issue here are not primarily academic. "'Tis Midnight" derives nearly all of its imagery from these two verses. So, from a practical standpoint, we may rightly question the value of a hymn based on a passage with uncertain canonical status. Do the dramatic elements of Luke 22.43–44 accurately reflect Jesus' ordeal, or do they exaggerate the moment of "weakness" that Jesus experienced? Is Tappan even able to draw valid conclusions from these verses in his hymn?

A full investigation of the relevant textual-critical issues here is beyond our scope and my ability. For purposes of this discussion, however, I am persuaded that (1) regardless of their origin, verses 43–44 are at least thematically and doctrinally consistent with the gospel accounts and with other Scriptures, and that (2) Tappan's hymn, while borrowing freely from Luke 22.43–44, offers us particularly useful insights about Jesus and prayer that do not depend on the canonicity of these verses.

3. Timothy Ashley, *The Book of Numbers,* The New International Commentary on the Old Testament (Grand Rapids: Eerdmans, 1993), 500.

4. *Nelson's New Illustrated Bible Dictionary,* ed. Ronald F. Youngblood (Nashville: Thomas Nelson, 1995), s.v. "Gethsemane."

5. Rikk Watts, "Mark," *Commentary on the New Testament Use of the Old Testament,* ed. G. K. Beale and D. A. Carson (Grand Rapids: Baker, 2007), 236.

6. Joel Green, *The Gospel of Luke,* New International Commentary on the New Testament (Grand Rapids: Eerdmans, 1997), 780.

7. *The American Heritage Dictionary of the English Language,* 4th ed.

8. Green, *Gospel of Luke,* 780.

9. For those who are still (understandably) skeptical that this nuance of *strains* was intended, I would simply point to the rhyme scheme of the stanza: *strains* rhymes with *plains* in line 1. Since there are more intuitive ways to say "from heaven" than *from ether plains,* one can assume that *strains* was an indispensable word for which Tappan needed to find a rhyme. That's my amateur attempt at literary analysis; don't worry, I'll keep my day job.

Night, With Ebon Pinion
1. On "Meek and Lowly," see Matthew 11.29.

Alas! And Did My Savior Bleed?
1. Isaac Watts, "Godly Sorrow Arising from the Sufferings of Christ," *Hymns and Spiritual Songs* (Project Gutenberg, 2004), http://www.gutenberg.org/etext/13341.

2. Elizabeth C. Clephane, "Beneath the Cross of Jesus."

3. Frances Jane Crosby, *Memories of Eighty Years* (Boston: James H. Earle, 1906), quoted in "Alas! and Did My Savior Bleed," *Cyberhymnal.org,* http://cyberhymnal.org/htm/a/l/a/alasand.htm.

O Sacred Head

1. As with any great work of poetry which remains great in a new language, the translator, James W. Alexander, deserves considerable credit.

2. *Hymns for Worship (Revised)*, ed. R. J. Stevens (Bowling Green, KY: Guardian of Truth, 1987).

I Come to the Garden Alone

1. "'In the Garden,'" *Cyberhymnal.org*, http://cyberhymnal.org/htm/i/t/g/itgarden.htm.

One Blest Chain of Loving Rite

1. Originally published in a Baptist hymnal in 1858, the hymn appeared subsequently in the 1876 collection of Rawson's *Hymns, Verses, and Chants*, published in London by Hodder and Stoughton. The hymn is quoted here from this 1876 version.

2. Although not discussing the Lord's Supper, Hebrews 9.28 uses a structure similar to that of the hymn, moving from the knowledge that Christ suffered (the past) to a triumphant affirmation that He will return (the future), which is then followed by a more subdued reminder of the Christian's responsibility (the present): "…so Christ, having been offered once to bear the sins of many, will appear a second time, not to deal with sin but to save those who are eagerly waiting for him."

Old Rugged Cross

1. *The American Heritage Dictionary of the English Language*, 4th edition.

2. For example, Ellis Crum, "The Breaking of the Bread" and Vana Raye, "'Tis Set, the Feast Divine."

3. Kenneth W. Osbeck, "The Old Rugged Cross," *101 Hymn Stories* (Grand Rapids: Kregel, 1982), 255-56.

4. Robert J. Morgan, "The Old Rugged Cross," *Then Sings My Soul: 150 of the World's Greatest Hymn Stories* (Nashville: Thomas Nelson, 2003), 275.

5. Isaac Watts, "When I Survey the Wondrous Cross."

6. *Ibid.*

Learning All the Worth of Pain

1. Tom Hamilton, "Portraits of the Messiah," in *Portraits in Isaiah*, ed. Daniel Petty (Temple Terrace: Florida College Bookstore, 2006), 174. Emphasis in original.

Sources and Acknowledgments

Essays
The original forms of "The Last Passover," "The Suffering Savior of Isaiah 53," and "Barabbas" were published in *Biblical Insights*. They are reprinted here with permission.

The original form of "The Greatest Devotional Aid" was published in *Truth Magazine*. It is reprinted here with permission.

Hymns
The lyrics to "Our God Reigns" ©1974, 1978 Leonard E. Smith are reprinted with permission.

The lyrics to "Come Share the Lord" ©1984 Fred Bock Music Co., Inc. are reprinted with permission.

All other hymns quoted are in the public domain. Lyrics are taken from Cyberhymnal.org.

Bible Quotations
Scripture quotations marked ASV are taken from the American Standard Version.

Scripture quotations marked KJV are taken from the King James Version.

Scripture quotations marked ESV are from The Holy Bible, English Standard Version®, copyright ©2001 by Crossway Bibles, a publishing ministry of Good News Publishers. Used by permission. All rights reserved.

Scripture quotations marked NASB taken from The New American Standard Bible®, Copyright ©1960, 1962, 1963, 1968, 1971, 1972, 1973, 1975, 1977, 1995 by The Lockman Foundation. Used by permission.

Scripture quotations marked NIV are taken from The Holy Bible, New

About the Authors

Wilson Adams preaches for the Carson Lane church in Murfreesboro, Tennessee, where he and his wife Julie live. Wilson also serves as editor for *Biblical Insights*, and wrote *Around the House* and *Around the House... Again*.

Joseph Bingham and his wife Lauren live in Chicago, where Joseph attends law school and Lauren takes pictures. They may be reached at teaforthetillerman@gmail.com.

Mark Bingham and his wife Melanie live in Seffner, Florida, and worship in nearby Plant City. Mark teaches English and Humanities courses at Florida College.

Andy Cantrell lives in Champlin, Minnesota with his wife Claire and sons Cade and Chayton. He assembles with the Christians who meet in New Hope, Minnesota.

Kenny ("Tack") Chumbley lives in Rantoul, Illinois and can be reached at KLChumbley@aol.com.

Kelly Cook lives in Georgetown, Indiana with wife Julie and their three children. Kelly can be reached at **kelly.cook@fscfsa.com**.

Jady Copeland lives in Tampa, Florida and worships with the Livingston Avenue church. He can be reached at **jadycopeland@gmail.com**.

Ken Craig and his wife live near Birmingham, Alabama, where he serves as an elder to the Helena church. His passion is spreading the gospel message, which he has all over the world, from the Seychelles Islands in the Indian Ocean to the Zulus in South Africa to various countries in Europe, Asia, and South America.

Edwin Crozier, the evangelist with the Franklin church of Christ in Franklin, Tennessee, and his wife Marita live in Spring Hill, Tennessee with their four children. He has been published in *Biblical Insights, Preceptor* and *Focus*. He has authored several books including *Walks with God* and *Plugged In: High Voltage Prayer* and produced the DVD *Your First 10 Days as a Christian*. Edwin can be reached at **ecroz@bellsouth.net.**

Melvin Curry and his wife Shirley live in Pasco County, north of Tampa, Florida. He preaches for the West Citrus congregation in Crystal River, Florida. Melvin taught biblical studies at Florida College for thirty-four years.

Daniel DeGarmo resides and works with the Lord's church in Chillicothe, Ohio. He and his wife Serena have three children, and a fourth on the way (at the time of publication). Dan serves his congregation and community as an evangelist.

Matt DeVore lives in Wooster, Ohio with his wife Rachel and two children Violet and Caleb. They assemble with the Northend church of Christ in Ashland, Ohio where Matt conducts Bible classes and shares the work of preaching with eight other men. Matt supports the computer network for a branch campus of The Ohio State University and also operates his own company helping churches set up web sites. Matt can be reached at **matt@devoredata.com.**

Gary Fisher and his wife, Sandra, live in New Salisbury, Indiana and are a part of the church there. They have two grown children, Laura and Kyle. Gary can be reached at **fisherg@insightbb.com.**

Ben Greiving and his wife Jenn recently moved to the Denver area. Ben graduated from the Florida State University College of Law in May. He can be reached at **ben.greiving@gmail.com.**

Patrick Halbrook, his wife Kaylie and their son John Luke live near Raleigh, North Carolina and worship with the Fuquay-Varina church of Christ where Patrick preaches periodically. Since 2006 he has taught middle school Bible and English classes at a local classical Christian school. Patrick can be reached at **patrickhalbrook@gmail.com.**

Sewell Hall lives in Atlanta and is, for the third time, a member of the Embry Hills Church. He has been preaching the gospel for more than 60 years and has contributed articles to several gospel papers. Sewell can be reached at **sewellhall@aol.com.**

Matt Harber and his wife Katie live in Pittsburgh. He can be reached at mattharb@gmail.com.

Jason Hardin lives in Reynoldsburg, Ohio and works with the Laurel Canyon church in Columbus. He and his wife Shelly have been blessed with three daughters: Chloe, Jadyn, and Emma. Much of Jason's work is shared at www.ThingsHopedFor.org. He is the author of the upcoming I.M.A.G.E. series of books for men (www.InGodsImage.com) and can be reached at jason@thingshopedfor.org.

Ben Hastings and his wife Stacey live on a small farm in Dayton, Ohio. Ben is a part-time evangelist for the West Carrollton church and supports his family working in Statistical Analysis and Quality Assurance for a large online publisher. He can be reached at ben.hastings@gmail.com.

Mark Hatfield, his wife Sharon, and two sons live in Chillicothe, Ohio. For the past nine years Mark has labored with churches in Barnesville, Ashland and Chillicothe, Ohio. He and his wife have been involved in mission work in Nicaragua. At this time, Mark is working with a newly planted church in Chillicothe.

Gary Henry preaches part-time for the Broadmoor church in Nashville, Tennessee. The remainder of his time is devoted to gospel meetings and writing. He is the author of *Diligently Seeking God* and *Reaching Forward.*

Mark Lloyd and his wife Diana live in Gainesville, Florida and assemble with the Glen Springs Road church, where Mark serves as an Elder. He has been in private practice in Gainesville since 1980. Mark can be reached at GatrDoc@aol.com.

Ethan Longhenry is the evangelist for the church of Christ in Norwalk, Ohio. Ethan is the editor of *Renewed in Spirit,* a contributor to various publications, and the author of *Churches of the New Testament.* He and his wife Sarah have three children: Julianna, Maia, and Nathaniel. Ethan can be reached at deusvitae@hotmail.com.

Reagan McClenny is an evangelist with the Lindale church of Christ in Lindale, Texas. He can be reached at reaganmcclenny@lindalechu rchofchrist.org.

David McClister and his wife Lisa live in Temple Terrace, Florida. David is a professor of Biblical studies, Greek and Latin at Florida College and preaches for the Antioch church in Thonotosassa.

Mark Moseley and his wife Mary live in Gainesville, Florida where he is an elder and evangelist for the Glen Springs Road congregation. Mark also serves the community as Circuit Judge of the Eight Judicial Circuit for the State of Florida.

Doy Moyer started preaching the gospel in 1986 and has worked in several states, including Louisiana, Kentucky, Ohio, and California. Doy presently works with the Cork church outside of Tampa, Florida and has been a professor of Biblical studies and philosophy at Florida College since 2001. He is married to Laurie (Teel) Moyer, and they have three children: Caleb, Lucas, and Audrey.

Robert Ogden preaches for the West Mobile congregation in Mobile, Alabama. He can be reached at **robert.ogden@gmail.com.**

Dan Petty and his wife Kathy have lived in Temple Terrace, Florida since 1989, when Dan joined the faculty at Florida College. He is a professor of Biblical studies and church history at Florida College, where he currently serves as chair of the Biblical studies department. The Pettys are members of the Lutz church, where Dan preaches and serves as an elder. Dan can be reached at **pettyd@floridacollege.edu.**

Martin Pickup and his wife Aimee live in Plant City, Florida and have three grown children. Marty serves as a preacher and elder for the Valrico church of Christ. He taught for 17 years in the Biblical studies department at Florida College, and has published articles in various popular journals, such as *Biblical Insights*, as well as numerous scholarly journals and books, including *Quest for the Historical Pharisees*. Marty can be reached at **mpickup@aol.com.**

Nathan Quinn lives in Lincoln, Nebraska where he preaches for the Eastside church. He has lived in Nebraska since 2003. Nathan can be reached at **quinners24@gmail.com.**

Jerold Redding and his wife Shirley live in Gainesville, Florida and worship with the Glen Springs Road congregation.

Hill Roberts and his wife Carol live in Huntsville, Alabama where he works for Mantech SRS Technologies as Chief Scientist. Hill is coauthor of Broadman-Holman's *Quicksource Guide to Creation* (Oct 2008). Hill can be reached through the **LordiBelieve.org** website.

John Trimble and his wife Jenny live in Orlando, Florida and assemble with the saints at South Bumby. John has written several hymns, one of which was published in the *Sumphonia Hymn Supplement*. He comes from a family of hymn writers and Christians who have instilled in him a love for music and meaningful hymns.

Ralph Walker and his wife Paula live in Temple Terrace, Florida. Ralph serves the Henderson Boulevard church as a shepherd and part-time preacher, and works as the Public Relations Director at Florida College. He and Paula help conduct summer marriage seminars with Mark and Judy Broyles. Ralph has preached since 1975.

Steve Wallace and his wife Jennifer work with the Glen Springs Road congregation in Gainesville, Florida, where he serves as a deacon. Steve has spoken at the Florida College Lectures on the subject of web design for congregations and can be reached at **sewallace@cox.net**.

Keith Ward and his wife Dene live in Lake Butler, Florida and worship with the Glen Springs Road congregation in Gainesville, where he serves as a deacon.

Lucas Ward lives in Gainesville, Florida and worships with the Glen Springs Road congregation. He can be reached at **pubdeli@yahoo.com**.

Nathan Ward and his wife Brooke live Tampa, Florida and assemble with the 58th Street church. He is the author of *The Growth of the Seed: Notes on the Book of Genesis*. Nathan can be reached at **nathan_ward@hotmail.com**.

Coulter A. Wickerham his wife Lauren, and two daughters live in Thomasville, Georgia. He is a full-time evangelist for the Moultrie Road congregation. Coulter can be reached at **coulterwickerham@yahoo.com**.

ALSO FROM DEWARD PUBLISHING:

The Growth of the Seed:
Notes on the Book of Genesis
Nathan Ward

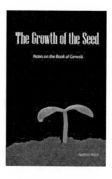

A study of the book of Genesis that emphasizes two primary themes: the development of the Messianic line and the growing enmity between the righteous and the wicked. In addition, it provides detailed comments on the text and short essays on several subjects that are suggested in, yet peripheral to, Genesis. 540 pages.

The Man of Galilee
Atticus G. Haygood

An apologetic for the deity of Christ using Jesus Himself as presented by the gospel records as its chief evidence. This is a reprint of the 1963 edition. The Man of Galilee was originally published in 1889. 108 pages.

COMING IN 2008:

The Big Picture of the Bible
Kenneth W. Craig

In this short book, the author summarizes the central theme of the Bible in a simple, yet comprehensive approach. Evangelists across the world have used this presentation to convert countless souls to the discipleship of Jesus Christ. Bulk discounts and special pricing for church orders will be available.

DEWARD
PUBLISHING COMPANY
dewardpublishing.com

CPSIA information can be obtained
at www.ICGtesting.com
Printed in the USA
FFOW02n0809020617
36164FF

9 780979 889332